Contents

Special fried rice with prawns & chorizo

Prep: 10 mins **Cook:** 18 mins

Serves 2

Ingredients

- 100g basmati rice or long-grain rice
- 85g frozen pea
- 1 tbsp sunflower oil
- 1 egg , beaten
- 50g finely diced chorizo , bacon or ham
- 1 garlic clove , chopped
- 3 spring onions , sliced on an angle
- ½ red pepper , deseeded and chopped
- good pinch five spice powder
- 1 tsp soy sauce
- 100g beansprout (optional)
- 50g peeled prawn

Method

STEP 1

Boil the rice following pack instructions, adding the peas for the final min. Drain.

STEP 2

Heat half the oil in a wok. Pour in the egg and stir-fry until scrambled. Tip onto a plate and set aside.

STEP 3

Wipe the wok with kitchen paper, then heat the remaining oil. Toss in the meat, garlic, spring onions and pepper, and stir-fry until the pepper starts to soften. Add the five-spice, rice, peas and soy, then stir-fry for 5 mins more. Finally add the beansprouts, if using, the egg and prawns, and stir-fry to heat through.

Halloween brownies

Prep: 25 mins **Cook:** 45 mins

Serves 12

Ingredients

- 200g butter
- 200g dark chocolate, roughly chopped
- 4 large eggs
- 350g caster sugar
- 100g plain flour
- cocoa powder

- milk chocolate, chopped
- white chocolate, chopped
- créme-filled chocolate sandwich cookies
- sugar-coated chocolates
- icing pens

Method

STEP 1

Heat the oven to 180C/160C fan/gas 4 and line a 24 x 20cm brownie tin with baking parchment. Melt the butter and dark chocolate in a heatproof bowl set over a small pan of just simmering water. Stir until completely smooth, then leave to cool for 10 mins.

STEP 2

Beat the eggs and sugar with an electric whisk until thick and pale – the mixture should double in volume and leave a trail when the beaters are lifted. Pour the cooled dark chocolate mixture around the edge of the bowl. Sift over the flour and cocoa, add the milk chocolate, and gently fold everything together with a spatula or large metal spoon. Pour into the prepared tin and bake for 35-40 mins.

STEP 3

Meanwhile, make the 'eyeballs'. Melt the white chocolate in a heatproof bowl over the pan of just simmering water. Stir until smooth. Dip each cookie into the chocolate to cover one side. Stick a sugar-coated chocolate in the centre of each, then leave to set. When the chocolate is fully dry, pipe a pupil and red veins onto each eyeball using the icing pens.

STEP 4

Remove the traybake from the oven, and immediately push the eyeballs into the surface in even rows – do this gently, so they're just pushed in slightly. Leave to cool completely. Cut into 12 squares.

Fruity sundae

Prep: 10 mins

Serves 1

Ingredients

- 80ml natural yogurt
- 25g strawberries
- 10g mixed berries

Method

STEP 1

Dollop the natural yogurt into an airtight container. Blend or mash the strawberries to a purée and swirl through the yogurt. Top with mixed berries.

RECIPE TIPS

TRY THIS

Add these extras: 1 baby cucumber cut into chunks and 2 tbsp houmous in a small pot.

Lunchbox pasta salad

Prep: 15 mins **Cook:** 11 mins

Serves 4

Ingredients

- 400g pasta
- 4-5 tbsp fresh pesto
- 1 tbsp mayonnaise
- 2 tbsp Greek yogurt
- ½ lemon , juiced

- 200g mixed cooked veg such as peas, green beans, courgette (chop the beans and courgette into pea-sized pieces)
- 100g cherry tomatoes , quartered
- 200g cooked chicken , ham, prawns, hard-boiled egg or cheese

Method

STEP 1

Cook the pasta in boiling water until it is al dente, so about 11 mins, but refer to the pack instructions. Drain and tip into a bowl. Stir in the pesto and leave to cool.

STEP 2

When the pasta is cool, stir through the mayo, yogurt, lemon juice and veg. Spoon into lunchboxes or on to pasta plates and put the cooked chicken or protein of your choice on top. Chill until ready to eat if intended for a packed lunch.

Snowflake biscuits

Prep: 25 mins **Cook:** 20 mins

Makes about 25-30

Ingredients

- 200g unsalted butter , softened
- 200g golden caster sugar
- 1 large egg
- ½ tsp vanilla extract
- 400g plain flour , plus extra

- 500g pack ready-to-roll fondant icing
- honey , for sticking
- 100g royal icing sugar
- silver balls and white sprinkles , to decorate

You will need

- snowflake cookie cutter

Method

STEP 1

Heat oven to 200C/180C fan/gas 6 and line a baking sheet with baking parchment. Put the butter in a bowl and beat it with electric beaters until soft and creamy. Beat in the sugar, then the egg and vanilla, and finally the flour to make a dough. If the dough feels sticky, add a little flour and knead it in. Chill for 20 mins in the fridge.

STEP 2

Roll the dough to about the thickness of a £1 coin on a lightly floured surface. Cut out snowflake shapes using a biscuit cutter, then re-roll the off-cuts and repeat.

STEP 3

Bake for 8-10 mins or until the edges are just beginning to brown. Leave to cool for 5 mins before trying to move them. Cool completely.

STEP 4

Roll out the fondant icing to the thickness of a 50p piece. Use the same cutter to stamp out the icing. If you have smaller cutter you can stamp out holes in the middles of some of them. Brush each biscuit with a tiny amount of honey and press an icing snowflake on top.

STEP 5

Mix the icing sugar with enough water to make a pipeable icing, and spoon it into a piping bag fitted with a straight piping nozzle. Pipe patterns onto the snowflakes and add silver balls and sprinkles as you decorate. Leave to dry completely.

Cranberry & orange hot cross buns

Prep:45 mins **Cook:**22 mins

Makes 16 small buns

Ingredients

For the buns

- zest of 2 oranges and juice of 1
- 100g dried cranberries
- 250ml milk
- 50g unsalted butter , diced
- 1 large egg
- 500g strong white bread flour , plus extra for kneading

- 1 tbsp fast-action dried yeast
- 2 tsp mixed spice
- 100g caster sugar
- a little oil , for greasing
- butter , to serve

For the crosses

- 75g plain flour
- juice 1 orange

- 5 tbsp apricot jam

Method

STEP 1

Put the orange zest in a bowl and set aside. Pour the juice into another bowl, add 75ml boiling water and the dried cranberries, then leave to soak.

STEP 2

Meanwhile, pour the milk into a saucepan, add the butter and heat over a low heat, stirring occasionally, until the butter has just melted. Turn off the heat and beat in the egg by hand.

STEP 3

Mix together the bread flour, yeast, 1 tsp salt, and the mixed spice and sugar in a large bowl. Make a well in the flour and pour in the milk mixture.

STEP 4

Drain the cranberries and add to the bowl with the orange zest, then mix into the dough with a wooden spoon until it comes together enough to handle without getting too sticky.

STEP 5

Tip out onto a floured surface and knead for 5 mins until smooth and elastic – you'll need to keep poking the cranberries into the mix as you go. Grease a bowl with a little oil, then add the dough and cover with cling film. Leave somewhere warm to rise for 1 hr.

STEP 6

Once risen to twice the size, turn out the dough onto a lightly floured surface. Knock it back by kneading for about 1 min – this will get all the large air holes out and give you nice even buns.

STEP 7

Divide the dough into 16 equal pieces, roll into balls and lay on baking sheets lined with parchment. Put a plastic bag over the baking sheets and leave to prove for 1 hr more.

STEP 8

Heat oven to 220C/200C fan/gas 7. Mix together the plain flour and 5 tbsp water in a bowl to a sticky consistency. Spoon into a piping bag with a small opening, or use a 2mm nozzle, and pipe crosses onto each risen bun. Put the buns in the oven for 20-22 mins until brown on top.

STEP 9

While the buns are baking, make the glaze. Pour the orange juice into a saucepan and mix in the jam. Bring to the boil over a low heat, then simmer for 3-5 mins – you'll need to keep an eye on this the whole time and stir it to stop it sticking. Once the buns are cooked, put them on a wire rack and immediately paint with the glaze. Leave to cool, then eat with butter. Will keep for up to 2 days in an airtight container.

Rainbow pancakes

Prep: 10 mins **Cook:** 20 mins

Serves 4

Ingredients

- 200g self raising flour
- 1 tsp baking powder
- 1 tbsp golden caster sugar

- ½ tsp vanilla extract
- 200ml milk
- 3 eggs

- 25g butter , melted, plus extra for frying
- red, yellow, green and blue gel food colouring
- To serve (optional)

- punnet raspberries
- punnet blueberries
- whipped cream or ice cream
- maple syrup

Method

STEP 1

Put all the pancake ingredients, except the dye, in a bowl and mix well with a whisk until smooth. Divide the batter into 5 bowls or disposable cups. Use the food colouring to dye 4 of them a different colour, leaving one plain.

STEP 2

Melt a small knob of butter in a large non-stick frying pan over a medium-low heat. Once foaming put spoonfuls of the pancake batter into the pan and shape into 4-5cm circles with the back of your spoon, you should have enough to make 4 pancakes from each coloured batter. Cook for 2-3 mins then flip over and cook the other side for another minute or until cooked through and ever so slightly golden.

STEP 3

Stack the pancakes so that everyone gets one of each colour. Serve with fresh fruit, cream or ice cream and a drizzle of maple syrup if you like.

RECIPE TIPS

USING GEL COLOURING

Gel food colouring will give you the brightest result but just add a tiny bit at a time as it's strong stuff.

STACK A RAINBOW

To create a full rainbow effect, we stacked our pancakes in the following order (from the bottom): blue, green, plain, yellow, red. You can mix them up however you like though.

Milk chocolate pots with citrus shortbread

Prep:20 mins **Cook:**30 mins

Serves 4

Ingredients

For the chocolate pots

- 200g good-quality milk chocolate , chopped
- 200ml double cream
- 2 large egg yolks , lightly whisked

For the shortbread

- 160g self-raising flour , plus extra for dusting
- zest 1 orange
- 110g butter , cut into cubes
- 60g golden caster sugar , plus extra for sprinkling
- 1 large egg yolk
- 100ml whipping cream

Method

STEP 1

Put the chocolate in a heatproof bowl. Heat the cream in a saucepan until it just boils, then pour it over the chocolate. Stir until smooth, then beat in the egg yolks. Tip the mixture into a jug, then pour into four individual pots and put in the fridge to set for at least 2 hrs.

STEP 2

Meanwhile, put the flour, orange zest and butter in a large bowl and rub together until it resembles fine breadcrumbs. Add the sugar and egg yolk, mix gently and bring the biscuit dough together with your hands. Roll the shortbread out on a lightly floured surface until 1cm thick, then transfer to a baking tray lined with baking parchment. Leave to rest for 10 mins in the fridge.

STEP 3

Heat oven to 160C/140C fan/ gas 3. Bake for 23-25 mins until golden brown, then sprinkle with sugar. While still warm, cut into eight x 2cm biscuits, trimming off any excess, and leave to cool.

STEP 4

When ready to eat, whip the cream to soft peaks, then spoon on top of the chocolate pots. Serve with the shortbreads on the side.

Chocolate chip hot cross buns

Prep:40 mins **Cook:**20 mins

Makes 8

Ingredients

- 400g strong white bread flour , plus extra for dusting
- 7g sachet fast-action dried yeast
- 50g golden caster sugar , plus 1 tsp
- 1 tsp mixed spice
- 1 tsp ground cinnamon
- 250ml warm milk

- 1 medium egg , beaten
- 50g butter , melted, plus extra for greasing
- 100g chocolate chip (milk or dark, whichever you prefer), or currants or raisins
- 50g plain flour

For the glaze (optional)

- 2 tbsp apricot jam

Method

STEP 1

KIDS the writing in bold is for you ADULTS the rest is for you. **Mix the bun ingredients.** Put the strong flour, yeast, caster sugar and 1 tsp salt in a bowl with the spices and mix. Make a well in the centre and pour in the milk, egg and butter. Start mixing with a plastic or wooden spoon and finish with your hands. If the dough is too dry, add warm water, or extra flour if it's wet.

STEP 2

Now stretch the dough – this is called kneading. Knead the dough on a floured surface for 10 mins until it becomes smooth and springy. This will be a bit too much work for children, so get them to start the kneading, then when they get tired, take over.

STEP 3

Leave the dough to rise until doubled in size because of the yeast. Transfer to a clean, lightly greased bowl and cover loosely with a clean, damp tea towel. Leave in a warm place to rise until roughly doubled in size – this will take about 1 hr depending on how warm the room is.

STEP 4

Add the chocolate chips and do some division. Tip the dough onto a lightly floured surface and flatten. Scatter over the chocolate chips (or dried fruit), and knead the dough a few more times.

Divide it into 8 even portions – halve the dough, then halve each portion twice more, and explain the maths.

STEP 5

Roll the dough into buns. Roll each portion into a smooth round and place on a greased baking sheet in 2 rows of 4, leaving some room between each bun for it to rise. Cover with a tea towel again and leave in a warm place to prove for 20 mins, until almost doubled in size again or just touching.

STEP 6

Make the crosses on the buns and bake them. Heat oven to 200C/180C fan/gas 6. Mix the plain flour with 1 tsp sugar and 4-5 tbsp water to give you a thick paste. Spoon into a piping bag and pipe white lines on the buns to make crosses. Bake for 20 mins until they are light brown.

STEP 7

Brush them with jam if you want them to be nice and shiny. If you want to enjoy the buns untoasted, gently heat the jam in a pan or the microwave, and brush over the buns using a pastry brush. If you are going to toast them, then don't glaze them as the jam will burn.

Magical reindeer cake

Prep: 2 hrs and 15 mins **Cook:** 1 hr

Serves 16 - 22

Ingredients

- 200g salted butter , softened, plus more for the tin
- 200g plain chocolate , chopped
- 240g light muscovado sugar
- 3 medium eggs and 3 medium egg yolks, beaten together

- 2 tsp vanilla bean paste
- 150g full-fat soured cream
- 180g self-raising flour
- 40g cocoa powder
- 1 tsp baking powder

For the chocolate ganache

- 200g dark chocolate
- 100g salted butter

- 50g double cream

For the buttercream

- 200g unsalted butter , very soft

- 2 tsp vanilla bean paste

- 400g unrefined Billington's icing sugar , sifted (this is a pale biscuit colour, not white)

For the antlers

- 200g light muscovado sugar
- 200g butter , softened
- 1 tsp vanilla bean paste
- 1 large egg
- 375g plain flour
- 2 tsp ground ginger
- 2 tsp cinnamon
- large pinch mixed spice

To decorate

- Brown, black, red, green and white ready-to-roll fondant icing

Method

STEP 1

Butter and line 3 x 15 or 16cm round tins (alternatively do the baking in batches if you only have one tin). Heat the oven to 170C/150C fan/gas 3.

STEP 2

Gently melt the chocolate, butter and sugar together in a large microwave-safe bowl on medium heat for a minute at a time, stirring until melted or, set a bowl over a pan of simmering water. Leave to cool a little.

STEP 3

Beat together the eggs with the vanilla and soured cream in a bowl. Sift the flour, cocoa and baking powder into another bowl and whisk to distribute. Stir the egg mix into the cooled melted chocolate, then fold in the flour mix and fold through until all the powder has disappeared.

STEP 4

Spoon a third of the mixture into each tin (if you weigh the tins, you can get it perfectly even and your cakes will cook at the same rate and to the same height). Level off each thin layer with the back of a spoon.

STEP 5

Bake until just cooked, so when a skewer poked into the centre of the sponge layer comes out with a few crumbs and the cakes are shrinking away from the tin a bit. This will take about 25-30 mins, but check after 20 to be safe as all ovens vary. Remove and cool in the tins on a wire rack, or on top of cold oven hob rings.

STEP 6

Meanwhile, to make the ganache, microwave all the ingredients together in 30 sec bursts until they have all melted, stirring at each interval. Or melt everything together in a bowl set over a pan of simmering water. Cool to room temperature before adding to the buttercream.

STEP 7

To make the buttercream, beat the butter and vanilla paste until pale and creamy. Gradually add the icing sugar, beating well between each addition. (Using unrefined sugar will give the buttercream a natural caramel flavour.) Beat in the cooled ganache.

STEP 8

To make the antlers, combine the sugar and butter with the vanilla paste until amalgamated but not creamed. Add the egg and combine. Mix the flour with the spices then tip that in and mix to form a dough. Wrap in cling film and chill in the fridge to firm up for 20 minutes. Roll out on a floured surface to a 5/6mm thickness. Lay the template on the dough and cut around it using a small sharp knife – make two sets in case of breakages (any additional dough can be saved). Push the lolly sticks up into the bottom of the antlers and bake for around 15-20 mins until cooked through and golden. Allow to cool.

STEP 9

Make the ears by pulling a little of the brown fondant icing off the block and kneading it with white fondant icing to make a pale brown. Roll the rest of the dark brown icing out thickly on a surface dusted with icing sugar. Roll the paler icing out thinly. Cut large teardrop shapes from the lighter icing to form the ears (about 6cm in size) and stick the lighter shape on top of the darker icing with a little water. Cut a larger teardrop around the lighter shape. Fold and pinch together at the base, push a cocktail stick into the bottom of each one and set aside to firm up.

STEP 10

Trim the cakes flat if they have a little hump where they have been baked. Put the first layer onto a 16cm cake board and use a little of the chocolate frosting to secure it to the board. Spread frosting over the first layer then add layer two. Sandwich together by pressing gently and add another layer of frosting to this layer. For the last layer, take the sponge and invert it on top of the other two cakes, so that the smooth part of the cake – that was on the bottom of the tin –becomes the top. This will make it nice and neat. Spread a very thin layer of icing over the whole cake to crumb coat it and chill to set for about 30 mins.

STEP 11

Add more buttercream to the cake to make a clean top coat – use a palette knife or side scraper to get a smooth finish (but do save a little of the buttercream for the final flourish). Mark out the eyes with a cutter so you can see where to add them. Roll little strips of black fondant icing for the eyes and lashes, then stick these onto the cake. Mould the nose with red fondant icing and stick it on with a cocktail stick, pushing one end into the nose and the other into the cake.

STEP 12

For the little collar, roll out about 100g of green fondant icing on a surface dusted with icing sugar and cut a thin strip for the bow that will fit around the base of the cake. Stick the ends together with a little water, then make a bow by folding another thin strip and stick this onto the collar with another dab of water. Scoop the leftover buttercream into a bag with a large star nozzle. Pipe some fluffy reindeer hair on top of the cake, then add the ears and biscuit antlers, pushing them in gently but firmly.

Easy chilli con carne

Prep: 20 mins **Cook:** 1 hr

Serves 4

Ingredients

- 2 tbsp olive oil
- 2 large onions, halved and sliced
- 3 large garlic cloves, chopped
- 2 tbsp mild chilli powder
- 2 tsp ground cumin
- 2 tsp dried oregano
- 1kg pack lean minced beef
- 400g can chopped tomato
- 2 beef stock cubes (we like Just Bouillon)
- 2 large red peppers, deseeded and cut into chunks
- 10 sundried tomatoes
- 3 x 400g cans red kidney beans, drained

Method

STEP 1

Heat oven to 150C/fan 130C/gas 3. Heat the oil, preferably in a large flameproof casserole, and fry the onions for 8 mins. Add the garlic, spices and oregano and cook for 1 min, then gradually add the mince, stirring well until browned. Stir in the tomatoes, add half a can of water, then crumble in the stock and season.

STEP 2

Cover and cook in the oven for 30 mins. Stir in the peppers and sundried tomatoes, then cook for 30 mins more until the peppers are tender. Stir in the beans.

STEP 3

To serve, reheat on the hob until bubbling. Serve with avocado or a big salad with avocado in it, some basmati rice or tortilla chips and a bowl of soured cream.

STEP 4

If you want to use a slow cooker, fry your onions in a pan for 8 mins, then add your garlic, spices and oregano and cook for a minute. Gradually add the mince until it's brown. Tip into your slow cooker with the tomatoes, peppers, sundried tomatoes and beans, crumble in the stock cubes and season to taste. Cook on Low for 8-10 hours, then serve as above.

Reindeer food

Prep: 15 mins **Cook:** 40 mins

Serves 6

Ingredients

- 150g porridge oats
- 150g jumbo oats
- 50g mixed nuts
- 25g pumpkin seeds
- 25g sunflower seeds
- 50g golden caster sugar
- 4 tbsp sunflower oil
- 2 tbsp maple syrup
- ½ tsp ground cinnamon
- ½ tsp mixed spice
- ½ tsp ground ginger
- 100g sultanas
- 100g apricots , chopped
- mixture of sweets (we used silver balls, chocolate beans, jelly sweets and hundreds and thousands)

Method

STEP 1

Heat oven to 140C/120C fan/gas 1. Put all the ingredients (except the apricots, sultanas and sweets) in a large bowl. Stir everything well, then spread out onto two baking trays in an even layer. Put the tray in the oven for 40 mins.

STEP 2

Leave the granola to cool on the tray, then break it up into small chunks and stir in the sultanas and apricots.

STEP 3

Put the granola in a jar ready for breakfast. To make it suitable for magic reindeer, put a few spoonfuls into a small paper bag and mix in some sweets.

STEP 4

Tie with string or a ribbon and add a fun label for Father Christmas to find.

Rainbow fruit skewers

Prep:15 mins

Serves 7

Ingredients

- 7 raspberries
- 7 hulled strawberries
- 7 tangerine segments
- 7 cubes peeled mango
- 7 peeled pineapple chunks

- 7 peeled kiwi fruit chunks
- 7 green grapes
- 7 red grapes
- 14 blueberries

Method

STEP 1

Take 7 wooden skewers and thread the following fruit onto each – 1 raspberry, 1 hulled strawberry, 1 tangerine segment, 1 cube of peeled mango, 1 chunk of peeled pineapple, 1 chunk of peeled kiwi, 1 green and 1 red grape, and finish off with 2 blueberries. Arrange in a rainbow shape and let everyone help themselves.

Mini top-your-own pizzas

Prep:1 hr and 25 mins **Cook:**20 mins

Makes 6

Ingredients

For the pizza base

- 300g strong white bread flour , plus extra for kneading
- 1 tbsp fast-action dried yeast

- 1 tsp caster sugar
- 1 tbsp olive oil , plus a little extra for greasing the bowl

For the pizza sauce

- 150ml passata

- small pack basil , leaves picked and finely chopped

- 1 tsp mixed herbs

For the toppings

- choose your favourites (we used black olives , yellow peppers, salami and grated cheddar)

- 200g ball mozzarella , torn into small pieces

Method

STEP 1

Put the flour in a large bowl. Add a little salt to one side of the bowl and the yeast to the other side. Sprinkle over the sugar, together with a spoon, and add the oil and 190ml warm water. Combine with a spoon until all the flour comes away from the sides of the bowl, then tip onto a floured surface. Knead for 5-10 mins or until smooth and elastic. Lightly oil a clean bowl, add the dough, cover with cling film and leave to rise for 1 hr.

STEP 2

Meanwhile, make the sauce. Pour the passata into a saucepan, add the basil and mixed herbs, then season and bring to the boil over a low heat. Simmer gently for 5 mins, then set aside to cool. Chop the toppings.

STEP 3

Once the dough has risen, tip it out, knock out the air and divide into 6 equal parts. Heat oven to 240C/220C fan/gas 9 and place 2 large baking sheets in the oven.

STEP 4

Roll out the dough on a lightly floured surface into a circle around 15cm in diameter. Pick up the circle of dough and toss about a metre up, spinning it in the air. Catch it on the back of your hand, so your fingers don't poke through the dough. Do this at least 3 times to achieve a thin central base and a thicker outside crust. Alternatively, you could carry on rolling, but it's not as much fun!

STEP 5

Lay the bases onto baking parchment (2 bases on 1 piece of parchment) and carefully slide each pair inside a plastic bag 'tent' for 15 mins to prove again.

STEP 6

After the second rise, spread the sauce over the bases and add the and mozzarella. Take the baking sheets out the oven and quickly slide the pizzas (still on their baking parchment) on top. You can cook 2-3 pizzas per tray. Return to the oven and bake for 12 mins. Take out, slice and eat.

Baked camembert kit

Prep:10 mins **Cook:**10 mins

Serves 2

Ingredients

- 100g sultana
- 5 tbsp Calvados , PX Sherry, rum or brandy

- 1 boxed camembert

To complete the kit

- small jar , string or ribbon and a label

Method

STEP 1

Heat sultanas and alcohol together until just simmering, then turn off the heat and cool completely. Spoon into a small jar and seal. Put the jar on top of the cheese and tie together with string or ribbon.

STEP 2

Keep in the fridge for up to a week until you are ready to give them away, then add a label with these instructions: 'Heat oven to 200C/fan 180C/gas 6. Unwrap the camembert, take off the wax wrapper and any other packaging. Put it back in the box but leave the lid off. Cook for 10 mins or until the centre of the cheese feels very soft. Cut a slashed cross in the centre of the cheese then tip in and over as many of the sultanas as you like. Serve with chunks of crusty bread.'

Caramel & coffee ice cream sandwich

Prep:5 mins

Serves 2

Ingredients

- 1 tbsp chocolate-coated coffee beans , roughly chopped

- 2 scoops coffee ice cream , softened
- 4 caramel wafers

Method

STEP 1

Mix the chocolate coffee beans into the softened ice cream until combined, then transfer to a small loaf tin and freeze for a few hours or until solid.

STEP 2

Use cookie cutters to cut the ice cream to the same size as the waffles, then sandwich between two waffles.

Puff pastry pizzas

Prep:20 mins **Cook:**25 mins

Serves 4 (or 3 adults and 2 children

Ingredients

- 320g sheet ready-rolled light puff pastry
- 6 tbsp tomato purée
- 1 tbsp tomato ketchup

- 1 tsp dried oregano
- 75g mozzarella or cheddar

For the topping

- sweetcorn , olives, peppers, red onion, cherry tomatoes, spinach, basil

Method

STEP 1

Heat the oven to 200C/180C fan/gas 6. Unroll the pastry, cut into six squares and arrange over two baking trays lined with baking parchment. Use a cutlery knife to score a 1cm border around the edge of each pastry square. Bake for 15 mins, until puffed up but not cooked through.

STEP 2

While the pastry cooks, make the sauce and prepare your toppings. Mix the tomato purée, tomato ketchup, oregano and 1 tbsp water. Grate the cheese and chop any veg or herbs you want to put on top into small pieces. Set aside.

STEP 3

Remove the pastry from the oven and squash down the middles with the back of a spoon. Divide the sauce between the pastry squares and spread it out to the puffed-up edges. Sprinkle with the cheese, then add your toppings. Bake for another 5-8 mins and serve.

Chewy cranberry choc-nut cookie kit

Total time 15 mins

Ready in 15 mins

Makes 1 gift jar

Ingredients

- 1 large (1 litre approx) jar - Kilner or with a good screw lid
- 100g caster sugar
- 100g light muscovado sugar
- 250g self-raising flour
- 85g macadamia nut , roughly chopped
- 85g dried cranberry
- 100g white chocolate chip , buttons, or roughly chopped chunks

Method

STEP 1

Clean the jar and dry well. Layer in the ingredients, starting with the caster sugar, followed by the muscovado, flour, nuts, cranberries and finally finishing with the white chocolate. Close the jar, then add a label with baking instructions, plus a ribbon or pretty cover if you like.

RECIPE TIPS

ON THE LABEL

Add the following instructions to your label: Beat 200g soft butter with 1 large egg, then tip in the contents of the jar. Mix together with a wooden spoon. Space about 25 blobs of dough well apart on baking sheets and cook for 12-14 minutes at 180C/160C fan/gas 4.

Eyeball snot-tail

Prep: 25 mins

Serves 10 - 15

Ingredients

- 135g pack lime jelly
- 700ml apple & pear juice (we used Copella)
- 300ml lemonade
- 425g can lychees in syrup
- 10-15 cocktail cherries from a jar
- 10-15 raisins

You will need

- 10-15 cocktail sticks

Method

STEP 1

Make the jelly following pack instructions and chill until set. Combine the apple & pear juice with the lemonade in a large jug and chill in the fridge.

STEP 2

To make the eyeballs, drain the lychees and poke a hole in each cherry with one of the cocktail sticks. Put the cherry inside the lychee, then push the raisin into the cherry. Press the eyeball onto the end of a cocktail stick and set aside until serving.

STEP 3

When the jelly has set, use a whisk to break it up into small chunks. Spoon into the cocktail glasses and top up with the apple juice mixture. Put an eyeball into each glass before serving.

Gravadlax kit

Ingredients

- 1 orange
- 1 dill plant
- small pot of black peppercorns
- 125g box of sea salt
- 500g bag of demerara sugar
- small pot of coriander seeds
- small pot of caraway seeds
- a fishmonger gift voucher (to buy a 500g boneless piece of salmon)
- pestle and mortar (optional)

Method

STEP 1

To use the kit: Write the following instructions on the gift tag:
To make the cure for your gravadlax, zest the orange and roughly chop a large bunch of dill. Using a pestle and mortar, grind 1 /2 tbsp peppercorns, then stir in 50g sea salt, 75g sugar, 1 tsp each coriander seeds and caraway seeds, and the zest.

STEP 2

Put half the dill on a large piece of cling film and place your salmon on top. Cover with all the cure and the remaining dill, then wrap tightly. Place in a dish with something heavy on top to weigh it down.

STEP 3

Leave to cure for 24-48 hrs, turning the salmon once, then rinse well and pat dry before serving. Will keep in the fridge for up to three days.

Satay chicken & mango wraps

Prep:15 mins **Cook:**15 mins

Serves 4

Ingredients

- 5 tbsp smooth peanut butter
- 160ml can coconut cream
- 1 tbsp soy sauce
- 2 tbsp mango chutney
- zest 1 lime , plus wedges to serve

- 4 skinless chicken breasts , cut into chunky pieces
- 300g pack chopped mango
- 2 carrots , grated or julienned
- handful coriander leaves (optional)
- 4 wraps , warmed

Method

STEP 1

In a large bowl, mix the peanut butter, coconut cream, soy, mango chutney and lime zest. Spoon half into a serving bowl and set aside. Add the chicken pieces to the large bowl and toss everything well to coat. Can be left to marinate in the fridge for up to 24 hrs.

STEP 2

Thread the chicken onto skewers (you should make 4-6), alternating the chunks with pieces of mango. Place on a baking tray lined with foil. Heat the grill to high and cook the skewers for 5 mins each side until the chicken is cooked through and starting to char on the edges. Serve in warm wraps with bowls of carrot, coriander, extra satay sauce and lime wedges for squeezing over.

RECIPE TIPS

IF YOUR KIDS DON'T LIKE SAUCE...

In general, lots of children don't like food to be covered in sauce, so having it in a little bowl on the side is a great way for them to try a little and still enjoy their dinner. Letting children assemble their own dinner gives them the choice of how much of this or how little of that they try.

Christmas tree pops

Prep:1 hr **Cook:**20 mins

Makes 8

Ingredients

- 100g butter at room temperature, plus extra for greasing
- 100g golden caster sugar
- 1 tsp vanilla extract
- 2 medium eggs
- 100g self-raising flour
- 3 tbsp cocoa powder

- 3 tbsp milk
- 300g icing sugar , sifted
- green food colouring
- sprinkles , for decorating (we used sugar snowflakes and mini Smarties)
- 8 lollipops or cake pop sticks, to serve

Method

STEP 1

Heat oven to 180C/160C fan/gas 4. Grease a 20cm round cake tin and line the base with a circle of baking parchment.

STEP 2

Put the butter in a big mixing bowl with the sugar and vanilla extract, and mix until it looks creamy. Crack in the eggs, one at a time, mixing after each one. Sift the flour and cocoa together, add to the bowl with the milk and stir everything together until smooth. Spoon into the cake tin and use the back of a wooden spoon to spread the top to make it as flat as you can. Bake for 20 mins until a skewer poked into the centre comes out clean, with just cake crumbs stuck to it, not wet batter. Leave the cake to cool completely in the tin on a wire rack.

STEP 3

Remove the cake from the tin and use a serrated knife to cut it into 8 wedges. Turn each one so that the round, outside edge is facing you, and push a lollipop or cake pop stick through the middle of the outside edge. Remember to leave enough of the stick poking out for you to hold.

STEP 4

Mix the food colouring and icing sugar with enough water to make an icing that is a bit runny, but still quite stiff. Try drizzling a bit on a spare piece of paper; you want it to stay in strips, not run all over the place.

STEP 5

Spoon some icing over each cake wedge (you can cover it completely or drizzle lines across them in a tree shape). Decorate with sugar snowflakes and mini Smarties, then lift onto a wire rack and leave to set completely (this will take a few hours). Iced cakes will keep in the tin for up to 2 days. The un-iced cake can be frozen for up to 6 months. Defrost completely before cutting and decorating.

Chocolate fudge Easter cakes

Cook: 15 mins

16

Ingredients

Chocolate fudge easter cakes

- 140g soft butter
- 140g golden caster sugar
- 3 medium eggs

- 100g self-raising flour
- 25g cocoa , sifted

For the frosting

- 85g milk chocolate , broken
- 85g soft butter
- 140g icing sugar , sifted

- 235g/1.5oz packs white chocolate maltesers, mini foil-wrapped chocolate eggs We use Fairtrade Divine milk chocolate eggs from Waitrose

Method

STEP 1

Heat oven to 190C/fan 170C/gas 5 and put 16 gold cases into a fairy-cake tin. Tip all the ingredients for the cake into a mixing bowl and beat for 2 mins with an electric hand-whisk until smooth. Divide between the cases so they are two-thirds filled, then bake for 12-15 mins until risen. Cool on a wire rack.

STEP 2

For the frosting, microwave the chocolate on High for 1 min. Cream the butter and sugar together, then beat in the melted chocolate. Spread on the cakes and decorate with Maltesers and chocolate eggs.

Sweet & sticky wings with classic slaw

Prep: 10 mins **Cook:** 40 mins

Serves 6

Ingredients

- 4 tbsp ketchup
- 4 garlic cloves , crushed
- 3 tbsp soft brown sugar
- 4 tbsp sweet chilli sauce
- 4 tbsp dark soy sauce

- 1kg chicken wings
- 1 small white cabbage , shredded
- 3 large carrots , grated
- 1 large onion , thinly sliced
- 8 tbsp light salad cream or mayonnaise

Method

STEP 1

Heat oven to 200C/180C fan/gas 6. In a large bowl, mix the ketchup, garlic, sugar, half the sweet chilli sauce and the soy sauce with some seasoning. Tip in the wings and toss to combine so that they are all coated. Transfer to a large roasting tray or two smaller ones, in a single layer. Roast for 35-40 mins until cooked through and golden.

STEP 2

Meanwhile, make the slaw. Mix the vegetables with remaining chilli sauce, salad cream or mayo and seasoning. Pile the wings onto a large platter and transfer the slaw to a serving bowl. Let everyone dig in and help themselves.

RECIPE TIPS

INDIAN WINGS

Mix 250g natural yogurt with 4 heaped tbsp tikka paste and seasoning. Add 1kg chicken wings and marinate for 20 mins. Cook at 220C/ 200C fan/gas 7 for 35-40 mins, until lightly charred. Serve with warmed naan.

Easter egg rocky road

Prep:25 mins **Cook:**5 mins

Makes 8-10 bars

Ingredients

- 225g dark chocolate , broken into pieces
- 100g unsalted butter , cubed
- 2 tbsp cocoa powder
- 2 tbsp golden syrup
- 100g rich tea biscuits
- 50g mini marshmallows
- 50g dried cranberries
- 200g chocolate mini eggs

Method

STEP 1

Line a 20 x 30cm traybake tin with 2 sheets of cling film (in a criss-cross pattern). Put the chocolate and butter in a large bowl set over a saucepan of gently simmering water, and melt until smooth and glossy.

STEP 2

Remove from the heat and add the cocoa powder and golden syrup. Mix together unti! fully combined and leave to cool at room temperature for about 15 mins.

STEP 3

Put the biscuits in a freezer bag and use a rolling pin to bash them, leaving some pieces chunkier than others. Stir into the cooled chocolate with the marshmallows, cranberries and 150g of the mini eggs.

STEP 4

Pour the mix into the tin and press down with the back of a spoon until even. Scatter over the remaining mini eggs, pressing them in a little, and leave to set in the fridge for 1 hr.

STEP 5

Remove from the tin and cut into bars to serve. Will keep for up to 1 week in an airtight container.

Icy kir

Prep: 5 mins

Serves 1

Ingredients

- 25ml vodka
- a scoop of blackcurrant or raspberry sorbet
- 100ml prosecco

Method

STEP 1

Pour the vodka into the bottom of a coupe glass. Chill for 30 mins, then top with the blackcurrant or raspberry sorbet and pour the Prosecco around it. Serve immediately.

Family meals: Mild chicken curry

Prep: 10 mins **Cook:** 1 hr and 20 mins

Serves 2 adults, 1 child

Ingredients

- 1-1½ tsp coconut oil (we used Fushi) or sunflower oil
- 1 large onion, finely chopped
- 2 fat garlic cloves, crushed
- 1cm fresh ginger, grated or finely chopped
- 1 tsp ground coriander
- 1 tsp yellow mustard seed
- 1 tsp garam masala
- ½ tsp ground cumin
- 1 x 500g pack chicken pieces (thighs and drumsticks), or thighs
- 1 chicken stock cube
- 1 cinnamon stick
- 250g Greek yogurt, at room temperature
- 2 tbsp sultana
- handful chopped coriander, to serve (optional)

Method

STEP 1

Heat the oil in a heavy-based pan. Fry the onions gently for 5 – 10 mins until soft. Add the garlic, ginger, coriander, mustard seeds, garam masala and cumin and cook for 1 - 2 min allowing the aromas to release.

STEP 2

Add the chicken and cook for 10 mins over a gentle heat, flipping occasionally and making sure the spices don't catch. Pour in around 300 ml boiling water until almost covering. Stir in the stock cube and cinnamon stick. Simmer for around 45 mins - 1 hour with the lid off so there is a small amount of thickened sauce at the bottom of the pan. Remove the cinnamon stick.

STEP 3

Stir in the yogurt and sultanas, heat through gently and serve. Scatter with coriander, if using.

Milkshake ice pops

Prep:10 mins

Makes 4

Ingredients

- 405ml can light condensed milk
- 1 tsp vanilla bean paste
- 1 ripe chopped banana

- 10 strawberries or 3 tbsp chocolate hazelnut spread

Method

STEP 1

Pour the light condensed milk into a food processor and add the vanilla bean paste and chopped banana. Whizz until smooth. Add either the strawberries or chocolate hazelnut spread and whizz again.

STEP 2

Divide the mixture between 4 paper cups, cover with foil, then push a lolly stick through the foil lid of each cup until you hit the base. Freeze for 4 hrs or until solid. Will keep in the freezer for 2 months.

Simple nutty pancakes

Prep:5 mins **Cook:**5 mins

makes 4

Ingredients

- 150g self-raising flour
- ½ tsp baking powder

- 1 large egg
- 150ml milk

- 2 tbsp agave syrup , plus extra to serve
- 50g mixed nuts , chopped
- 2 tbsp rapeseed oil , for frying

Method

STEP 1

Tip the flour and baking powder into a large bowl with a pinch of salt. Make a well in the centre, then add the egg, milk and syrup. Whisk until smooth, then fold in half the nuts.

STEP 2

Heat 1 tbsp oil in a large, non-stick frying pan over a medium-high heat. Spoon two ladles of the mixture into the pan and cook for 1 min each side. Repeat to make two more.

STEP 3

Serve with a drizzle of agave syrup and the remaining nuts for extra crunch.

Breakfast bar

Prep:20 mins **Cook:**25 mins

Makes 12

Ingredients

- 50g mixed dried fruit (a mixture of raisins, sultanas and apricots is nice)
- 50g mixed seed
- 140g oats
- 25g multi-grain hoop cereal
- 100g butter
- 100g light muscovado sugar
- 100g golden syrup

Method

STEP 1

Grease and line a 20cm square cake tin with baking parchment.

STEP 2

Put the dried fruit in a mixing bowl. Add the seeds, oats and cereal, and mix well.

STEP 3

Put the butter, sugar and golden syrup in the saucepan. Cook gently on the hob, stirring with the spatula, until the butter and sugar are melted.

STEP 4

Remove from the heat and pour the dry ingredients into the saucepan. Mix well until all the ingredients are coated with the syrup mix.

STEP 5

Fill the baking tin with the mixture. Use the spatula to press the mix down evenly. Bake at 160C/140C fan/gas 3 for 20 mins, then leave to cool completely before cutting into squares or fingers. Store in an airtight tin for up to 3 days – if they last that long!

Rudolph shortbread

Prep: 35 mins **Cook:** 25 mins

Makes 8 big biscuits

Ingredients

- 200g salted butter , softened
- 2 tsp vanilla extract
- 85g golden caster sugar
- 85g ground rice
- 225g plain flour , plus extra for dusting
- 3 tbsp icing sugar

- 8 red Smarties
- 16 white sweets or white chocolate buttons, for the eyes (we used Waitrose Cooks' Homebaking Meringue pieces)
- black writing icing tube

You will also need

- 8 cellophane bags (15 x 25cm) or 8 x 40cm cellophane squares
- 8 brown pipe cleaners

- labels and string or ribbon
- 22-23cm round plate, cake tin or cardboard template

Method

STEP 1

Put the butter, vanilla and sugar in a big mixing bowl and stir together with a wooden spoon until really smooth. Stir in the ground rice first, then the flour. If it starts to get dry, you might need to use your hands to squish everything together to make a smooth dough.

STEP 2

Put a piece of baking parchment on a baking sheet. Make the dough into a round ball in the middle of the parchment, then use your hands to push it down and flatten it. Get a rolling pin and dust it with some flour so it doesn't stick to the dough. Use the rolling pin to roll the dough out to a big circle.

STEP 3

Get your 22-23cm round plate, cake tin or cardboard template and place on top of the dough when you've rolled it big enough. Use a cutlery knife to trim round the edges to make a neat circle. Use the offcuts to make smaller biscuits or freeze the dough for another time.

STEP 4

Use a knife to mark the giant biscuit into 8 smaller wedge-shaped biscuits – pretend you are cutting a pizza into slices but don't actually cut it. Prick lines from the edge to the centre of the dough. Use the back of a fork to press all around the top of the circle along the edge to make a line pattern (it's going to be hair for your reindeer!)

STEP 5

Cover with cling film and put the tray in the fridge for 30 mins to get cold. Heat oven to 180C/160C fan/gas 4. Cook the chilled shortbread for 25 mins until golden. Cool completely on the tray, then use a sharp knife to follow the lines you made with a fork and cut into 8 wedges.

STEP 6

Mix the icing sugar with 1-2 tsp of water to make a thickish icing. Dunk each Smartie in and use like glue to stick one on the pointy end of each biscuit to make red noses. Dunk in your white sweets or chocolate buttons and stick them 2cm in from the edge at the other end to be eyes. Use the black writing icing tube to add dots to the white eyes, then let all the icing dry and go hard.

STEP 7

Carefully wrap each biscuit in a square of cellophane or put in a cellophane bag. Twist the middle of a pipe cleaner in a loop around the top of the bag or gathered cellophane to enclose the biscuit. Now twist each end of the pipe cleaner so it looks like the reindeer's antlers. Add labels and give to your friends and family, or hang on the tree. Will keep for up to 3 days in a cool, dry place.

Crispy chocolate fridge cake

Prep: 15 mins **Cook:** 5 mins

Easy

Makes 16-20 chunks

Ingredients

- 300g dark chocolate , broken into chunks
- 100g butter , diced
- 140g golden syrup
- 1 tsp vanilla extract
- 200g biscuit , roughly chopped
- 100g sultana
- 85g Rice Krispies
- 100-140g mini eggs (optional)
- 50g white chocolate , melted

Method

STEP 1

Line a 20 x 30cm tin with baking parchment. Melt the chocolate, butter and golden syrup in a bowl set over a pan of simmering water, stirring occasionally, until smooth and glossy. Add the vanilla, biscuits, sultanas and Rice Krispies, and mix well until everything is coated.

STEP 2

Tip the mixture into the tin, then flatten it down with the back of a spoon. Press in some mini eggs, if using, and put in the fridge until set. When hard, drizzle all over with the melted white chocolate and set again before cutting into chunks.

Flowerpot chocolate chip muffins

Prep:10 mins **Cook:**12 mins - 15 mins

Makes 10 mini muffins

Ingredients

- 3 tbsp vegetable oil
- 125g plain flour
- 1 tsp baking powder
- 25g cocoa powder
- 100g golden caster sugar
- 1 large egg
- 100ml milk
- 150g milk chocolate chips
- 25g chocolate cake decorations such as vermicelli sprinkles or chocolate-coated popping candy
- 20 rice paper wafer daisies (these come in packs of 12, so get 2 packs)

You will need

- 10 mini teracotta pots (see tip)

Method

STEP 1

Heat oven to 180C/160C fan/gas 4. Lightly oil the inside of the terracotta pots with a little vegetable oil and place on a baking tray. Place a paper mini muffin case in the bottom of each pot.

STEP 2

Put the flour, baking powder and cocoa in a bowl and stir in the sugar.

STEP 3

Crack the egg into a jug and whisk with the milk and remaining oil. Pour this over the flour and cocoa mixture, and stir in with 50g of the chocolate chips. Be careful not to overmix – you want a loose but still quite lumpy mixture. Spoon into the pots up to three-quarters full. Place in the middle of the oven and bake for 12-15 mins until risen and firm. Transfer to a wire rack (still in the pots) and leave to cool.

STEP 4

Put the rest of the chocolate chips in a small bowl and melt over a small pan of gently simmering water (don't let the water touch the bowl), or put in a microwave-proof bowl and heat on High for 1 min until melted.

STEP 5

Spread the tops of the muffins with the melted chocolate. Sprinkle over the chocolate decorations and add 2 rice paper wafer daisies to each pot to serve. Will keep for 2 days in an airtight container.

Pea hummus

Prep: 10 mins

Serves 4

Ingredients

- 200g cooked peas
- 1 garlic clove , crushed
- 1 tbsp tahini
- squeeze of lemon

- 1 tbsp cooked cannellini beans , from a can
- 2 tbsp olive oil
- strips of pitta bread , to serve
- raw vegetable sticks, to serve

Method

STEP 1

Blitz all the ingredients together using a hand blender or food processor. Add 1-2 tbsp water, then blitz again. Transfer a portion to a pot and add to a lunchbox with pitta bread strips and veg sticks. Keep the rest chilled for up to 3 days.

Flatbreads with brunch-style eggs

Prep: 20 mins **Cook:** 15 mins

Serves 6

Ingredients

- 110g self-raising flour , plus extra for dusting
- 110g atta or plain wholemeal flour

- 3 tbsp rapeseed oil , plus extra for the bowl and frying
- small knob of butter , melted

For the eggs

- 1 tbsp olive oil
- 12 cherry tomatoes , halved
- 4 large eggs

- 25g grated cheddar
- 2 tbsp double cream

Method

STEP 1

Sift the flours and 1 tsp salt into a large bowl. Add 1 tbsp of the oil and 150ml warm water. Bring together into a soft but not too sticky dough (you may need up to 175ml water). If it feels too wet, add some flour. If it's too dry, add water.

STEP 2

Tip onto a floured surface and knead for 4-5 mins, or until smooth. Put the dough in an oiled bowl, cover and leave for 30 mins.

STEP 3

Tip onto a floured surface. Divide into six balls and roll each out into a thin, 18-20cm wide circle using a rolling pin. If you prefer, you can divide again into twelve balls to make smaller flatbreads.

STEP 4

Brush a heavy-based pan with oil and cook one flatbread over a high heat for 1-2 mins on each side, or until golden and starting to puff. Put on a plate and brush with butter. Repeat with the rest of the dough.

STEP 5

Meanwhile, for the eggs, heat the oil in a small non-stick pan and cook the tomatoes briefly until just softened. Season. Crack the eggs into the pan, add the cheese and cream, cover and cook for 2 mins. Remove the lid. Cook until the egg whites are set, then serve from the pan with the flatbreads, making sure the pan has cooled a little first.

Green burgers

Prep:30 mins **Cook:**20 mins

makes 8 (4 for now, 4 for the freezer)

Ingredients

- 2 tbsp olive oil
- 2 onions , finely chopped
- 250g bag spinach
- 5 slices white bread , blitzed into breadcrumbs (or 150g dried breadcrumbs)

- good grating of fresh nutmeg
- 100g mature cheddar , grated
- 40g parmesan , finely grated
- 1-2 large eggs , beaten
- 3 tbsp plain flour

To serve

- 6 crusty bread rolls
- 4 ripe, juicy tomatoes , thickly sliced

- good-quality ketchup or other relish
- sweet potato fries (optional)

Method

STEP 1

Heat half the oil in a frying pan and gently fry the onions for about 10 mins until pale and soft, then leave to cool a little.

STEP 2

Finely chop the spinach in a food processor and tip into a bowl. Add the cooled onion, breadcrumbs, nutmeg, cheddar and Parmesan, and mash together. Add the beaten egg, a little at a time (you may not need all of it), until the mixture holds together. Divide into eight (see tip below) and shape into fat burgers.

STEP 3

Put the flour in a shallow bowl, season well and dip the burgers into the flour to coat. Store in a plastic container between layers of baking parchment. Either chill until ready to cook, or freeze.

STEP 4

Heat the remaining oil in the frying pan and fry for about 5 mins each side until browned all over. Serve in the crusty rolls, with a couple of slices of tomato, ketchup and sweet potato fries on the side, if you like.

RECIPE TIPS

BURGER PATTIES

Flouring your hands helps stop the mixture from sticking to your fingers.

Vegan Thai green curry

Prep: 10 mins **Cook:** 20 mins

Serves 4

Ingredients

- 200g baby potatoes, halved
- 100g green beans, trimmed and halved
- 1 tbsp rapeseed oil
- 1 garlic clove, finely sliced
- 1 tbsp Thai green curry paste (check the label to make sure it's vegetarian/ vegan)
- 400g can light coconut milk
- 1 lime, zest pared in thick strips
- 80g sugar snap peas, halved lengthways
- 150g cherry tomatoes, halved
- 100g firm tofu, chopped into small cubes
- small bunch coriander, chopped
- 200g jasmine rice, cooked following pack instructions

Method

STEP 1

Cook the potatoes in boiling water for 8 mins. Add the green beans and cook for a further 3 mins, then drain.

STEP 2

Heat the oil in a wok or pan, fry the garlic for 1 min, add the curry paste and cook for 1 min, or until it starts to darken a little and smell fragrant. Stir in the coconut milk and bring to a simmer, drop in the lime zest and gently bubble for 5 mins to thicken the sauce a little.

STEP 3

Add the potatoes and beans followed by the sugar snap peas and cook for 1 min before stirring in the cherry tomatoes and tofu.

STEP 4

Cut the lime in half and squeeze the juice into the pan, then stir in the coriander and serve over the rice.

Simple stir-fry

Prep:20 mins **Cook:**10 mins

Serves 4-5

Ingredients

- 500g vegetables such as carrots, baby corn, broccoli, courgettes, red peppers and cabbage or pak choi
- 1 tbsp rapeseed oil
- 1 garlic clove, sliced
- 1cm fresh ginger, grated

- 1½ tbsp reduced salt soy sauce
- 2 tbsp sweet chilli sauce (optional)
- 200g cooked prawns, salmon (flaked) or chicken breast (shredded)
- 200g egg noodles, cooked

Method

STEP 1

Finely chop or slice the vegetables into pieces roughly the same size. Slice the carrots diagonally, slice the baby corn, cut the broccoli into small florets, then slice the stem, and finely slice the peppers, cabbage or pak choi. Heat the oil in a large frying pan or wok, then fry the garlic and ginger for 1 min.

STEP 2

Add the veg and toss to coat. Fry for 2-3 mins, then add the soy sauce and chilli sauce, if using, and mix well. Cook for 2-3 mins more until the veg is tender. Stir in the prawns, salmon or chicken and heat through. Serve over the noodles.

Chocolate Rice Krispie cakes

Prep:15 mins **Cook:**5 mins

Makes 9

Ingredients

- 100g milk chocolate, broken up

- 50g dark chocolate, broken up

- 100g butter
- 4 tbsp golden syrup
- 100g rice pops (we used Rice Krispies)

To decorate

- 50g milk chocolate, melted
- sprinkles, mini marshmallows, nuts, Smarties, dried fruit or white chocolate buttons

Method

STEP 1

Put the chocolate in a heatproof bowl with the butter and golden syrup and gently melt in 10-second bursts in the microwave, or melt it over a pan of simmering water, making sure the bowl doesn't touch the water. Stir until smooth, then take off the heat and stir in the rice pops, coating them gently with the chocolate until they are all completely covered.

STEP 2

Divide the mixture between nine cupcake or 12 fairy cake paper cases – it's easier if you slide these into a muffin tin as it will help them hold their shape. Leave to set. If you want them to set faster, put in the fridge for 1 hr.

STEP 3

Drizzle with a little melted chocolate and decorate with sweets, dried fruit or nuts while they are still wet enough to stick them on. Will keep in an airtight container for five days.

Gingerbread people

Prep: 45 mins **Cook:** 12 mins - 15 mins

Serves 15 - 20

Ingredients

- 175g dark muscovado sugar
- 85g golden syrup
- 100g butter
- 350g plain flour, plus extra for dusting
- 1 tsp bicarbonate of soda
- 1 tbsp ground ginger
- 1 tsp ground cinnamon
- 1 egg, beaten

To decorate

- ready-made writing icing
- chocolate buttons or small sweets (optional)

Method

STEP 1

Melt the sugar, golden syrup and butter in a saucepan, then bubble for 1-2 mins. Leave to cool for about 10 mins.

STEP 2

Tip the flour, bicarbonate of soda and spices into a large bowl. Add the warm syrup mixture and the egg, stir everything together, then gently knead in the bowl until smooth and streak-free. The dough will firm up once cooled. Wrap in cling film and chill for at least 30 mins.

STEP 3

Remove the dough from the fridge, leave at room temperature until softened. Heat the oven to 200C/180C fan/gas 6 and line two baking trays with baking parchment.

STEP 4

Roll out the dough to the thickness of a £1 coin, then cut out gingerbread people with a cutter. Re-roll the excess dough and keep cutting until it's all used up.

STEP 5

Lift the biscuits onto the trays and bake for 10-12 mins, swapping the trays over halfway through cooking. Leave to cool on the trays for 5 mins, then transfer to a wire rack to cool completely. Use the icing to decorate the biscuits as you wish, and stick on chocolate or sweets for buttons. Leave to dry for 1-2 hrs. Will keep for up to three days in an airtight container.

Salmon egg-fried rice

Prep: 10 mins **Cook:** 10 mins

Serves 2 - 3

Ingredients

- thumb-sized piece ginger, grated
- 1-2 garlic cloves, grated
- 2 tbsp low-salt soy sauce
- ½ tbsp rice wine or sherry vinegar
- 2 tbsp vegetable oil
- 1 large carrot, chopped into chunks
- 175g pack baby corn & mangetout or sugar snap peas, chopped
- 2 skinless salmon fillets
- 250g pouch cooked brown basmati rice
- 2 eggs
- hot sauce, to serve

Method

STEP 1

Mix the ginger, garlic, soy and vinegar, and set aside. Heat a large pan or wok and add 1 tbsp oil, the vegetables and salmon. Fry the salmon for 2 mins each side until it begins to turn opaque. Tip in the rice and stir, flaking the fish into large pieces, then move everything to the side of the pan.

STEP 2

Add the remaining oil to the pan, crack in the eggs and stir to roughly scramble them. Once cooked, stir through the rice and pour over the soy marinade. Season and leave to bubble away for a few mins more, so that all the rice is coated in the sauce. Serve in bowls with hot sauce for drizzling.

Three-minute blender banana pancakes

Prep:1 min **Cook:**2 mins

Serves 2

Ingredients

- small knob of butter , for frying
- 1 banana
- 1 egg
- 1 heaped tbsp self-raising flour
- ½ tsp baking powder
- chopped strawberries and banana, to serve (optional)
- maple syrup , to serve (optional)

Method

STEP 1

Melt the butter in a non-stick frying pan over a low-medium heat. Meanwhile, add the banana, egg, flour and baking powder to a blender and blitz for 20 seconds.

STEP 2

Pour three little puddles straight from the blender into the frying pan. Cook for 1 min or until the tops start to bubble, then flip with a fork or a fish slice and cook for 20-30 seconds more. Repeat with the rest of the mixture to make three more pancakes.

STEP 3

Serve the pancakes with chopped strawberries or banana and a splash of maple syrup, if you like.

Butternut squash & chickpea tagine

Prep: 5 mins **Cook:** 25 mins

Serves 2 adults + 2 children

Ingredients

- 1 tbsp oil
- 1 red onion, finely chopped
- 2 garlic cloves, crushed
- 1 tsp grated ginger
- ½ tsp ground cumin
- 1 tsp ground coriander
- 1 tsp cinnamon

- ¼ tsp mild chilli powder
- 500g bag frozen butternut squash chunks
- 2 carrots, cut into small dice
- 1 courgette, cut into small dice
- 2 x 400g cans chopped tomatoes
- 1 x 400g can chickpeas, drained
- cooked couscous or rice, to serve

Method

STEP 1

Heat the oil in a heavy-based pan, then slowly cook the onions for around 10 mins until starting to caramelise. Stir in the garlic, ginger and spices and cook for a further 2 mins. Add the vegetables and canned tomatoes and bring to a simmer. Put the lid on and simmer for around 15 mins or until all the veg are tender. Stir in the chickpeas, heat through and serve with couscous or rice.

Sticky pork lettuce wraps

Prep: 20 mins **Cook:** 10 mins

Serves 4

Ingredients

- 2 tbsp soy sauce
- 2 tbsp honey
- 2 tbsp brown sugar
- pinch cinnamon
- pinch five-spice powder
- 4 thin-cut pork loin steaks
- 1 carrot , sliced into matchsticks

- 1 lime , juiced
- pinch golden caster sugar
- 1 tbsp rapeseed oil
- ½ cucumber , cut into matchsticks
- 16 soft lettuce leaves (we used Butterhead lettuce)
- sweet chilli sauce , to serve

Method

STEP 1

Make the marinade by mixing the soy with the honey, brown sugar, spices and 1 tbsp water. Put the pork in a shallow bowl, pour the marinade over, turning to make sure the steaks are well coated, then leave to marinate for at least 30 mins.

STEP 2

Mix the carrot with the lime juice and caster sugar. Brush a piece of foil with oil and line the grill pan. Grill the pork steaks (or griddle if you prefer) for 4 mins each side. Keep an eye on them in case the sugar in the marinade starts to blacken. When cooked, cut the pork into strips.

STEP 3

Put the lettuce leaves out on a board and divide the pork between them. Add some carrot and cucumber, then fold in both ends of the lettuce leaf and roll up from one side to contain the filling. Serve with sweet chilli sauce, if you like.

Watermelon lemonade

Prep: 35 mins

Serves 8

Ingredients

- 1 large or 2 small watermelons
- 250ml lemon juice (from a bottle or squeeze your own)
- 100g golden caster sugar
- 1l bottle soda water
- 1 lime , cut into slices
- small handful mint
- crushed ice

Method

STEP 1

Cut the top off the watermelon and hollow it out using a large spoon, fishing out any pips along the way. Mash the flesh through a sieve into a bowl. Put the flesh in a blender (or use a tall jug and hand blender) with the lemon juice and sugar, whizz to a purée, then stir in the soda.

STEP 2

Heap some ice into the hollowed-out watermelon and fill it with the lemonade mixture. Serve the rest in a jug with the lime slices and mint. Have a bowl of extra crushed ice on the side so people can help themselves.

HOW TO MAKE WATERMELON COCKTAILS

A dash of booze will turn this summer soft drink into a refreshing cocktail. Add one shot of tequila and some ice to a tall glass and top with the watermelon lemonade. White rum would work equally well.

One-pan egg & veg brunch

Prep:5 mins **Cook:**25 mins

Serves 2 adults + 2 children

Ingredients

- 300g baby new potatoes , halved
- ½ tbsp rapeseed oil
- 1 knob of butter
- 1 courgette , cut into small chunks
- 1 yellow pepper , cut into small chunks
- 1 red pepper , cut into small chunks

- 2 spring onions , finely sliced
- 1 garlic clove , crushed
- 1 sprig thyme , leaves picked
- 4 eggs
- toast , to serve

Method

STEP 1

Boil the new potatoes for 8 mins, then drain.

STEP 2

Heat the oil and butter in a large non-stick frying pan, then add the courgette, peppers, potatoes and a little salt and pepper. Cook for 10 mins, stirring from time to time until everything is starting to brown. Add the spring onions, garlic and thyme and cook for 2 mins more.

STEP 3

Make four spaces in the pan and crack in the eggs. Cover with foil or a lid and cook for around 4 mins, or until the eggs are cooked (with the yolks soft for dipping into). Sprinkle with more thyme leaves and ground black pepper if you like. Serve with toast.

Quick banana ice cream sandwiches

Prep:15 mins **Cook:**12 mins

Serves 4

Ingredients

- 200g peanut butter (crunchy or smooth is fine)
- 175g golden caster sugar

For the ice cream

- 3 bananas , peeled, chopped and frozen in advance

- 75g dark chocolate , chopped into chunks
- 1 large egg

- 2 tbsp double cream
- 1 tsp vanilla essence

Method

STEP 1

Heat oven to 180C/fan 160C/gas 4 and line two large baking sheets with baking parchment. Put the peanut butter, sugar, ¼ tsp fine table salt and chocolate chunks in a bowl and mix well with a wooden spoon. Crack in the egg and mix again until the mixture clumps together and forms a dough.

STEP 2

Break off chunks of dough (about the size of a cherry tomato) and arrange them, spaced apart, on the sheets. Press the cookies down with the back of a fork to squash them a little. (The cookies can be frozen for up to two months – to cook from frozen, add an extra 1-2 mins to the cooking time.) Bake for about 12 mins until golden around the edges and paler in the centre. Leave to cool on the trays for 5 mins.

STEP 3

Meanwhile, put the bananas, cream and vanilla in a food processor and blend until they make a thick ice cream. Scoop into balls with an ice cream scoop, and sandwich between the cookies. Serve immediately.

RECIPE TIPS

BANANAS

Make sure the bananas are frozen solid before blitzing. If the ice cream consistency is too soft to scoop, put it back in the freezer for 10 mins.

Elf & Santa cupcakes

Prep: 40 mins **Cook:** 18 mins

Serves 16

Ingredients

For the cupcakes

- 175g butter , softened
- 175g golden caster sugar
- 3 eggs
- 200g self-raising flour

- 1 orange , zested and 1/2 juiced
- pinch of cinnamon
- 1 tsp vanilla extract

For the icing

- 100g unsalted butter , softened
- 2 tsp vanilla extract

- 250g icing sugar , sifted

For the legs

- fondant icing sugar
- candy canes
- strawberry pencil sweets

- black, green and white fondant icing
- gold and silver balls

You will need

- our template for

Method

STEP 1

Heat the oven to 190C/170C fan/gas 5. Line bun tins with paper cake cases. Put all the ingredients for the cupcakes in a large bowl using 4 tbsp of the orange juice, then beat together for 1-2 mins until smooth.

STEP 2

Spoon the cake mix into the cases, so they are three-quarters full. Bake for 15-18 mins or until golden and firm to the touch. Cool in the tin for 5 mins, then transfer to a wire rack.

STEP 3

For the icing, beat the butter, vanilla and icing sugar until pale and creamy, adding 1-2 tbsp warm water to loosen, if needed. Ice the cakes with a palette knife or use a piping bag to create swirls deep enough to hold the Santa and elf legs.

STEP 4

For the legs, make a batch of fondant icing following the pack instructions. Cut the candy canes and pencil sweets into 4cm lengths. Use green fondant icing to mould elf boots around the candy cane legs and black fondant icing to mould Santa boots around the strawberry pencil legs. Add some white fondant around the top of Santa boots. Use the made-up fondant icing to stick a silver or gold ball onto each toe of the elf boots. Let the boots dry completely. Use our chimney template, to make paper sleeves to wrap around the cupcake cases. Push the legs into the cupcakes just before serving.

Simple iced biscuits

Prep:30 mins **Cook:**20 mins

Makes 40-45

Ingredients

- 200g unsalted butter , softened
- 200g golden caster sugar
- 1 large egg

- ½ tsp vanilla extract or 1 lemon, zested
- 400g plain flour , plus extra for dusting

To decorate

- 8-12 x 19g coloured icing pens , or fondant icing sugar mixed with a little water and food colouring

Method

STEP 1

Heat oven to 200C/180C fan/gas 6. Put the butter in a bowl and beat it using an electric whisk until soft and creamy. Beat in the sugar, then the egg and vanilla or lemon, and finally the flour to make a dough. If the dough feels a bit sticky, add a little more flour and knead it in.

STEP 2

Cut the dough into six pieces and roll out one at a time to about 5mm thickness on a floured surface. The easiest way to do this is to roll the mixture out on a baking mat. Cut out letter and number shapes (we used 7 x 4cm cutters) and peel away the leftover dough at the edges. Re-roll any off-cuts and repeat.

STEP 3

Transfer the whole mat or the individual biscuits to two baking sheets (transfer them to baking parchment if not using a mat) and bake for 7-10 mins or until the edges are just brown. Leave to cool completely and repeat with the rest of the dough. You should be able to fit about 12 on each sheet. If you are using two sheets, then the one underneath will take a minute longer.

STEP 4

Ice the biscuits using the pens to make stripes or dots, or colour in the whole biscuit if you like. They will keep for five days in an airtight container.

Giant cookie

Prep: 15 mins **Cook:** 20 mins

Serves 6 - 8

Ingredients

- 200g butter at room temperature, plus extra for the pan
- 250g light brown sugar
- 2 egg yolks
- ½ tsp vanilla extract
- 275g plain flour
- 1 tsp baking powder
- 150g chocolate chips
- 100g other cookie fillings, such as pretzels, chopped nuts, pieces of fudge or toffee, marshmallows
- vanilla ice cream, to serve (optional)

Method

STEP 1

Heat oven to 180C/160C fan/gas 4. Tip the butter and sugar into a large mixing bowl, beat until combined, then stir in the yolks and vanilla. Tip in the flour, baking powder, chocolate chips, a pinch of sea salt and any other fillings you want to add. Mix until a crumbly dough forms.

STEP 2

Lightly butter a 25cm ovenproof frying pan. Spoon in and flatten the cookie mixture. For a gooey dessert, bake for 20 mins, leave to rest for 5 mins, then scoop straight from the pan and serve with ice cream, if you like. For a firmer cookie you can cut, bake for 30 mins, then leave to cool completely before cutting into wedges.

Chicken, sweet potato & coconut curry

Total time35 mins

Ready in 25-35 minutes

Serves 2 adults and 2 children

Ingredients

- 1 tbsp sunflower oil
- 2 tsp mild curry paste
- 2 large boneless, skinless chicken breasts, cut into bite-size pieces
- 2 medium-sized sweet potatoes, peeled and cut into bite-size pieces

- 4 tbsp red split lentils
- 300ml chicken stock
- 400ml can coconut milk
- 175g frozen peas

Method

STEP 1

Heat the oil in a deep frying pan or wok, stir in the curry paste and fry for 1 minute. Add the chicken, sweet potatoes and lentils and stir to coat in the paste, then pour in the stock and coconut milk. Bring to the boil, then simmer for 15 minutes.

STEP 2

Tip in the peas, bring back to the boil and simmer for a further 4-5 minutes. Season to taste before serving.

Christmas truffles

Prep:30 mins **Cook:**5 mins

plus 7 hrs chilling

Makes 35

Ingredients

- 150g dark chocolate, chopped
- 150g milk chocolate, chopped
- 150ml double cream

- 50g unsalted butter
- cocoa powder, sprinkles, lustre powder, icing sugar, chopped nuts, for coating

- flavourless oil (such as sunflower), for shaping

Method

STEP 1

Put the dark and milk chocolate in a bowl, then put the cream and butter in a pan and bring to a simmer. Pour the hot cream over the chocolate and stir until it melts. Leave to cool, then chill in the fridge for 7 hrs.

STEP 2

Put the coatings into separate bowls. To shape the truffles, lightly rub your hands with flavourless oil and roll teaspoons of the truffle mix between your palms – this can get messy!

STEP 3

Gently roll the truffles in the bowl until evenly coated, then put in a box and chill. Store in the fridge in an airtight container for three days, or freeze for up to a month. Defrost in the fridge overnight.

RECIPE TIPS

ROLL THE TRUFFLES WITH COLD HANDS

It's less messy if you have cold hands – just rinse them under a cold tap first!

Easy classic lasagne

Prep: 15 mins **Cook:** 1 hr

Serves 4 - 6

Ingredients

- 1 tbsp olive oil
- 2 rashers smoked streaky bacon
- 1 onion , finely chopped
- 1 celery stick, finely chopped
- 1 medium carrot , grated
- 2 garlic cloves , finely chopped
- 500g beef mince
- 1 tbsp tomato purée
- 2 x 400g cans chopped tomatoes
- 1 tbsp clear honey
- 500g pack fresh egg lasagne sheets
- 400ml crème fraîche
- 125g ball mozzarella , roughly torn
- 50g freshly grated parmesan
- large handful basil leaves , torn (optional)

Method

STEP 1

Heat the oil in a large saucepan. Use kitchen scissors to snip the bacon into small pieces, or use a sharp knife to chop it on a chopping board. Add the bacon to the pan and cook for just a few mins until starting to turn golden. Add the onion, celery and carrot, and cook over a medium heat for 5 mins, stirring occasionally, until softened.

STEP 2

Add the garlic and cook for 1 min, then tip in the mince and cook, stirring and breaking it up with a wooden spoon, for about 6 mins until browned all over.

STEP 3

Stir in the tomato purée and cook for 1 min, mixing in well with the beef and vegetables. Tip in the chopped tomatoes. Fill each can half full with water to rinse out any tomatoes left in the can, and add to the pan. Add the honey and season to taste. Simmer for 20 mins.

STEP 4

Heat oven to 200C/180C fan/gas 6. To assemble the lasagne, ladle a little of the ragu sauce into the bottom of the roasting tin or casserole dish, spreading the sauce all over the base. Place 2 sheets of lasagne on top of the sauce overlapping to make it fit, then repeat with more sauce and another layer of pasta. Repeat with a further 2 layers of sauce and pasta, finishing with a layer of pasta.

STEP 5

Put the crème fraîche in a bowl and mix with 2 tbsp water to loosen it and make a smooth pourable sauce. Pour this over the top of the pasta, then top with the mozzarella. Sprinkle Parmesan over the top and bake for 25–30 mins until golden and bubbling. Serve scattered with basil, if you like.

Creamy lentil & veggie curry

Prep:10 mins **Cook:**30 mins

Serves 4

Ingredients

- 2 tbsp rapeseed oil
- 1 onion , chopped
- 1 tsp ground cumin
- 1 tbsp Madras curry powder
- 200g red lentils

- 2 sweet potatoes , peeled and cut into cubes
- 1l veg stock
- 400g canned peeled cherry tomatoes

- 200g green beans , trimmed and cut into short lengths
- 4 tbsp Greek yogurt plus more for the top if you like
- ½ small bunch coriander , chopped
- ¼ cucumber , finely chopped (optional)
- naan bread and rice to serve

Method

STEP 1

Heat the oil in a large pan and fry the onion for a few mins until softened. Add the spices and cook for 1 min, then stir in the lentils, sweet potatoes, stock and the cherry tomatoes.

STEP 2

Bring to the boil, then cover and simmer for 20 mins until the lentils and sweet potatoes are tender. Add the beans and cook for 2 mins then stir in the yogurt and some seasoning. Sprinkle over the coriander and chopped cucumber if using and serve with naan bread and rice.

RECIPE TIPS

HOW TO MAKE CURRIED LENTIL SOUP

You can add more stock to this and blend it to make a soup if you like.

Pastry snakes

Prep:27 mins **Cook:**14 mins

Serves 20

Ingredients

- 320g pack ready-rolled puff pastry
- 50g grated parmesan or vegetarian alternative
- flour , for dusting
- 1 egg , beaten
- poppy seeds , nigella seeds, sesame seeds or celery seeds, to decorate
- black or green peppercorns

Method

STEP 1

Heat the oven to 220C/200C fan/ gas 7. Unroll the pastry and top with a couple of handfuls of parmesan, then fold in half. On a lightly floured surface, roll the pastry out to a thickness of 2mm. Cut into 1cm strips, then twist each strip several times to form a snake.

STEP 2

Lay out the snakes on a baking sheet, then brush each one with egg and sprinkle with more cheese. To decorate, scatter over the seeds. Flatten one end of each snake and press in two peppercorns for eyes. Bake for 12-14 mins, or until golden. Leave to cool. Will keep for two days in an airtight container.

Omelette in a bun

Prep:5 mins **Cook:**20 mins

Serves 3

Ingredients

- 1 tbsp olive oil
- 1 medium potato , cut into cubes
- 1 spring onion , finely sliced
- handful baby spinach leaves

- 4 eggs
- 9 small cherry tomatoes , halved
- handful crumbled feta or grated cheddar
- 3 rolls

Method

STEP 1

Heat the oil in a small non-stick frying pan and fry the potato over a low heat until it is browned and tender, this will probably take about 10 mins in all. Add the spring onion and fry for a minute then stir in the spinach.

STEP 2

Whisk the eggs lightly with a little seasoning and then pour them into the pan and cook until set on the base. Dot on the tomatoes, sprinkle on the cheese and grill until the top browns. Cool a little then slide out of the pan and cut into thirds.

STEP 3

Split the rolls and stuff them with a piece of omelette, sandwich together and halve.

Jammy star cookies

Prep: 1 hr **Cook:** 15 mins - 30 mins

Makes 15-20

Ingredients

- 175g cold unsalted butter, cubed
- 250g plain flour, plus extra for dusting
- 100g golden icing sugar

- 1 tsp vanilla extract
- 1 egg yolk

For the filling

- 50g unsalted butter, softened
- 160g icing sugar

- 120g seedless raspberry or strawberry jam

You will need

- 2 star cutter, around 6cm and 3cm

Method

STEP 1

Blitz the butter, flour and a pinch of salt in a food processor until the mixture resembles fine breadcrumbs. Add the sugar and blitz again. Add the vanilla and egg yolk and blend until balls of dough have formed. Tip the dough onto a work surface and knead briefly to make a smooth ball. Cut into two equal pieces, pat them into discs, then wrap and chill for at least 30 mins. Line two baking sheets with baking parchment.

STEP 2

Remove the dough from the fridge 15 mins before you roll it out. Lightly flour your work surface and rolling pin. Unwrap 1 piece of dough and roll it out to the thickness of a 50p coin. Use a 6cm star cutter to stamp out stars (you should get about 15) and transfer to a baking sheet.

STEP 3

Unwrap and roll out the other piece of dough. Stamp out 15 more stars and transfer to the second baking sheet. Stamp holes from the middle of 15 of the biscuits using the smaller cutter. Cover and chill for 15 mins. Heat the oven to 180C/160C fan/gas 4. Bake for 10-15 mins (the stars with a hole need less time), cool for 5 mins, then transfer to a wire rack to cool completely.

STEP 4

Meanwhile, make the filling. Whisk the butter, sugar and 50g of the jam with an electric whisk. Transfer to a piping bag with a small round nozzle, or snip off the end to make a ½cm opening. Put the remaining jam in another piping bag and snip off the end to make a slightly smaller hole.

STEP 5

Pipe blobs of the filling around the edge of each whole biscuit, leaving a space in the centre. Fill the space with jam, then sandwich a biscuit with a hole cut out on top of each one. Will keep in an airtight container for up to three days.

Pick & mix pesto pasta salad bar

Prep:10 mins **Cook:**15 mins

Serves 6

Ingredients

- 400g of your favourite pasta (shells or butterflies work well)
- 3 tbsp olive oil
- 3 tbsp pesto
- 100g frozen peas , defrosted

- 100g sweetcorn from a can, drained (or use defrosted frozen sweetcorn)
- 290g pack baby mozzarella
- 100g cherry tomatoes , halved
- 50g pitted black olives , halved
- 3 spring onions , trimmed and chopped

Method

STEP 1

Cook the pasta following pack instructions, then drain and toss in 1 tbsp oil. Transfer to a large bowl and set aside to cool, tossing occasionally so the pasta doesn't stick. Mix the remaining olive oil with the pesto and set aside. Both can be prepared up to two days ahead, then covered and chilled.

STEP 2

Put all the ingredients into individual bowls and serve with a large empty bowl and wooden spoon for mixing individual portions of pasta salad with your choice of ingredients.

Chicken & chickpea rice

Prep: 15 mins **Cook:** 25 mins

Serves 2-3

Ingredients

- 25g butter
- 1 shallot , finely chopped
- 1 skinless chicken breast (about 180g), cut into strips
- 1 carrot (about 100g), cut into thin batons
- 1 cinnamon stick
- 1 strip lemon zest
- 125g basmati rice
- 2 heaped tbsp raisins or sultanas
- 250ml chicken stock
- 215g can chickpeas (drained weight 130g)

Method

STEP 1

Melt half the butter in a frying pan with a lid. Fry the shallot for a couple of minutes, then add the chicken and carrot. Fry the veg until starting to brown, then add the cinnamon and lemon, and season well. Stir in the rice and raisins, then add the stock and bring to a simmer.

STEP 2

Scatter the chickpeas on top, then cover with the lid. Cook for 15 mins over a low heat until the rice has absorbed all the stock – if the rice is still firm, add 50ml water. Stand for 5 mins, then fluff up the rice. Dot over the remaining butter, then serve.

Crumpet pizzas

Prep: 20 mins **Cook:** 10 mins

Serves 6

Ingredients

- 6 crumpets
- 4 tbsp passata
- 4 tbsp ketchup
- ½ tsp dried oregano
- toppings of your choice (peppers, cherry tomatoes, red onion, sweetcorn, olives, ham and basil all work well)
- 75g cheddar cheese , grated

Method

STEP 1

Heat the grill to high. Lightly toast the crumpets in a toaster or under the grill. Meanwhile, mix the passata, ketchup and oregano together in a bowl. Season. Chop your chosen toppings into small pieces – young children can tear basil, or chop soft veg in a cup using safety scissors.

STEP 2

Line a baking tray with foil. Spread the sauce over the crumpets, then top with the veg and cheese. Arrange on the tray and grill for 3-4 mins, until the cheese is golden and bubbling. Leave to cool slightly before eating.

Chicken & mushroom hot-pot

Prep: 35 mins **Cook:** 25 mins

Serves 4

Ingredients

- 50g butter or margarine, plus extra for greasing
- 1 onion, chopped
- 100g button mushrooms, sliced
- 40g plain flour
- 1 chicken stock cube or 500ml fresh chicken stock

- pinch of nutmeg
- pinch of mustard powder
- 250g cooked chicken, chopped
- 2 handfuls of a mixed pack of sweetcorn, peas, broccoli and carrots, or pick your favourites

For the topping

- 2 large potatoes, sliced into rounds

- knob of butter, melted

Method

STEP 1

Heat oven to 200C/180C fan/gas 6. Put the butter in a medium-size saucepan and place over a medium heat. Add the onion and leave to cook for 5 mins, stirring occasionally. Add the mushrooms to the saucepan with the onions.

STEP 2

Once the onion and mushrooms are almost cooked, stir in the flour – this will make a thick paste called a roux. If you are using a stock cube, crumble the cube into the roux now and stir well. Put the roux over a low heat and stir continuously for 2 mins – this will cook the flour and stop the sauce from having a floury taste.

STEP 3

Take the roux off the heat. Slowly add the fresh stock, if using, or pour in 500ml water if you've used a stock cube, stirring all the time. Once all the liquid has been added, season with pepper, a pinch of nutmeg and mustard powder. Put the saucepan back onto a medium heat and slowly bring it to the boil, stirring all the time. Once the sauce has thickened, place on a very low heat. Add the cooked chicken and vegetables to the sauce and stir well. Grease a medium-size ovenproof pie dish with a little butter and pour in the chicken and mushroom filling.

STEP 4

Carefully lay the potatoes on top of the hot-pot filling, overlapping them slightly, almost like a pie top.

STEP 5

Brush the potatoes with a little melted butter and cook in the oven for about 35 mins. The hot-pot is ready once the potatoes are cooked and golden brown.

5-a-day Bolognese

Prep: 20 mins **Cook:** 1 hr

Serves 2

Ingredients

- 1 ½ tbsp olive oil
- 150g beef mince
- 2 onions , finely chopped
- 2 leeks , finely sliced
- 1-2 garlic cloves , crushed
- 1 red pepper , chopped into small pieces
- 1 large courgette , chopped into small pieces

- 1 can chopped tomatoes
- 2 tbsp tomato purée
- 50ml chicken or beef stock
- ½ tsp dried oregano
- 150g spaghetti
- 25g parmesan , finely grated
- a few basil leaves (optional)

Method

STEP 1

Put ½ tbsp of the oil in a large saucepan over a medium-high heat, add the beef and fry until well browned. Tip out into a dish and put the pan back on the heat with the remaining oil. Turn the heat down and cook the onions and leeks for 8-10 mins or until very soft, then add the garlic, pepper and courgette. Fry until the veg is starting to char at the edges and any water that's been released has evaporated.

STEP 2

Tip the meat back into the pan and add the tinned tomatoes, purée, stock and oregano. Stir everything together, cover and simmer over a low heat, stirring occasionally, for 35 mins. Meanwhile cook the spaghetti following pack instructions, then towards the end of cooking, stir half the parmesan into the Bolognese. Put a spoonful of the pasta water into the sauce to loosen it, if it looks too thick, then drain the spaghetti. Tip the pasta onto the sauce, toss everything together to coat and season well. Garnish with the remaining parmesan and a few basil leaves.

Kiwi slime pies

Prep:25 mins **Cook:**30 mins**Serves:**8

Ingredients

- 320g shop-bought ready-rolled shortcrust pastry
- 4 egg yolks , plus 1 egg white (freeze the remaining whites to make meringues another day)
- 400ml milk

- 35g golden caster sugar
- 1 heaped tbsp plain flour
- 5 cubes green jelly
- 2-3 green and golden kiwi fruit , peeled and sliced

Method

STEP 1

Heat the oven to 190C/170C fan/gas 5. Divide the pastry into eight equal pieces. Roll each out until large enough to line deep 7-8cm fluted tartlet tins or eight holes of a large muffin tin. Line the tins with the pastry, leaving a little sticking up above the rims, then line with paper cases and baking beans. Put the tins on a baking tray and bake for 10 mins, then remove the paper and beans, brush with the egg white and bake for 5-10 mins more until crisp and golden. Leave to cool for 5 mins, then remove from the tins and leave to cool completely.

STEP 2

Put the milk in a pan and bring almost to the boil, then remove from the heat. Put the egg yolks, sugar and flour in a bowl and whisk with an electric whisk until pale and fluffy – it should leave a trail that stays on the surface momentarily when the whisk is lifted. Pour a third of the hot milk into the bowl, slowly whisking all the time, until it has all been mixed in. Whisk in the remaining milk.

STEP 3

Return the mixture to the pan, scraping it out using a rubber spatula. Bring slowly to the boil, stirring, until the custard is thick, smooth and glossy. At first, it will look a bit lumpy, but keep stirring and it will become smooth. Reduce the heat and simmer for 2 mins, stirring. Stir in the jelly until the cubes have dissolved. Leave the mixture to cool until just warm, then divide it between the baked tart cases. Top each with a slice of kiwi and leave to cool completely.

Noodle stir-fry with crunchy peanuts

Prep: 10 mins **Cook:** 10 mins

Serves 3

Ingredients

- 2 tbsp crunchy peanut butter
- 1 tbsp soy sauce
- 1 tbsp roasted unsalted peanuts , chopped, plus extra to serve
- 300g pack ready to eat egg noodles

- 1 tbsp oil
- 2 eggs , lightly beaten
- 300g pack stir-fry vegetables
- sweet chilli sauce , to serve (optional)

Method

STEP 1

Mix the peanut butter with the soy sauce and 50ml water, then add the peanuts. Put the noodles in a bowl and cover them with boiling water. Stir them gently so they separate, then drain.

STEP 2

Heat ½ tbsp oil in a wok or large frying pan, and pour in the egg. Leave the egg to set, then chop it up with your spatula and tip it onto a plate. Heat the remaining oil in the wok. Stir-fry the veg until starting to wilt, then add the noodles and keep cooking. Return the egg to the wok, then spoon in the peanut mixture and toss. Divide between bowls, then sprinkle over more peanuts. Serve with sweet chilli sauce, if you like.

Healthy Easter bunny pancakes

Prep:15 mins **Cook:**30 mins

Serves 4-6

Ingredients

- 50g self-raising flour
- 50g wholemeal flour
- 2 small eggs , separated
- 150ml skimmed milk
- oil , for frying

- a few raisins for bunny paws, to serve (optional)
- 30g banana , sliced into rounds for the tails
- extra chopped fruit , to serve

Method

STEP 1

Put both the flours into a large bowl and whisk to break up any lumps. Add the egg yolks and a little of the milk, whisking to a thick paste. Add the remaining milk, a splash at a time, to loosen the batter. (Use whole or semi-skimmed milk if cooking for under fives, dependent on age.)

STEP 2

In a separate bowl and using a clean whisk, whisk the egg whites until they hold stiff peaks. Gently fold the egg whites into the batter with a spatula, trying to keep in as much air as possible.

STEP 3

Heat a large non-stick pan over a medium heat and carefully wipe it with some oiled kitchen paper. Using a large spoon, add a generous dollop of batter to the pan in a round, for the bunny body. Add a smaller round for the head, two small ovals for feet, and two long thin strips for ears. Fit all the bunny components into the pan, or cook them in batches.

STEP 4

Flip the pancakes after a minute or two, once the edges are set, the base is golden brown and bubbles start to pop on the surface. Cook for another min until golden brown.

STEP 5

Put the bunny body in the middle of the plate, position the head, ears and feet just overlapping to look like the back of a bunny. Add a banana slice for the tail, and raisins (if using) for the feet pads.

STEP 6

Repeat with the remaining batter. Decorate with extra chopped fruit, if you like.

Salmon & spaghetti supper in a parcel

Prep: 10 mins **Cook:** 30 mins

Serves 4

Ingredients

- 200g spaghetti
- 2 courgettes , grated
- 100g red cherry tomatoes , halved
- 100g yellow cherry tomatoes , halved

- 4 salmon fillets or 2 chicken breasts
- 4 tbsp olive oil
- 1 garlic clove , finely sliced

Method

STEP 1

Heat oven to 180C/160C fan/gas 4. Cook the spaghetti following pack instructions and drain. Cut 4 rectangles of baking parchment off a roll, each twice as long as it is wide. Lay them on a work surface. Toss the spaghetti with the grated courgettes. Divide the spaghetti between the pieces of parchment, then divide the cherry tomatoes between each pile.

STEP 2

If using salmon, slice lengthways, but keep the fillet together. Place on top of the veg and press sideways so the slices move apart a little. If using chicken, halve each breast through the middle horizontally to give four pieces, then cut each into strips and tip a pile of chicken strips onto each pile of spaghetti.

STEP 3

Heat the oil and fry the garlic for 1 min, then pour a little garlic oil over each pile. Season with black pepper if your children like it. Bring the two longer sides of parchment up to meet in the middle and fold the ends over and over, working down towards the filling, leaving a little room for the steam to expand the parcel. Flatten the seam down and then fold in each end. Use paper clips to hold the folds, if you like. Lift the parcels onto a baking tray and bake for 10-15 mins. The parcels should puff up as they cook.

STEP 4

Serve each person a puffed parcel in a shallow bowl and snip it open at the table, staying clear of any steam (and removing any paperclips).

Traffic light chicken shish kebabs

Prep: 20 mins **Cook:** 10 mins

Serves 6

Ingredients

- 6 chicken breasts, chopped into large chunks
- 2 each red, orange and green peppers , deseeded and chopped into large chunks
- warmed flatbreads , chopped
- tomato and lemon wedges, to serve

For the marinade and sauce

- 2 garlic cloves , finely grated
- 300g natural or Greek yogurt
- 1 tbsp paprika
- 3 tbsp ketchup

Method

STEP 1

Make the marinade by mixing all of the ingredients together in a large bowl. Spoon a third of the mixture into a smaller bowl, then cover and chill until needed. Stir the chicken into the marinade and set aside for 20 mins. Can be chilled for up to two days, covered.

STEP 2

If using wooden skewers, soak them in water for 1 hr before using. Alternately thread the peppers and chicken onto the skewers until you have 6-8 kebabs. You can do this in advance if you like, and chill the kebabs until needed.

STEP 3

Heat a barbecue to medium, or until a thin layer of coals has turned grey. Cook the kebabs for 10 mins, turning occasionally, until the chicken is charred and cooked through. Serve the kebabs with the reserved yogurt sauce, warmed flatbreads, chopped tomatoes and lemon wedges on the side.

RECIPE TIPS

RAIN OR SHINE

The kebabs can also be cooked indoors under a hot grill on a tray lined with foil for 15-20 mins.

Spider biscuits

Prep: 25 mins **Cook:** 12 mins

Makes 20

Ingredients

- 70g butter, softened
- 50g peanut butter
- 150g golden caster sugar
- 1 medium egg
- 1 tsp vanilla extract

- 180g plain flour
- ½ tsp bicarbonate of soda
- 20 peanut butter cups, Rolos or Maltesers
- 100g milk chocolate, chopped
- icing eyes, or make your own

Method

STEP 1

Heat oven to 180C/160C fan/gas 4 and line two baking sheets with parchment. Using an electric hand whisk, cream the butter, peanut butter and sugar together until very light and fluffy, then beat in the egg and vanilla. Once combined, stir in the flour, bicarb and ¼ tsp salt.

STEP 2

Scoop 18-20 tbsps of the mixture onto the trays, leaving enough space between each to allow for spreading. Make a thumbprint in the centre of the cookies. Bake for 10-12 mins or until firm at the edges but still soft in the middle – they'll harden a little as they cool. Leave to cool on the tray for a few mins before topping each biscuit with a peanut butter cup, Rolo or Malteser. Transfer to a wire rack to cool completely.

STEP 3

Heat the chocolate in the microwave in short bursts, or in a bowl set over a pan of simmering water, until just liquid. Scrape into a piping bag and leave to cool a little. Pipe the legs onto each spider, then stick two eyes on each. Leave to set. Will keep for three days in an airtight container.

Gingerbread stained glass biscuits

Prep:40 mins **Cook:**5 mins - 6 mins

Makes 30

Ingredients

- 175g dark soft brown sugar
- 85g golden syrup
- 100g unsalted butter
- 2-3 tsp ground ginger
- 350g plain flour, plus extra to dust

- 1 tsp bicarbonate of soda
- 1 large egg, lightly beaten
- clear fruit-flavoured boiled sweets (don't use anything with a soft centre)
- white icing, to decorate

You will need

- star or snowflake cutters

Method

STEP 1

Heat the sugar, golden syrup and butter in a pan until melted. Mix the ginger and flour in a large bowl and make a well in the centre. Add the bicarbonate of soda to the melted mixture and stir – it will fizz a little – then pour into the flour mixture with the egg. Stir to combine. The mix will be soft but will firm up as it cools.

STEP 2

Scoop the mixture into a box or fridge bag and chill for at least 1 hr until firm enough to roll out. The dough can be kept in the fridge for up to a week or frozen for three months.

STEP 3

Heat oven to 190C/170C fan/gas 5. Turn the dough out onto a lightly floured surface and cut in half. Briefly knead the first piece, then roll it on a lightly floured surface to 2mm thick. Cut into shapes with snowflake or star cutters about 12cm across, then transfer to lined baking sheets, leaving a little room for them to spread. Cut a window out of each biscuit using another cutter about about 6cm across, then add a sweet to the centre.

STEP 4

If the sweets are large, chop them up first – you'll have to judge by the size of the hole. (Don't be tempted to add too much or it will spill over the edge.) If you plan to hang the biscuits, make a small hole in the top of each one using the end of a piping nozzle (the hole will close up a little so make sure it's big enough). Repeat with remaining dough.

STEP 5

Bake in batches for 5-6 mins or until they darken slightly and the sweets have melted. If the holes have closed up, remake them while the biscuits are warm. Leave to cool and harden up completely before moving them. Don't forget to bake the parts you've cut out, too! You can decorate the biscuits further by using white piped icing, if you like.

Unicorn poo meringues

Prep:20 mins **Cook:**1 hr and 20 mins

Makes 44

Ingredients

- 4 large egg whites , at room temperature
- 100g caster sugar
- 100g icing sugar , sifted

- 4 food colouring gels or pastes (we used pink, yellow, blue and green)
- small amount of white and black ready-to-roll fondant icing for the eyes and mouth

You will also need

- 4cm round cutter or circle to drawn around
- 1 large piping bag fitted with a large open star nozzle (1cm)

- 4 small paintbrushes

Method

STEP 1

Heat oven to 120C/100C fan/gas ½. Line 2 baking sheets with parchment. Using a 4cm round cutter as a guide, draw 22 circles on each piece of parchment in pencil. Turn the parchment over.

STEP 2

Whip up the egg whites in a stand mixer or with an electric hand whisk until they form stiff peaks. Gradually add the caster sugar in, a spoonful at a time, whisking in completely between each addition. Repeat with the icing sugar until the mixture is glossy and stiff.

STEP 3

Put the piping bag nozzle down in a tall glass or jug. Roll down the top of the bag a little, over the rim, then paint a thin stripe of each coloured food gel from the nozzle all the way up to the top of the bag. Spoon in the meringue mixture.

STEP 4

Pipe swirls of meringue onto the trays using the circles as a guide. Bake for 20 mins then turn down to 100C/80C fan/gas ¼ and cook for a further hour, or until they are completely cooked through and sound hollow when tapped on the base. Leave to cool in the oven.

STEP 5

Mould small pieces of white and black fondant icing to create eyes and mouths. Stick these on the cooled meringues with a small dab of royal icing (if they don't stick by themselves).

Loaded open sandwiches

Prep:20 mins

Makes 20-24 small sandwiches

Ingredients

- 12 small slices rye bread or 6 slices thin, firm bread
- softened butter , for spreading
- 6 tbsp mayonnaise
- 2 tsp cucumber relish or piccalilli
- 2 slices ham , shredded
- 2 tbsp cream cheese
- ¼ cucumber , halved, peeled and thinly sliced
- 2 boiled eggs , halved and sliced
- 100g frozen north Atlantic prawns , defrosted
- sliced radishes , dill sprigs and cress, to garnish

Method

STEP 1

Trim the crusts from the bread if you like and cut each slice into smaller pieces. Spread each slice with butter and lay out on a board.

STEP 2

Mix 2 tbsp mayonnaise with the cucumber relish and spread over a quarter of the buttered bread slices. Arrange the ham and the radishes over the top. Spread the cream cheese over another quarter and arrange the cucumber and dill on top. Mash the egg with 2 tbsp mayonnaise and spread over another quarter, then top with the cress. Mix the prawns with the remaining mayonnaise and spoon over the remaining bread slices, then grind over a little black pepper. Add a garnish of dill, if you like.

Chicken skewers with tzatziki

Prep:10 mins **Cook:**15 mins

Serves 8

Ingredients

- 4 skinless chicken breasts
- 1 lemon
- 2 tsp oregano
- 1 garlic clove
- 1 small yellow pepper

- 1 small red pepper
- wholemeal tortilla wraps, to serve
- baby spinach leaves, to serve
- few sprigs flat-leaf parsley , to serve

For the tzatziki

- ½ cucumber
- ¼ garlic clove

- 4 tbsp Greek yogurt
- 1 tbsp extra virgin olive oil

You will need

- eight bamboo skewers

Method

STEP 1

Soak eight bamboo skewers in water. Using sharp kitchen scissors, chop the chicken into small pieces. Pop into a plastic box with a lid. Pare strips of lemon zest from the lemon using a vegetable peeler, then juice the lemon as well. Add both the peel and the juice to the chicken in the box along with the oregano and the garlic, crushed in. Season generously, mix and put in the fridge for 15 mins with the lid on. Deseed and chop the peppers into similar-sized pieces to those of the chicken.

STEP 2

Heat a griddle pan to high while you get the chicken out. Discard the lemon zest and thread the chicken onto the skewers, alternating every few bits of chicken with a piece of red pepper followed by a piece of yellow pepper. Griddle for 10 mins, turning halfway.

STEP 3

While the skewers are cooking, make the tzatziki. Get a box grater and a bowl. Cut the cucumber into long lengths, discarding the watery seedy core. Grate into the bowl, then grate the ¼ garlic clove. Season generously and stir in the Greek yogurt. Drizzle with a little extra virgin olive oil.

STEP 4

Serve the skewers hot off the griddle with the dip, or take the chicken and peppers off the skewers, leave to cool and pack into wholemeal wraps spread with a little tzatziki and rolled up with baby spinach and a few picked leaves of parsley.

Salmon tacos with lime dressing

Prep: 15 mins **Cook:** 10 mins

Serves 4

Ingredients

- olive oil , for the foil
- 500g piece salmon fillet
- 8 soft corn tacos
- 2 limes , zested and juiced
- 200g natural yogurt

- 2 ripe avocados , peeled and cubed
- 10 cherry tomatoes , halved
- 1 small red chilli , deseeded and sliced (optional)

Method

STEP 1

Cut a piece of foil big enough to wrap the salmon in and brush with oil. Put the salmon on top, season and sprinkle with some of the lime zest and juice. Fold up the foil around the salmon so it all meets at the top and makes a handle to lift the parcel with.

STEP 2

Heat a barbecue until the coals are glowing white hot. Make sure the grill is set high above the coals and put the foil parcel on. Cook for 10 mins and then open it and have a look. The salmon should be opaque – if it isn't, wrap it up and continue cooking.

STEP 3

Wrap the tacos in foil and warm them at the side of the barbecue. Mix the remaining lime zest and juice with the yogurt and season. When the salmon is cooked, open out the foil and flake it into pieces. Serve the tacos with the salmon, tomato, avocado, chilli and sauce so people can stuff their own. Napkins are necessary.

RECIPE TIPS

SERVE WITH SALSA

Serve with a spicy salsa if adults or older children like a bit of heat.

CHOOSING YOUR SALMON

You can use four individual salmon fillets instead of a whole fillet for this if you prefer – lay them up against each other on the foil so they cook through at the same rate as the whole piece.

Unicorn biscuits

Prep:15 mins **Cook:**30 mins

around 20

Ingredients

- 250g plain flour
- 150g butter
- 100g caster sugar
- 1 egg
- ½ tsp vanilla extract
- pink food colouring

- 50g icing sugar
- 1 lemon , juice only
- your choice of coloured sprinkles (we used hundreds and thousands, pink and yellow sugar and some white chocolate stars)

Method

STEP 1

Rub the flour and butter together with your fingertips until it looks and feels like fresh breadcrumbs then add a pinch of salt. In another bowl, mix together the sugar, egg and vanilla extract then pour it over the butter and flour mixture. Gently knead it together then separate the dough into 2 equal blocks. Knead some pink food colouring into one of them and keep the other plain. Wrap both types of dough in sheets of cling film and chill in the fridge for 20-30 mins.

STEP 2

Roll the plain dough out onto a lightly floured surface until it's about 25cm long and 20cm wide. Do the same with the pink dough and lay one on top of the other. Lightly roll over the surface once or twice with your rolling pin just to press them together. Trim off all the edges so they're straight then carefully roll them up from one of the short edges to make a tight spiral. Wrap tightly in cling film and chill for 1hr or overnight.

STEP 3

Heat oven to 180C/160C fan/gas 4 and line 2 trays with baking parchment. Unwrap the dough, trim the end and cut the rest into 20 slices and lay them cut side down on your prepared baking tray. Bake for 15-17 mins or until ever so slightly golden at the very edges. Allow them to cool on the tray before transferring them to a wire rack to cool completely.

STEP 4

Mix the icing sugar with enough lemon juice to make it the consistency of smooth peanut butter and pour the sprinkles into a shallow bowl or plate. Dip the outside edges of the biscuits into the icing (or spread it onto the edges using the back of a teaspoon) and then into the sprinkles, turning to coat. Leave to set before serving.

Vegan nuggets

Prep:20 mins

Cook:40 mins

MAKES 30

Ingredients

- 300g cauliflower florets (or 3/4 small cauliflower)
- 2 carrots , chopped (about 165g)
- ½ medium onion , chopped
- 1 tbsp olive oil
- 1 garlic clove , crushed

For the coating

- 100g gram flour , plus a little extra
- 100g breadcrumbs (use gluten-free if necessary)

- 2 tbsp nutritional yeast
- 2 tsp yeast extract
- 400g can cannellini beans , drained
- 50g gram (chickpea) flour
- olive oil , for the baking tray

Method

STEP 1

Pulse the cauliflower, carrots and onion in a food processor until very finely chopped, like rice. Heat the oil in a large frying pan and gently fry the mix for 12-15 mins until softened. Add the garlic and fry for a further 1 min, then take off the heat and stir in the nutritional yeast and yeast extract. Set aside.

STEP 2

Blend the beans into a mushy purée in a food processor, then add to the veggie mix and combine well. Stir in the flour and season. Put in the fridge to firm up for 1 hr.

STEP 3

Heat the oven to 220C/200C fan/gas 7. Line a large baking tray with baking parchment and coat with a little olive oil. To make the coating, mix the gram flour with 150ml water using a fork so it resembles beaten egg, then season. Scatter the extra gram flour on a plate and fill a second with the breadcrumbs.

STEP 4

Roll the bean mixture into walnut-sized pieces, then flatten to form nugget shapes. Dip the pieces first in the gram flour, then in the gram batter, and finally roll in the breadcrumbs – handle carefully as they will be a little soft. When the nuggets are fully coated, lay them out on the prepared tray.

STEP 5

Bake for 20 mins, then use tongs to turn each nugget over and bake for a further 15 mins until they are dark golden and crisp. Leave to cool for 20 mins before serving with your choice of dipping sauces.

Egg-less mayo sandwiches

Prep:5 mins

plus 30 mins draining

Makes 16-20 sandwiches

Ingredients

- 400g block of medium-firm tofu in water
- 6 tbsp vegan mayo
- ½ tsp Dijon mustard
- ¼ tsp ground turmeric
- 1 tbsp nutritional yeast

- 2 tsp finely chopped chives
- 1 large white sandwich or wholemeal loaf (10-12 slices), or 12 mini rolls (use gluten-free bread if necessary)
- 1 punnet cress (optional)

Method

STEP 1

Remove the tofu from the pack and press out the excess water, either between sheets of kitchen paper or a clean tea towel, weighed down with a plate for about 30 mins.

STEP 2

Mix the mayo, mustard, turmeric and nutritional yeast together with a little salt and pepper.

STEP 3

Crumble the tofu into a bowl, leaving large chunks to create a chopped egg texture. Gently stir in the chives. If you want it looser you can add more mayo.

STEP 4

Spread the mixture on the bread to make four or five rounds of sandwiches (depending on how much filling you want), then add cress, if you like. Use a sharp knife to cut into triangles.

RECIPE TIPS

GET THE EGGY FLAVOUR

If you want to replicate an eggy flavour in these sandwiches, try adding a pinch of black salt (also called kala namak or Himalayan black salt) which has a distinctive sulphurous flavour.

Mexican-style stuffed peppers

Prep:15 mins **Cook:**35 mins

Serves 2 adults, 2 children

Ingredients

- 3 large mixed peppers , halved
- oil , for drizzling
- 2 x 250g pouches lime & coriander rice , cooked
- 400g can black beans , drained and rinsed
- 6 Mexican-style chilli cheese slices (use regular cheddar or monterey jack, if you like)
- 150g fresh guacamole

Method

STEP 1

Heat the oven to 220C/200C fan/gas 7. Remove the seeds and any white pith from the peppers and arrange, cut-side up, in a roasting tin. Drizzle with oil and season, then bake for 20 mins.

STEP 2

Combine the rice and beans. Remove the peppers from the oven and fill with the rice mixture. Top each with a slice of cheese and bake for 10-15 mins more, until the rice has melted and the filling is hot. Top with spoonfuls of guacamole.

RECIPE TIPS

SERVE THE LEFTOVERS

If you have any leftover rice and beans that won't fit into the peppers, warm it up and serve on the side.

Chocolate brownie cake

Prep: 15 mins

Serves 6 - 8

Ingredients

- 100g butter
- 125g caster sugar
- 75g light brown or muscovado sugar
- 125g plain chocolate (plain or milk)
- 1 tbsp golden syrup

- 2 eggs
- 1 tsp vanilla extract/essence
- 100g plain flour
- ½ tsp baking powder
- 2 tbsp cocoa powder

Method

STEP 1

Heat oven to 180C/fan 160C/gas 4. Grease and line a 20cm cake tin.

STEP 2

Place the butter, caster sugar, brown sugar, chocolate and golden syrup in the pan and melt gently on a low heat until it is smooth and lump-free.

STEP 3

Remove the pan from the heat.

STEP 4

Break the eggs into the bowl and whisk with the fork until light and frothy. 5 Add the eggs, vanilla extract or essence, flour, baking powder and cocoa powder to the chocolate mixture and mix thoroughly.

STEP 5

Put the mixture into the greased and lined cake tin and place on the middle shelf of the oven. Bake for 25-30 mins.

STEP 6

Remove and allow to cool for 20-30 mins before cutting into wedges and serving.

STEP 7

Serve with cream or ice cream and plenty of fresh fruit.

Sticky plum flapjack bars

Prep: 20 mins **Cook:** 1 hr

Makes 18

Ingredients

- 450g fresh plum , halved, stoned and roughly sliced
- ½ tsp mixed spice
- 300g light muscovado sugar
- 350g butter , plus extra for greasing
- 300g rolled porridge oats (not jumbo)
- 140g plain flour
- 50g chopped walnut pieces
- 3 tbsp golden syrup

Method

STEP 1

Heat oven to 200C/180C fan/gas 6. Tip the plums into a bowl. Toss with the spice, 50g of the sugar and a small pinch of salt, then set aside to macerate.

STEP 2

Gently melt the butter in a saucepan. In a large bowl, mix the oats, flour, walnut pieces and remaining sugar together, making sure there are no lumps of sugar, then stir in the butter and golden syrup until everything is combined into a loose flapjack mixture.

STEP 3

Grease a square baking tin about 20 x 20cm. Press half the oaty mix over the base of the tin, then tip over the plums and spread to make an even layer. Press the remaining oats over the plums so they are completely covered right to the sides of the tin. Bake for 45-50 mins until dark golden and starting to crisp a little around the edges. Leave to cool completely, then cut into 18 little bars. Will keep in an airtight container for 2 days or can be frozen for up to a month.

Lemon curd & blueberry loaf cake

Prep:20 mins **Cook:**1 hr and 15 mins

Cuts into 8-10 slices

Ingredients

- 175g softened butter , plus extra for greasing
- 500ml tub Greek yogurt (you need 100ml/3.5fl oz in the cake, the rest to serve)
- 300g jar good lemon curd (you need 2 tbsp in the cake, the rest to serve)
- 3 eggs
- zest and juice 1 lemon , plus extra zest to serve, if you like
- 200g self-raising flour
- 175g golden caster sugar
- 200g punnet of blueberries (you need 85g/3oz in the cake, the rest to serve)
- 140g icing sugar
- edible flowers , such as purple or yellow primroses, to serve (optional)

Method

STEP 1

Heat oven to 160C/140C fan/gas 3. Grease a 2lb loaf tin and line with a long strip of baking parchment. Put 100g yogurt, 2 tbsp lemon curd, the softened butter, eggs, lemon zest, flour and caster sugar into a large mixing bowl. Quickly mix with an electric whisk until the batter just comes together. Scrape half into the prepared tin. Weigh 85g blueberries from the punnet and sprinkle half into the tin, scrape the rest of the batter on top, then scatter the other half of the 85g berries on top. Bake for 1 hr 10 mins-1 hr 15 mins until golden, and a skewer poked into the centre comes out clean.

STEP 2

Cool in the tin, then carefully lift onto a serving plate to ice. Sift the icing sugar into a bowl and stir in enough lemon juice to make a thick, smooth icing. Spread over the top of the cake, then decorate with lemon zest and edible flowers, if you like. Serve in slices with extra lemon curd, Greek yogurt and blueberries.

Easter chocolate bark

Prep:20 mins **Cook:**5 mins

Makes enough for 6-8 gift bags

Ingredients

- 3 x 200g bars milk chocolate
- 2 x 90g packs mini chocolate eggs
- 1 heaped tsp freeze-dried raspberry pieces – or you could use crystallised petals

Method

STEP 1

Break the chocolate into a large heatproof bowl. Bring a pan of water to a simmer, then sit the bowl on top. The water must not touch the bottom of the bowl. Let the chocolate slowly melt, stirring now and again with a spatula. For best results, temper your chocolate (see tip).

STEP 2

Meanwhile, lightly grease then line a 23 x 33cm roasting tin or baking tray with parchment. Put three-quarters of the mini eggs into a food bag and bash them with a rolling pin until broken up a little.

STEP 3

When the chocolate is smooth, pour it into the tin. Tip the tin from side to side to let the chocolate find the corners and level out. Scatter with the smashed and whole mini eggs, followed by the freeze-dried raspberry pieces. Leave to set, then remove from the parchment and snap into shards, ready to pack in boxes or bags.

RECIPE TIPS

TEMPERING CHOCOLATE

Tempering is the process of heating then cooling chocolate to form a specific type of crystals in the cocoa butter. If we simply melt and cool shop- bought chocolate, it will quickly 'bloom', with dots and streaks of cocoa butter. It melts quickly when touched too. Tempered chocolate will quickly set hard and shiny, won't bloom, and shrinks as it cools, making it easy to remove from a mould. Here's a simple method: Break up 3/4 of the chocolate into a heatproof bowl. Melt until it is flowing and smooth. White chocolate should reach 43C, milk and dark 45C. Add the remaining chocolate, chopped into small pieces. Stir with a spatula until the pieces have melted and the thermometer shows 28C for milk and white, 30C for dark. This can take a while, so have patience and keep stirring. Use as soon as possible. If the chocolate starts to get too cold and thick as you use it, heat for just a few seconds and stir well.

Family meals: Easy lamb tagine

Prep: 10 mins **Cook:** 2 hrs and 10 mins

Serves a family of 4-6 or makes 6-8 toddler meals

Ingredients

- 2 tbsp olive oil
- 1 onion, finely diced
- 2 carrots, finely diced (about 150g)
- 500g diced leg of lamb
- 2 fat cloves garlic, crushed
- ½ tsp cumin
- ½ tsp ground ginger
- ¼ tsp saffron strands
- 1 tsp ground cinnamon

- 1 tbsp clear honey
- 100g soft dried apricot, quartered
- 1 low-salt vegetable stock cube
- 1 small butternut squash, peeled, seeds removed and cut into 1cm dice
- steamed couscous or rice, to serve
- chopped parsley and toasted pine nuts, to serve (optional)

Method

STEP 1

Heat the olive oil in a heavy-based pan and add the onion and carrot. Cook for 3- 4 mins until softened.

STEP 2

Add the diced lamb and brown all over. Stir in the garlic and all the spices and cook for a few mins more or until the aromas are released.

STEP 3

Add the honey and apricots, crumble in the stock cube and pour over roughly 500ml boiling water or enough to cover the meat. Give it a good stir and bring to the boil. Turn down to a simmer, put the lid on and cook for 1 hour.

STEP 4

Remove the lid and cook for a further 30 mins, then stir in the squash. Cook for 20 – 30 mins more until the squash is soft and the lamb is tender. Serve alongside rice or couscous and sprinkle with parsley and pine nuts, if using.

Really easy roast chicken

Prep: 25 mins **Cook:** 1 hr and 20 mins

Serves 4 with leftover chicken

Ingredients

- 1 whole chicken , about 1.5kg
- 1 lemon , halved
- 2 garlic cloves
- thyme or rosemary sprig, if you have it
- 50g soft butter
- 800g very small salad potato , such as Charlotte, halved if you can only find large ones

- 350g small Chantenay carrot , or 3-4 regular carrots. cut into chunks
- 1 tbsp olive oil
- 300ml chicken stock
- 1 tbsp low-salt soy sauce

Method

STEP 1

KIDS: The writing in bold is for you. ADULTS: The rest is for you. **Cut the string off the chicken.** Heat oven to 220C/200C fan/gas 7. Get your child to use a pair of scissors to cut the elastic or string holding the chicken together.

STEP 2

Stuff the chicken. Stuff the lemon halves in the cavity of the chicken with the garlic and herb sprig (if using).

STEP 3

Time to get your hands mucky. Sit the chicken in a large roasting tin and use your hands to smear the butter all over it.

STEP 4

Easy-peasy vegetables. Tip the carrots and potatoes into a large bowl, drizzle over the oil and toss everything together with your hands.

STEP 5

Scatter the vegetables around the chicken. Scatter the vegetables in an even layer around the chicken, then season everything. Put the chicken in the oven and roast for 30 mins. Remove from the oven and give the vegetables a stir, reduce the heat to 200C/180C fan/gas 6, then return to the oven for 50 mins more.

STEP 6

Test if the chicken is cooked. Remove the chicken from the oven. Using a cloth, pull the leg – if it easily comes away from the body, there is no sign of pink and the juices run clear, the chicken is cooked. If you have a digital cooking thermometer, it should read above 70C. Take the chicken out of the tin.

STEP 7

Make a lemony sauce. Scoop the vegetables into a serving dish. Using a spoon or a pair of tongs, remove the garlic, lemon and herbs from the chicken and put them in the roasting tin. Squash them down well with a potato masher to release all the juice from the lemons.

STEP 8

Strain the sauce. Pour in the chicken stock and soy sauce and give it all a good stir. Get the child to hold a sieve over a jug while you lift up the pan and strain the juices into the jug. If you want it piping hot, reheat in a pan or in the microwave.

RECIPE TIPS

WHAT KIDS LEARN FROM MAKING REALLY EASY ROAST CHICKEN

Roasting: At its most basic, roasting is nothing more than putting something in the oven to cook. Seeing the process happen from start to finish gives a child a greater understanding of how so many family meals end up cooked and on the table. **Using the oven:** As there is no direct flame, using the oven is the first way kids will progress to cook alone. It's good for them to know how it works and how hot it can get – if your oven has a clear glass door, then they can even watch things as they cook.

Strawberry & cream roly-polys

Prep:35 mins **Cook:**15 mins - 20 mins

plus 1 hr 30 mins chilling

Makes 24

Ingredients

- 2 x 7g packs freeze-dried strawberry pieces (available from Waitrose, Sainsbury's or online)
- 140g cold slightly salted butter , cubed
- 250g plain flour , plus extra for dusting
- 100g icing sugar
- 1 tsp vanilla extract
- 1 large egg yolk
- 2 tbsp double cream
- good splash or squeeze of red or pink food colouring

Method

STEP 1

Tip the freeze-dried strawberries into a food processor and whizz to a powder. Transfer to a bowl, then wash the bowl of the food processor.

STEP 2

Put the butter and flour in the food processor with a good pinch of salt and blend until the mixture resembles breadcrumbs. Add the icing sugar and whizz again. In a small bowl, whisk together the vanilla extract, egg yolk and cream, then add to the mixture in the food processor and whizz again until the dough clumps around the blade and most of the small crumbs have been worked into the dough.

STEP 3

Scoop about half the dough out of the processor (being careful not to cut yourself on the sharp blade) and briefly knead it on a work surface to bring it together. Shape into a puck, then wrap in cling film and chill. Add the strawberry powder and a few drops of food colouring to the remaining dough in the blender, and whizz again until evenly coloured and combined – it should be bright pink (add more colouring if needed). Tip onto the work surface, flatten to roughly the same shape as the other dough, then wrap and chill for 30 mins.

STEP 4

Remove both pieces of dough from the fridge 10-15 mins before you want to roll them. Dust the work surface with a little flour and unwrap the doughs. Place 1 piece of dough on top of the other, squashing the sides until they are roughly the same shape. Flour your rolling pin, then roll the dough into a rectangle, roughly 25cm x 20cm – this is easiest if you first 'notch' the dough, which means pressing the rolling pin firmly over the surface in one direction to make a long indentation in one direction, then turning the dough 90 degrees and repeating the process.

STEP 5

From one of the longer sides, roll the dough into a tight coil, as you would a Swiss roll. Wrap the dough in cling film and chill for 1 hr. Or you can freeze it for up to 2 months. About 10 mins before you are ready to bake the biscuits, heat oven to 180C/160C fan/gas 4 and line 2 baking sheets with baking parchment.

STEP 6

When the dough is firm, cut off and discard the end pieces, then slice into discs about the thickness of a £1 coin. Lay the biscuit dough out on your baking trays, spaced a little apart, and bake for 15-17 mins, swapping the trays over halfway through cooking, until the biscuits are firm and starting to turn pale golden around the edges. Leave to cool on the trays for 5 mins, then transfer to a wire rack to cool completely. Stores in a biscuit tin for 3 days.

Blueberry & lemon pancakes

Prep:10 mins **Cook:**20 mins

Makes 14-16

Ingredients

- 200g plain flour
- 1 tsp cream of tartar
- ½ tsp bicarbonate of soda
- 1 tsp golden syrup
- 75g blueberry
- zest 1 lemon
- 200ml milk
- 1 large egg
- butter , for cooking

Method

STEP 1

First, put the flour, cream of tartar and bicarbonate of soda in the bowl. Mix them well with the fork. Drop the golden syrup into the dry ingredients along with the blueberries and lemon zest.

STEP 2

Pour the milk into a measuring jug. Now break in the egg and mix well with a fork. Pour most of the milk mixture into the bowl and mix well with a rubber spatula. Keep adding more milk until you get a smooth, thick, pouring batter.

STEP 3

Heat the frying pan and brush with a little butter. Then spoon in the batter, 1 tbsp at a time, in heaps. Bubbles will appear on top as the pancakes cook – turn them at this stage, using the metal spatula to help you. Cook until brown on the second side, then keep warm on a plate, covered with foil. Repeat until all the mixture is used up.

Bread in four easy steps

Prep: 15 mins **Cook:** 35 mins

Cuts into 8 thick slices

Ingredients

- 500g granary, strong wholewheat or white bread flour (I used granary)
- 7g sachet fast-action dried yeast

- 1 tsp salt
- 2 tbsp olive oil
- 1 tbsp clear honey

Method

STEP 1

Tip the flour, yeast and salt into a large bowl and mix together with your hands. Stir 300ml hand-hot water with the oil and honey, then stir into the dry ingredients to make a soft dough.

STEP 2

Turn the dough out onto a lightly floured surface and knead for 5 mins, until the dough no longer feels sticky, sprinkling with a little more flour if you need it.

STEP 3

Oil a 900g loaf tin and put the dough in the tin, pressing it in evenly. Put in a large plastic food bag and leave to rise for 1 hr, until the dough has risen to fill the tin and it no longer springs back when you press it with your finger.

STEP 4

Heat oven to 200C/fan 180C/gas 6. Make several slashes across the top of the loaf with a sharp knife, then bake for 30-35 mins until the loaf is risen and golden. Tip it out onto a cooling rack and tap the base of the bread to check it is cooked. It should sound hollow. Leave to cool.

Chocolate fudge cupcakes

Prep: 30 mins **Cook:** 25 mins - 30 mins

Makes 12

Ingredients

- 200g butter

- 200g plain chocolate , under 70% cocoa solids is fine
- 200g light, soft brown sugar
- 2 eggs , beaten

For the icing

- 200g plain chocolate
- 100ml double cream , not fridge-cold

- 1 tsp vanilla extract
- 250g self-raising flour
- Smarties , sweets and sprinkles, to decorate

- 50g icing sugar

Method

STEP 1

Heat oven to 160C/140C fan/gas 3 and line a 12-hole muffin tin with cases. Gently melt the butter, chocolate, sugar and 100ml hot water together in a large saucepan, stirring occasionally, then set aside to cool a little while you weigh the other ingredients.

STEP 2

Stir the eggs and vanilla into the chocolate mixture. Put the flour into a large mixing bowl, then stir in the chocolate mixture until smooth. Spoon into cases until just over three-quarters full (you may have a little mixture leftover), then set aside for 5 mins before putting on a low shelf in the oven and baking for 20-22 mins. Leave to cool.

STEP 3

For the icing, melt the chocolate in a heatproof bowl over a pan of barely simmering water. Once melted, turn off the heat, stir in the double cream and sift in the icing sugar. When spreadable, top each cake with some and decorate with your favourite sprinkles and sweets.

Bespoke martini kit

Ingredients

- 700ml bottle rye vodka
- small pot of juniper berries
- small pod of green cardamom pods
- small pot of dried rose petals
- small pot of coriander seeds

- 1 lemon
- 1 coffee filter paper
- bottle of vermouth
- small jar of green olives

Optional extras

- 2 martini glasses
- shot measure

- tall glass
- cocktail stirrer

- cocktail strainer

Method

STEP 1

To use the kit: Write the following instructions on the gift tag:
Open the bottle of vodka and add 2 tbsp juniper berries, 6 cardamom pods, a pinch of dried rose petals, 1 tsp coriander seeds and a strip of lemon peel. Put the lid back on and leave in a cool dark place for 24 hrs.

STEP 2

Strain the infused mixture through the coffee filter paper into a jug, then pour back into the bottle to store.

STEP 3

To make a martini, chill 2 martini glasses in the fridge for 30 mins. Put 50ml vermouth in a tall glass, add 150ml infused vodka and a large handful of ice. Stir well until the outside of the glass feels cold, then strain into the chilled glasses. Garnish with an olive.

Cheese, ham & grape kebabs

Prep:10 mins

Serves 1

Ingredients

- 6 bocconcini (mini mozzarella balls)
- 6 grapes (a combination of red and green looks nice),
- 6 cubes of ham

Method

STEP 1

Using 3 short wooden skewers, thread on the mini mozzarella balls, grapes, and cubes of ham. Place in a sealable container or wrap in cling film and pop in a lunchbox.

White rabbit biscuits

Prep: 1 hr and 10 mins **Cook:** 45 mins

Makes 30-35 biscuits or 15 bunnies

Ingredients

- 200g unsalted butter , at room temperature
- 400g plain flour
- 280g caster sugar
- 1 egg

- ¼ tsp vanilla extract
- a pinch of salt
- ½ tsp cream of tartar

For the icing:

- 600g icing sugar
- pink food colouring gel

- 170g pack of desiccated coconut
- 15 mini marshmallows

You will also need:

- 1 x rabbit head-shaped cookie cutter
- 1 x 7cm round cookie cutter

- 1 x 3cm round cookie cutter

Method

STEP 1

Heat oven to 180C/160C fan/gas 4. Lightly rub the butter and flour together with your fingertips until the mixture looks like fresh breadcrumbs.

STEP 2

Mix the sugar and egg together in another in a bowl with a whisk and when it is really well combined and runny add it to the flour mixture.

STEP 3

Add all the other ingredients and squish it together with your hands, keep working the dough until it's smooth, soft and comes together in one piece.

STEP 4

Roll the dough out on a lightly floured surface with a rolling pin until it is about half a centimetre thick. Cut into shapes. We did 15 rabbit heads, 15 large circles and 30 mini circles.

STEP 5

Place your biscuits on baking sheets lined with baking paper and bake in batches for about 15 mins (or until they are lightly golden at the edges).

STEP 6

Let them cool in the tin for a few minutes before carefully transferring them to a wire rack to cool completely and become crisp.

STEP 7

While the biscuits cool mix enough cold water with the icing sugar to create a thick icing. Place a quarter of the icing in another bowl and add a very small amout of pink gel food colouring. Transfer both the white icing and the pink icing into disposable piping bags and snip off the end to make a very small nozzle on the pink icing and a wider one on the white icing.

STEP 8

Pipe white icing over the small round biscuits and leave to dry. Then pipe white icing to cover all of the large circular biscuits and the rabbit biscuits (be fairly sparing and spread it out with the back of a spoon – it doesn't have to be neat on these ones). Once you've iced each one sprinkle generously with dessicated coconut before the icing dries.

STEP 9

Take the pink icing and use to create paws on the smaller circles then stick 2 of them onto each of the large circles using icing like glue. With the icing you have left, coat the marshmallows and cover those in coconut too before sticking them onto the middle of the larger circles to create a fluffy tail. Leave to set completely for about 15-20 mins then serve.

Winter warmer hearty risotto

Prep:10 mins **Cook:**50 mins

Serves 4

Ingredients

- 1 medium butternut squash
- 2 tbsp olive oil
- pinch of nutmeg , or pinch of cinnamon
- 1 red onion , finely chopped
- 1 vegetable stock cube
- 2 garlic cloves , crushed

- 500g risotto rice (we used arborio)
- 100g frozen peas
- 320g sweetcorn , drained
- 2 tbsp grated parmesan (or vegetarian alternative)

- handful chopped mixed herbs of your   choice

Method

STEP 1

Heat oven to 200C/180C fan/gas 6. Peel the butternut squash, slice it in half, then scoop out and discard the seeds.

STEP 2

Cut the flesh of the butternut squash into small cubes and put in a mixing bowl. Drizzle 1 tbsp olive oil over the squash, and season with black pepper, and nutmeg or cinnamon. Transfer the squash to a roasting tin and roast in the oven for about 25 mins until cooked through, then set aside.

STEP 3

Heat the remaining oil in a large saucepan over a low heat. Add the onion and cover the pan with a tight-fitting lid. Allow the onion to cook without colouring for 5-10 mins, stirring occasionally.

STEP 4

In a measuring jug, make up 1.5 litres of stock from boiling water and the stock cube. Stir well until the stock cube has dissolved. When the onion is soft, remove the lid and add the garlic to the onion pan. Leave it to cook for 1 min more.

STEP 5

Rinse the rice under cold water. Turn up the heat on the pan and add the rice to the onion and garlic, stirring well for 1 min. Pour a little of the hot stock into the pan and stir in until the liquid is absorbed by the rice.

STEP 6

Gradually add the rest of the stock to the pan, a little at a time, stirring constantly, waiting until each addition of stock is absorbed before adding more. Do this until the rice is cooked through and creamy – you may not need all the stock. This should take 15-20 mins. Take the roasting tin out of the oven – the squash should be soft and cooked.

STEP 7

Add the squash, peas and sweetcorn to the risotto and gently stir it in. Season to taste. Take the risotto pan off the heat and stir in the Parmesan and herbs. Put the lid back on the pan and let the risotto stand for 2-3 mins before serving.

Sausage plait

Prep:30 mins **Cook:**40 mins

Serves 4

Ingredients

- a little oil, for greasing
- 400g pack pork and apple sausage - about 6 fat sausages
- 1 roasted red pepper from a jar, patted dry with kitchen paper
- 1 large egg

- ½ tsp chilli flakes (optional)
- 2 tbsp tomato purée
- flour, for dusting
- 250g ready-made puff pastry
- baked beans or salad, to serve

Method

STEP 1

Heat oven to 200C/180C fan/ gas 6. Grease a baking tray with oil using a pastry brush, then cover it with baking parchment. Put to one side. Remove the meat from the sausage skins by snipping off the ends, then squeezing the sausagemeat into a bowl (see step 1).

STEP 2

Cut the pepper into small pieces with scissors. Break the egg into the cup, beat with a fork, and save 2 tbsp for glazing. Add the red pepper and remaining egg to the sausagemeat with the chilli flakes, if using, and purée. Mix well with a fork or clean hands (step 2).

STEP 3

Sprinkle some flour on the work surface. Using a rolling pin, roll out the pastry into a rough square shape, about 30 x 30cm. Put the pastry on the lined baking tray (step 3).

STEP 4

Now spoon the filling down the middle of the pastry in a sausage shape – leave a little gap at the top and bottom (about 3cm) (step 4).

STEP 5

Cut the pastry at a slight diagonal, on either side of the filling, into 1.5cm strips, the same number each side – we cut 12 strips each side. Brush the pastry all over with most of the saved egg (step 5).

STEP 6

Tuck the top and bottom edges of the pastry over the filling. Starting at the top, lay the pastry strips over the filling, taking one from each side, to cross like a plait. Now brush the top all over with the last of the egg. Bake for 35-40 mins or until golden. Serve hot or cold with baked beans or salad (step 6).

RECIPE TIPS

FOR PARENTS

This is an excellent recipe for children of all ages, as it doesn't require any sharp knives. Smaller children may need help using scissors and rolling the pastry to the desired shape, but don't worry if it doesn't look perfect – it will still taste great!

EQUIPMENT YOU NEED

Baking tray Pastry brush Baking parchment Kitchen scissors Large mixing bowl Kitchen paper Cup Fork, large spoon and cutlery knife Measuring spoons Rolling pin Ruler Oven gloves

BEFORE YOU START

Wash your hands, tie back long hair, if necessary, and put on an apron.

Simple sushi

Prep: 40 mins **Cook:** 15 mins

Makes enough sushi for 6 as a main, or 4 with leftovers for lunchboxes

Ingredients

For the rice

- 300g sushi rice
- 100ml rice wine vinegar
- 2 tbsp golden caster sugar

For the Japanese mayonnaise

- 3 tbsp mayonnaise
- 1 tbsp rice wine vinegar
- 1 tsp soy sauce

For the sushi

- 25g bag nori (seaweed) sheets
- choose from the following fillings: cucumber strips, smoked salmon, white crabmeat, canned tuna, red pepper, avocado, spring onion

To serve with all styles of sushi

- wasabi (optional - and fiery!)
- pickled ginger
- soy sauce

Method

STEP 1

KIDS the writing in bold is for you. ADULTS the rest is for you. TO MAKE SUSHI ROLLS: **Pat out some rice.** Lay a nori sheet on the mat, shiny-side down. Dip your hands in the vinegared water, then pat handfuls of rice on top in a 1cm thick layer, leaving the furthest edge from you clear.

STEP 2

Spread over some Japanese mayonnaise. Use a spoon to spread out a thin layer of mayonnaise down the middle of the rice.

STEP 3

Add the filling. Get your child to top the mayonnaise with a line of their favourite fillings – here we've used tuna and cucumber.

STEP 4

Roll it up. Lift the edge of the mat over the rice, applying a little pressure to keep everything in a tight roll.

STEP 5

Stick down the sides like a stamp. When you get to the edge without any rice, brush with a little water and continue to roll into a tight roll.

STEP 6

Wrap in cling film. Remove the mat and roll tightly in cling film before a grown-up cuts the sushi into thick slices, then unravel the cling film.

STEP 7

TO MAKE PRESSED SUSHI: **Layer over some smoked salmon.** Line a loaf tin with cling film, then place a thin layer of smoked salmon inside on top of the cling film.

STEP 8

Cover with rice and press down. Press about 3cm of rice over the fish, fold the cling film over and press down as much as you can, using another tin if you have one.

STEP 9

Tip it out like a sandcastle. Turn block of sushi onto a chopping board. Get a grown-up to cut into fingers, then remove the cling film.

STEP 10

TO MAKE SUSHI BALLS: **Choose your topping.** Get a small square of cling film and place a topping, like half a prawn or a small piece of smoked salmon, on it. Use damp hands to roll walnut-sized balls of rice and place on the topping.

STEP 11

Make into tight balls. Bring the corners of the cling film together and tighten into balls by twisting it up, then unwrap and serve.

Blackberry & apple loaf

Total time2 hrs

Cuts into 10 chunky slices

Ingredients

- 250g self-raising flour
- 175g butter
- 175g light muscovado sugar
- ½ tsp cinnamon
- 2rounded tbsp demerara sugar

- 1 small eating apple, such as Cox's, quartered (not cored or peeled)
- 2 large eggs, beaten
- 1 orange, finely grated zest
- 1 tsp baking powder
- 225g blackberry

Method

STEP 1

Preheat the oven to 180C/gas 4/fan 160C. Butter and line the bottom of a 1.7 litre loaf tin (see tip below). In a large bowl, rub the flour, butter and muscovado sugar together with your fingers to make fine crumbs. Measure out 5 level tbsp of this mixture into a small bowl for the topping, and mix in to it the cinnamon and demerara sugar. Set aside.

STEP 2

Coarsely grate the apple down to the core and mix in with the eggs and the zest. Stir the baking powder into the rubbed-in mixture in the large bowl, then quickly and lightly stir in the egg mixture until it drops lightly from the spoon. Don't overmix.

STEP 3

Gently fold in three quarters of the berries with a metal spoon, trying not to break them up. Spoon into the tin and level. Scatter the rest of the berries on top. Sprinkle over the topping and bake for 1¼ -1 hour 20 minutes. Check after 50 minutes and cover loosely with foil if it is browning too much. When done the cake will feel firm, but test with a skewer.

STEP 4

Leave in the tin for 30 minutes before turning out, then cool on a wire rack. Peel off the paper before cutting. Will keep wrapped in foil or in a tin for up to 2 days.

RECIPE TIPS

WATCHING THE TIME

A 9x20x13cm loaf tin is ideal, but if yours is shallower, the cake may cook faster, so test after an hour.

Prawn & mango salad

Prep:10 mins

Serves 2

Ingredients

- ½ avocado , peeled and cut into cubes, see tip, below left
- squeeze of lemon juice
- 50g small cooked prawns
- 1 mango cheek, peeled and cut into cubes
- 4 cherry tomatoes , halved
- finger-sized piece cucumber , chopped
- handful baby spinach leaves
- couple of mint leaves , very finely shredded
- 1-2 tsp sweet chilli sauce

Method

STEP 1

Mix the avocado with the lemon juice, then toss with the prawns, mango, tomatoes, cucumber, spinach and mint. Pack into a lunchbox and drizzle over the sweet chilli sauce, then chill until ready to eat.

Chocolate marble pancakes

Prep:10 mins **Cook:**10 mins

makes 12

Ingredients

- 200g self-raising flour
- 2 eggs
- 2 tbsp caster sugar
- 300ml whole milk

- 1 tsp vanilla extract
- 2 tbsp cocoa powder
- oil for frying
- chocolate sauce , to serve

Method

STEP 1

Put the flour, eggs and sugar into a bowl. Pour in the milk and whisk until you have a smooth batter, then divide in half. To one half of the batter, whisk in the vanilla extract, and to the other half, whisk in the cocoa powder.

STEP 2

Lightly oil a non-stick pan, set over a medium heat. Using two spoons, alternately drop the white and dark batter on top of each other, a little off centre, so that the colours very slightly spread until you have 4 concentric circles. Cook until the underside is bubbly then flip and cook for 30 seconds more. Repeat the process with the rest of the batter. Serve drizzled with chocolate sauce.

Pirate ship and treasure island cake

Prep:2 hrs and 30 mins **Cook:**45 mins

Serves 20 - 24

Ingredients

- 200g butter , cubed
- 300g dark plain chocolate , broken into pieces
- 200g plain flour
- ¾ tsp baking powder
- ¾ tsp bicarbonate of soda

- 250g light muscovado sugar , plus extra for decoration
- 3 eggs
- 200g soured cream
- 1 ½ tsp vanilla extract

For the icing and decoration

- 150g sieved apricot jam , warmed
- 650g brown ready-to-roll icing
- 18 mini Toblerones
- 6 malt chocolate balls
- 6 chocolate caramels (we used Rolos)
- 8 mini chocolate fingers
- 100g white marzipan
- gold covered chocolate coins
- chocolate skull (optional)
- 250g royal icing made from packet royal icing sugar (use 250g sugar)
- blue food colouring
- 1 chocolate stick (we used Mikado) (optional)

Equipment

- 30 x 20cm cake tin
- 30cm square cake board (preferably blue)
- 2 sheets black, white or blue paper
- 2 drinking straws
- 2 sandwich flags

Method

STEP 1

Heat the oven to 160C/140C fan/gas 3. Grease and line a 30x20cm cake tin with baking parchment.

STEP 2

Put the butter and 200g of the chocolate into a saucepan and heat gently until melted. Remove from the heat. Sieve the flour, baking powder and bicarbonate of soda into a large bowl. Mix in the sugar. Beat together the eggs, soured cream and vanilla extract. Pour the chocolate and egg mixtures into the flour and sugar and beat well until smooth. Pour into the prepared tin and bake in the oven for about 40 minutes. Leave until completely cold before cutting and shaping.

STEP 3

Cut the cake in half lengthways. Place one complete half on the 30cm cake board. Cut the remaining half into 3 rectangles, 13x10cm, 7x10cm and 10x10cm. Attach the 10x10cm piece to one end of the base cake using a little warm jam. Cut a 'V' shape to represent the prow of the ship. Place the 13x10 piece at the other end of the base cake, attaching with jam. Using jam again attach the 7x10 piece on top of the 13x10 piece to make the upper deck. Slice the back of the ship at a very slight angle.

STEP 4

Brush the whole cake with jam. Roll out about 550g of the ready-to-roll icing and cover the cake. Trim the edges at the base and keep any trimmings.

STEP 5

Melt the remaining 100g chocolate in the microwave or in a heatproof bowl over a saucepan of barely simmering water. Use melted chocolate to stick the mini Toblerones to the edges of the two decks and to the 'V' shape of the prow. Trim any to fit exactly. Use the chocolate to stick on the chocolate balls for canon balls, finger biscuits stacked up as canons and chocolate caramels for port holes. Using a little of the marzipan, roll out and cut four windows. Make window frames from brown icing trimmings, rolling out to thin sausages to form a cross and sticking with chocolate. Attach to the sides of the ship with chocolate. Poke the chocolate stick out of the front of the prow, if using.

STEP 6

Arrange the chocolate coins in a little pile on the cake board, reserving 3 or 4 coins for the top. Roll out the remaining brown icing and cover the coins completely. Brush with melted chocolate and sprinkle with muscovado sugar. Push 3 or 4 coins into the sand along with the chocolate skull if using.

STEP 7

Put a little of the royal icing in a bowl. Colour the remainder blue. Spread the icing on the cake board around the ship and the island. Use the white icing to make 'surf' around the edge of the island.

STEP 8

Using the remaining marzipan and brown icing, make three barrels. Place one on the deck of the ship and the others in the sea. Cut out sails from the paper and make holes in them so you can push the straws through. Attach the sails to the ship and poke sandwich flags out of the top to finish.

Sweet sushi

Prep: 40 mins **Cook:** 5 mins

Makes 24

Ingredients

- 45g butter
- 280g marshmallows
- 340g Rice Krispies

To decorate

- 10 cola belts
- 50g dark or milk chocolate , melted
- 50g millions
- 50g apricot jam
- 2 red pencil sweets
- 2 green pencil sweets

- 100g ready-to-roll fondant icing
- orange, red and purple food colouring
- white and green food colouring powder
- 25g black treacle

Method

STEP 1

To make your bases melt the butter and marshmallows in a large saucepan. Once melted, gently stir in the Rice Krispies. Pour the mixture onto a lined 30cm x 20cm tray and press down firmly to compact the Rice Krispies and make flat. Leave to set for 1-2 hours.

STEP 2

Once set, cut out 12 small circles with a small round cutter using a small sharp knife to cut all the way through to the bottom if needed. Use the rest of the mix to make 10 rectangular pieces.

STEP 3

Cut your cola belts to size, measuring them around the cutter. Stick them with a small smudge of melted chocolate. Repeat on all 10 and leave to set. Mix the millions and jam together and put small heaps on 6 of the circles to look like caviar. On the remaining 6 pieces, get a chopstick and make 4 indents in the centre of the rice. Cut your pencil sweets into small pieces and poke them into the indents alternating in colour.

STEP 4

To decorate the rectangles, split your fondant icing in half and colour half orange and half a purple/red colour so they look like salmon and tuna. Roll each out to 5mm thick. Use a knife to cut out shapes that will fit on top of the rectangles and use the back of a knife to make fine imprints to make the pieces more flesh-like. On the orange 'salmon' pieces, paint the imprints with the white colouring powder. Place all the bits of decorated icing on top of the rectangular bases, moulding them to look as natural as possible.

STEP 5

Use the green food colouring powder to brush the cola belts and create a seaweed effect.

STEP 6

Finally to make your 'soy sauce' heat the black treacle and 50ml water in a pan until combined. Brush over the 'tuna' and 'salmon' sushi pieces and put the rest in a bowl as a dipping sauce.

Marshmallows dipped in chocolate

Prep: 10 mins **Cook:** 5 mins

Makes 26 approx

Ingredients

- 50g white chocolate
- 50g milk chocolate
- selection of cake sprinkles

- 1 bag marshmallows (about 200g)
- 1 pack lollipop sticks

Method

STEP 1

Heat the chocolate in separate bowls over simmering water or on a low setting in the microwave. Allow to cool a little.

STEP 2

Put your chosen sprinkles on separate plates. Push a cake pop or lolly stick into a marshmallow about half way in. Dip into the white or milk chocolate, allow the excess to drip off then dip into the sprinkles of your choice. Put into a tall glass to set. Repeat with each marshmallow.

Barbecued chicken fajita skewers

Prep: 30 mins **Cook:** 10 mins

Makes 6-8 skewers

Ingredients

For the fajitas

- 2 limes , plus wedges to serve
- 1 tsp dried oregano
- 1 tsp ground cumin
- 1 tsp smoked paprika
- 1 tsp olive oil

- 2 garlic cloves , crushed or finely grated
- 4 chicken breasts
- 3 mixed coloured peppers
- 1 red onion

For the guacamole

- 2 ripe avocados
- 1 lime

- 6 cherry tomatoes , halved

- warmed tortillas , chopped coriander, soured cream or yogurt, plus chilli sauce

for the grown-ups, to serve

Method

STEP 1

Make the marinade. In a large bowl, juice both the limes. Add the oregano, spices, olive oil and garlic, and mix together. Dice the chicken, then get your child to stir it through the marinade, and set aside.

STEP 2

Prepare the vegetables. Deseeding the peppers and halving the onion is tricky, so do this yourself. Children aged from about seven or above can cut them into chunks using a child-friendly knife.

STEP 3

Make your skewers. Carefully thread alternate pieces of chicken, peppers and onion onto your skewers. Smaller children might find this a little hard, so the best way is to stab the ingredients and push them up the skewers. When you've used up all the ingredients, set aside. Can be made several hours ahead and chilled until ready to cook.

STEP 4

Prepare the guacamole. Stone and peel the avocados, then tip into a bowl with the other ingredients. Get your child to use a potato masher to mash everything together and tip into a serving dish.

STEP 5

Cook the skewers. Heat a barbecue or griddle pan. Cook the skewers for 10-12 mins, turning, until they are cooked all the way through. A child from the age of eight can watch over a griddle and turn the skewers with a pair of tongs. Serve the skewers on heated tortillas with the guacamole, soured cream, chopped coriander, lime wedges on the side and chilli sauce for those who like a touch of spice.

Happy lion birthday cake

Prep: 20 mins **Cook:** 25 mins

Serves 16-18 or more if cut into rectangles

Ingredients

- 250g pack unsalted butter

- 50ml whole milk

- 150g whole natural yogurt
- ½ tsp vanilla paste or extract
- 3 large eggs

- 250g white caster sugar
- 300g self-raising flour
- 2 tsp baking powder

To fill and cover

- 200g unsalted butter , very well softened
- 300g icing sugar
- 1 tsp vanilla paste or extract

- 2 tsp whole milk
- 2 heaped tbsp raspberry jam (or lemon curd)

To decorate the cake

- 25cm cake board , or cake plate
- yellow or orange food colouring paste (we used Sugarflair Egg Yellow)
- about 350g white sugar paste
- a few strands of spaghetti , snipped into finger lengths

- a little icing sugar , sifted, for rolling out
- 2 liquorice Catherine wheels with blue middles
- about 2 tsp chocolate sprinkles

Method

STEP 1

Heat the oven to 180C/fan 160C/gas 4. Use a little of the butter to grease the sides and bases of two 20cm sandwich tins. Melt the rest of the butter in a small saucepan. Off the heat, add the milk, yogurt and vanilla, followed by the eggs. Beat well with a fork.

STEP 2

Put the dry ingredients plus ¼ tsp salt into a large bowl. Whisk to combine – this aerates and saves sifting. Tip in the wet ingredients and whisk to a smooth, silky batter.

STEP 3

Don't hang around at this point. Pour the batter evenly into the prepared tins and put onto the middle shelf in the oven. Bake for 25 mins or until risen and a skewer inserted into the middle of the cakes comes out clean. Cool for 10 mins in the tins, then carefully invert the cakes and leave to cool upside down on a cooling rack.

STEP 4

Make the buttercream. Put the butter into a large bowl and sift the icing sugar on top. Add the vanilla and milk and a pinch of salt then beat for a few mins with electric beaters until creamy, pale and spreadable.

STEP 5

Place one of the cakes onto the board or plate, and use a dab of buttercream underneath the cake to stop it slipping about. Spread with 1/4 of the buttercream and then all of the jam, if using.

STEP 6

Sandwich the second cake on top. Set aside 1 tsp buttercream to affix the ears later, then mound the rest on top of the cake. Use a palette knife to paddle it evenly over and down the sides. Set aside.

STEP 7

For the lion's mane and cheeks, use a little of the colouring paste to colour the sugarpaste yellow or orange, then split the paste in half. Add more colouring paste to one half and knead again to make it a shade darker. Roll two walnut-size balls of the darker paste to make the cheeks. Poke in the spaghetti to make whiskers, then set aside.

STEP 8

Using a little icing sugar, roll out the rest to about 2 x £1 coin thickness then cut into 12 squares measuring about 4 x 4cm. Re-roll any trimmings. Shape two small blobs into ears.

STEP 9

Position the squares around the cake, alternating lighter and darker yellow. Let the squares overhang the cake slightly with only the innermost corners meeting. Scatter the chocolate sprinkles into the gaps in-between.

STEP 10

Unroll a Catherine wheel. Cut two lengths of 20cm. Loop one end of each piece, then position on the cake to make the eyes and sides of the lion's nose. Poke into the buttercream. Add another strip of liquorice down the centre of the nose and a wiggly line to one side to give it some shadowing, if you like.

STEP 11

Make the bottom of the nose by snipping ever-decreasing lengths of liquorice and poking them into the buttercream.

STEP 12

Add two more curls for his mouth and two for eyebrows. Position the round cheeks to the sides. Put the middles of the Catherine wheels towards the bottom of the eyes to make pupils.

STEP 13

Put the cheeks onto the lion's face. Fix the ears on top using a small blob of leftover buttercream. Leave the cake to set for an hour before cutting. If the sponges are used fresh or within a day of baking (wrap well once cooled), the finished cake will keep in a cool place (not the fridge) for 3 days.

Winter wonderland cake

Prep: 1 hr **Cook:** 35 mins

Serves 12

Ingredients

- 175g unsalted butter , softened, plus more for the tin
- 250g golden caster sugar
- 3 large eggs
- 225g plain flour
- 2 tsp baking powder
- 50g crème fraîche

For the angel frosting

- 500g white caster sugar
- 1 tsp vanilla extract
- 1 tbsp liquid glucose

- 100g dark chocolate , melted and cooled a little
- 3 tbsp strawberry jam
- 8-10 candy canes , red and white
- mini white meringues and jelly sweets, to decorate

- 2 egg whites
- 30g icing sugar , sifted

Method

STEP 1

Heat oven to 180C/160C fan/gas 4. Butter and line three 18cm (or two 20cm) cake tins. Beat the butter and sugar together until light and fluffy. Add the eggs, beating them in one at a time. Fold in the flour, baking powder and a pinch of salt, then fold in the crème fraîche and chocolate and 100ml boiling water.

STEP 2

Divide the cake mixture between the tins and level the tops of the batter. Bake for 25-30 mins or until a skewer inserted into the middle comes out clean. Leave to cool for 10 mins in the tin, then tip out onto a cooling rack and peel off the parchment. Set aside to cool completely.

STEP 3

To make the angel frosting, put the sugar, vanilla and liquid glucose in a pan with 125ml water. Bring to the boil and cook until the sugar has melted – the syrup turns clear and the mixture hits 130C on a sugar thermometer (be very careful with hot sugar). Take off the heat. Meanwhile, beat the egg whites until stiff then, while still beating, gradually pour in the hot sugar syrup in a steady stream. Keep beating until the mixture is fluffy and thick enough to spread – this might take a few mins as the mixture cools. Beat in the icing sugar.

STEP 4

Spread two of the sponges with jam and some of the icing mixture, then sandwich the cakes together with the plain one on top. Use a little of the frosting to ice the whole cake (don't worry about crumbs at this stage). Use the remaining icing to ice the cake again, smoothing the side, and swirling it on top. Crush four of the candy canes and sprinkle over the cake, then add the remaining whole candy canes, meringues and sweets.

Bacon bolognese

Prep:10 mins **Cook:**12 mins

Serves 4

Ingredients

- 400g spaghetti
- 1 tsp olive oil
- 2 large carrots , finely diced
- 3 celery sticks, finely diced

- 200g pack smoked bacon lardon
- 190g jar sundried tomato pesto
- 8-12 basil leaves , shredded (optional)

Method

STEP 1

Boil the spaghetti following pack instructions. Meanwhile, heat the oil in a non-stick pan. Add the carrots, celery and bacon, and stir well. Cover the pan and cook, stirring occasionally, for 10 mins until the veg has softened.

STEP 2

Tip in the pesto, warm through, then stir through the drained spaghetti with the basil, if using.

Nutty cinnamon & yogurt dipper

Prep: 5 mins

Serves 1

Ingredients

- 100g natural Greek yogurt
- 1 tbsp nut butter (try almond or cashew)
- ¼ tsp ground cinnamon
- 1 tsp honey

To serve

- apple wedges (tossed in a little lemon juice to prevent them turning brown)
- celery sticks
- carrot sticks
- mini rice cakes or crackers (choose gluten-free brands if necessary)

Method

STEP 1

In a small tub, mix together the yogurt, nut butter, cinnamon and honey. Serve with apple wedges (tossed in a little lemon juice to prevent them turning brown), celery or carrot sticks, and mini rice cakes or crackers.

Vanilla chick biscuit pops

Prep: 15 mins **Cook:** 6 mins - 7 mins

Makes 15-18 biscuits

Ingredients

- 200g unsalted butter , at room temperature
- 100g golden caster sugar
- 1 medium egg , beaten
- 1 tsp vanilla extract
- 200g plain flour , plus extra for dusting
- 200g icing sugar
- 2 tbsp milk
- few drops yellow food colouring
- 75g unsweetened desiccated coconut
- 50g small chocolate chips
- 25g orange or white fondant icing , plus a few drops orange food colouring

You will need

- 15-18 lolly sticks (see tip)
- ribbon , to decorate (optional)

Method

STEP 1

Put half the butter and all the sugar in a bowl. Using an electric whisk or wooden spoon, beat together until smooth and creamy. Beat in the egg and half the vanilla extract until thoroughly combined.

STEP 2

Tip the flour into the mixture and mix on a low speed until it comes together to form a dough. Gather up into a ball, wrap in cling film and chill in the fridge for 20 mins.

STEP 3

Heat oven to 180C/160C fan/gas 4. Line 2 baking trays with baking parchment. Put the biscuit dough on a lightly floured surface and roll out until about 5mm thick. Cut out the biscuits using a 6cm round cutter. Transfer the biscuits to the prepared trays and insert the lolly sticks into the sides, just a quarter of the way through. Bake for 6-7 mins until the edges are golden brown, then carefully transfer to a wire rack and allow to cool completely before decorating.

STEP 4

Meanwhile, make some buttercream frosting. Place the remaining softened butter in a bowl and beat with a wooden spoon. Slowly add the icing sugar, 1 tbsp at a time, until thoroughly incorporated and you have a smooth, creamy mixture. Add a little milk and the remaining vanilla extract with a few drops of food colouring to give a pale yellow colour. Chill for 5 mins.

STEP 5

Put the desiccated coconut in a small bowl, add a few drops of yellow food colouring and mix well until the coconut is coloured pale yellow.

STEP 6

Spread the buttercream frosting over one side of the biscuit and sprinkle with the coconut. Add 2 chocolate chip eyes to each. Pinch a little orange fondant icing and shape into a beak and press into the mixture. Decorate with a ribbon, if you like, and serve. Will keep for 2 days in an airtight container.

Pressed picnic sandwich

Prep: 25 mins **Cook:** 3 mins

Serves 8

Ingredients

- long ciabatta loaf, sliced in half lengthways
- 3 tbsp olive oil
- 1 tbsp balsamic vinegar
- 2 garlic cloves , finely chopped
- 1 tsp Dijon mustard
- 2 big handfuls of baby spinach
- 8 marinated artichoke hearts from a jar, quartered
- 250g roasted red pepper from a jar
- 8 slices prosciutto
- big handful of basil
- 125g ball mozzarella , cut into slices
- ½ red onion , very finely sliced

Method

STEP 1

Ask an adult to slice the ciabatta loaf in half lengthways and heat the oven to 200C/180C fan/gas 6.

STEP 2

Put the ciabatta loaf halves, crust-side down, on a large baking tray and drizzle with a little olive oil. Pop them in the oven for a few mins until just golden and lightly toasted.

STEP 3

Put the olive oil, balsamic vinegar, garlic and mustard in a bowl, then whisk them together with a fork.

STEP 4

Remove the toasted ciabatta halves from the tray and drizzle the bottom slice with about half of the dressing.

STEP 5

Arrange the rest of the ingredients in layers. Start with a large handful of baby spinach, then a few artichoke hearts.

STEP 6

Next add the slices of pepper, the prosciutto, basil, mozzarella and, finally, the red onion.

STEP 7

Drizzle over the rest of the dressing and pop the other slice of ciabatta on top.

STEP 8

Press down on the sandwich to squash all the layers together.

STEP 9

Wrap the sandwich in baking parchment and tie it together with a couple of pieces of string.

STEP 10

Place a heavy baking tray on top of your sandwich and top it with weights or loaf tins filled with baking beans. Pop it all in the fridge overnight or until you are ready to eat it. Cut and serve in slices for the perfect picnic snack.

RECIPE TIPS

EQUIPMENT YOU WILL NEED

Chopping board, knife, 2 baking trays, oven gloves, small bowl, fork, spoon, baking parchment, ball of string, weights or loaf tins filled with baking beans.

ADAPTING FLAVOURS

If your kids aren't keen on some of the flavours, simply swap them for fillings they do like. Try, for example, ham, cheddar & tomato or tuna, watercress & cucumber.

Christmas pudding Rice Krispie cakes

Prep:30 hrs **Cook:**5 mins

Makes 10 - 12

Ingredients

- 50g rice pops (we used Rice Krispies)
- 30g raisin , chopped
- 50g butter
- 100g milk chocolate , broken into pieces
- 2 tbsp crunchy peanut butter
- 30g mini marshmallow
- 80g white chocolate
- ready-made icing holly leaves (we used Sainsbury's Christmas cake decorations)

Method

STEP 1

Put the rice pops and raisins into a bowl. Put the butter, milk chocolate, peanut butter and marshmallows into a small saucepan. Place on a medium to low heat and stir until the chocolate and butter have melted but the marshmallows are just beginning to melt.

STEP 2

Pour onto the rice pops and stir until well coated. Line an egg cup with cling film. Press about a tablespoon of the mixture into the egg cup. Press firmly and then remove, peel off the cling film and place the pudding into a cake case, flat-side down. Repeat with the remaining mixture. Chill until firm.

STEP 3

Melt the white chocolate in the microwave or in bowl over a saucepan of barely simmering water. Spoon a little chocolate over the top of each pudding. Top with icing holly leaves.

Whisky & pink peppercorn marmalade kit

Ingredients

- 500g mix of oranges , clementines and lemons
- 1kg demerara sugar

Optional extras

- jam pan
- muslin
- large wooden spoon

To use kit

see tip

- small pot of pink peppercorns
- small bottle of whisky

- small jars and labels (makes about 1kg jam)

Method

STEP 1

To use the kit: Write the following instructions on the gift tag:
Halve the fruits and squeeze the juices into a large saucepan. Remove all the peel and set aside. Put the flesh in the pan with 1 litre water and boil for 15 mins. Push through a sieve lined with muslin and return the liquid to the pan.

STEP 2

Shred the peel and tip into a heatproof bowl. Add enough water to just cover and microwave for 3-4 mins until soft. Add the peel to the pan, then add the sugar. Boil for 35-45 mins until the marmalade has reached setting point (keep an eye on it so it doesn't bubble over).

STEP 3

Remove from the heat and add 1 tsp pink peppercorns. Allow the mixture to cool a little, then stir in 50ml whisky. Ladle into sterilised jars and seal. Will keep for up to one year.

Yummy chocolate log

Prep:30 mins **Cook:**10 mins

Serves 8

Ingredients

For the cake

- 3 eggs
- 85g golden caster sugar
- 85g plain flour (minus 2 tbsp)
- 2 tbsp cocoa powder
- ½ tsp baking powder

For the filling & icing

- 50g butter, plus extra for the tin
- 140g dark chocolate , broken into squares
- 1 tbsp golden syrup
- 284ml pot double cream
- 200g icing sugar, sifted
- 2-3 extra strong mints, crushed (optional)
- icing sugar and holly sprigs to decorate - ensure you remove the berries before serving

Method

STEP 1

Heat the oven to 200C/180C fan/gas 6. Butter and line a 23 x 32cm Swiss roll tin with baking parchment. Beat the eggs and golden caster sugar together with an electric whisk for about 8 mins until thick and creamy.

STEP 2

Mix the flour, cocoa powder and baking powder together, then sift onto the egg mixture. Fold in very carefully, then pour into the tin. Tip the tin from side to side to spread the mixture into the corners. Bake for 10 mins.

STEP 3

Lay a sheet of baking parchment on a work surface. When the cake is ready, tip it onto the parchment, peel off the lining paper, then roll the cake up from its longest edge with the paper inside. Leave to cool.

STEP 4

To make the icing, melt the butter and dark chocolate together in a bowl over a pan of hot water. Take from the heat and stir in the golden syrup and 5 tbsp double cream. Beat in the icing sugar until smooth.

STEP 5

Whisk the remaining double cream until it holds its shape. Unravel the cake, spread the cream over the top, scatter over the crushed extra strong mints, if using, then carefully roll up again into a log.

STEP 6

Cut a thick diagonal slice from one end of the log. Lift the log on to a plate, then arrange the slice on the side with the diagonal cut against the cake to make a branch. Spread the icing over the log and branch (don't cover the ends), then use a fork to mark the icing to give the effect of tree bark. Scatter with unsifted icing sugar to resemble snow, and decorate with holly.

Pudsey bear cake

Prep:1 hr and 15 mins **Cook:**30 mins

Serves 10 - 12

Ingredients

- 225g softened butter
- 225g golden caster sugar
- 4 large eggs
- ½ lemon , zested

- 1 tsp vanilla extract
- 225g self-raising flour
- splash of milk

For the filling and covering

- 200g icing sugar
- 100g butter , softened
- 2 tsp milk

- 50g raspberry jam or strawberry jam, plus extra for sticking
- icing sugar for dusting
- 250g white fondant

To decorate

- 200g black sugar paste

- 100g yellow sugar paste

- 25g white fondant
- red, green and blue, fondant or coloured icing pens

Method

STEP 1

Heat oven to 180C/160C fan/gas 4, butter and line the base of two 20cm spring-form cake tins with baking parchment.

STEP 2

Using an electric whisk, beat the butter and sugar together until pale and fluffy. Crack the eggs in one at a time and whisk well, scraping down the sides of the bowl after each addition. Add the lemon zest, vanilla, flour, milk and a pinch of salt. Whisk until just combined then divide the mixture between the two tins.

STEP 3

Bake in the centre of the oven for 25-30 mins until a skewer inserted into the middle of each cake comes out clean. After 10 mins remove the cakes from their tins and leave to cool completely on a wire rack.

STEP 4

While the cakes cool, stir together the icing sugar, butter and milk for the filling. Once roughly mixed switch to using electric beaters until smooth and pale. When the cake is cold spread one third of the buttercream over one of the sponges and top with the jam. Smooth it over evenly then top with the other sponge. Spread the buttercream all over the outside of the sandwiched cake in an even thin layer and chill in the fridge until needed.

STEP 5

Dust your work surface with icing sugar and roll out 250g white fondant so that it is big enough to cover the cake. Lay it over the chilled cake, smooth down the surface and trim off any excess. Now roll out the black sugar paste so it's approx. 5mm thick then cut into the shape of Pudsey's head (it's easier to do this if you draw a template first then draw around it). Use a little buttercream or water to stick this on top of the cake. Roll out the yellow sugar paste and cut a slightly smaller version of Pudsey's head to stick on top in the same way so that the black sugar paste becomes the outline.

STEP 6

Roll out the remaining fondant to make the eyepatch, nose, mouth and eye and eyebrow and stick all the pieces on with a little bit of water. Use coloured sugar paste or writing icing to create polka

117

dots on the eye patch. Use a clean paintbrush dipped in water to remove any excess icing sugar from your design. Will keep covered for 2-3 days in a cool place.

Easy Easter nests

Prep:25 mins **Cook:**8 mins

Makes 12

Ingredients

- 200g milk chocolate , broken into pieces
- 85g shredded wheat , crushed

You'll also need

- cupcake cases

- 2 x 100g bags mini chocolate eggs

Method

STEP 1

Melt the chocolate in a small bowl placed over a pan of barely simmering water. Pour the chocolate over the shredded wheat and stir well to combine.

STEP 2

Spoon the chocolate wheat into 12 cupcake cases and press the back of a teaspoon in the centre to create a nest shape. Place 3 mini chocolate eggs on top of each nest. Chill the nests in the fridge for 2 hrs until set.

Coconut bauble truffles

Prep:45 mins

plus at least 2 hrs chilling, no cook

Makes about 20

Ingredients

- 250g madeira cake
- 85g ready-to-eat dried apricots , finely chopped

To decorate

- 25g desiccated coconut
- 125ml light condensed milk

- 140g desiccated coconut
- different food colourings , we used yellow, pink, blue and purple

Method

STEP 1

In a big mixing bowl, crumble the cake with your fingers – try to get the bits as small as possible.

STEP 2

Tip in the apricots and coconut. Using your hands again, mix together with the cake crumbs. Use a wooden spoon to stir in the condensed milk. After you've mixed it in a bit, use your fingers to pull off any bits stuck to the spoon. Squidge everything together with your hands until it is well mixed and all the cake crumbs are sticky. Rub your hands together over the bowl so any bits that are stuck drop off.

STEP 3

Line some trays that fit in your fridge with baking parchment. Roll the sticky cake mixture into small balls (about the size of a conker or gobstopper) between your hands. Line them up on the trays, then put them in the fridge while you get the decorations ready.

STEP 4

Decide on how many different food colourings you are going to use, then split the coconut into the same number of piles. Put each pile of coconut into a plastic sandwich bag, add a few drops of food colouring to each, and tie a knot in the top. Shake the bags and scrunch between your fingers until all the coconut is coloured – if it's not bright enough, open the bag and add a few more drops of colouring.

STEP 5

Open all the bags of coloured coconut and take the truffles from the fridge. Put 1 tbsp of water in a small bowl and lightly coat each truffle in it so the coconut can stick to the outside of each bauble.

STEP 6

One by one, drop each truffle into one of your bags. Shake it and roll it around until the outside is covered in coconut. Carefully put each truffle back onto the trays and chill for at least another 2 hrs until they are really cold and firm.

STEP 7

If you like, put some of the truffles in gift bags or boxes and tie with ribbons to give as presents. Will keep in the fridge for up to 1 week.

No-fuss fish pie

Prep: 30 mins **Cook:** 25 mins

Serves 4

Ingredients

- 400ml milk
- 1 bay leaf
- 1 garlic clove , finely chopped
- 1 medium onion , thinly sliced
- 300g skinless, boneless fish (we used a mix of salmon, smoked haddock and cod)
- 5 medium potatoes
- 3 parsnips , peeled
- 2 eggs
- 125g (drained weight) can sweetcorn
- 125g frozen peas
- 2 tbsp mixed chopped herbs (lemon thyme, coriander and chives are nice)
- zest 0.5 lemon
- small pack of cooked small prawns (optional)
- 4 tsp crème fraîche
- pinch of ground nutmeg
- pinch of white pepper
- 1 tsp wholegrain mustard
- 25g butter
- 50g grated cheese
- steamed carrots , to serve
- steamed broccoli , to serve

Method

STEP 1

Heat oven to 190C/170C fan/gas 5. Put the milk in a saucepan with the bay leaf, garlic and onion. Add the fish and poach on a medium heat for 15 mins. The milk should be just covering the fish, if not, add a little more.

STEP 2

Cut the potatoes and parsnips into equal-sized pieces and put in a saucepan. Cover with cold water and a lid, bring to the boil, then simmer on a medium heat for 10 mins, or until the potatoes and parsnips are soft (not falling apart).

STEP 3

Meanwhile, gently put the eggs in a small pan of water and bring to the boil. Cook for 7 mins, then transfer to a bowl of cold water and leave to cool. Once cool, peel and chop them.

STEP 4

When the fish is cooked (it should be firm to the touch and flake easily), remove from the milk, along with the onion, using a slotted spoon. Strain the milk into a jug and keep it for the mash.

STEP 5

Flake the fish into bite-sized chunks (checking for bones) and place in the bottom of a casserole dish, then add the onion, sweetcorn and peas.

STEP 6

Add the herbs, lemon zest, prawns (if using), hard-boiled eggs and the crème fraîche. Season and mix well.

STEP 7

Drain the parsnips and potatoes in a colander, and return to the saucepan. Add the nutmeg, white pepper, mustard and a knob of butter and mash well.

STEP 8

Taste to check the seasoning. Cover the fish filling with the mashed potato and, using a fork, create a wavy pattern, if you like. Sprinkle over the grated cheese.

STEP 9

Place in the oven for 20 mins or until the cheese is melted and golden brown, remove from the oven using oven gloves and serve with steamed crunchy carrots and broccoli.

Best ever pesto & potato pasta

Prep:20 mins **Cook:**11 mins

Serves 4 - 6

Ingredients

- 150g green bean
- 300g new potato
- 300g short dried pasta like fusilli or a long pasta like linguine
- For the pesto
- large bunch basil

- 50g pine nuts
- 50g parmesan (or vegetarian alternative), grated, plus extra to serve (optional)
- 2 garlic cloves
- 100ml olive oil

Method

STEP 1

KIDS: the writing in bold is for you. GROWN-UPS: the rest is for you. **Pick the basil for the pesto.** Get your child to pick the basil leaves off the stalks. Ask them to look at and smell the leaves as you tell them the name of the herb until they remember it – try to do this with all herbs when you can.

STEP 2

Make the pesto. Toast the pine nuts in a pan over a low heat. A child of seven years plus can stir the nuts in the pan. Tip into a mini chopper (or use a pestle and mortar) with the basil, parmesan, garlic and olive oil. Blitz or pound into a green sauce, then set aside.

STEP 3

Chop up the beans. Using a child-friendly knife, get children from the age of five to chop the green beans into shorter lengths, and quarter the potatoes. Younger children can snap the beans into short lengths while you prepare the potatoes.

STEP 4

Cook the vegetables and pasta. Bring a large pan of water to the boil, add the potatoes and boil for 3 mins. Remove from the heat and ask the child to tip in the pasta and give it a stir. Put the pan back on the heat, boil the pasta for 5 mins, add the beans and cook for a final 3 mins.

STEP 5

Mix everything together. Drain everything well and tip into a bowl. Spoon most of the pesto into the pasta and stir everything together to coat. Bring the large bowl of pasta to the table and serve with extra parmesan, more basil and remaining pesto, if you like.

RECIPE TIPS

WHAT SKILLS CAN KIDS LEARN FROM MAKING PESTO PASTA?

As well as making a family meal, this recipe requires a couple of key skills that will help younger children become more confident cooks. COOKING PASTA: Pasta has become such a staple part of the family diet that it's really useful for children to know how to cook it. It's one of the first lessons of everyday cooking and the sooner they understand it, the better. IDENTIFYING HERBS/INGREDIENTS: Every time you cook with an aromatic ingredient, encourage your child to smell or taste it and repeat the name of the ingredient. this can start from a very early age, before they actually start cooking properly. It's such a little thing, but it helps children to feel comfortable around food and excited about trying new ingredients.

Carrot cake traybake

Prep: 30 mins **Cook:** 30 mins

Makes 6-12

Ingredients

- 200g carrots , peeled
- 175g soft brown sugar
- 200g self-raising flour
- 1 tsp bicarbonate of soda

- 2 tsp cinnamon
- zest 1 orange
- 2 eggs
- 150ml sunflower oil

For the icing

- 50g softened butter
- 75g icing sugar

- 200g soft cheese
- sprinkles (optional)

Method

STEP 1

Line an 18cm square tin with baking parchment. **Ask your grown-up helper** to turn the oven on to 180C/160C fan/gas 4. Grate the carrots on the fine side of the grater, then tip them into a large bowl.

STEP 2

Sift the sugar, flour, bicarb and cinnamon on top of the carrot, then add the orange zest and mix everything around a bit.

STEP 3

Break the eggs into a bowl (scoop out any bits of shell), then add them to the bowl along with the oil. Mix everything together well.

STEP 4

Scoop the cake mix into your tin and level the top. **Ask a grown-up** to put it in the oven for 30 minutes or until the cake is cooked. Cool.

STEP 5

To make the icing, mix the butter and icing sugar together, then stir in the soft cheese until smooth.

STEP 6

When the cake is cool, spread the top with the icing and cut into squares. Decorate with sprinkles, if you like.

Simnel muffins

Prep: 45 mins - 55 mins

Makes 12

Ingredients

- 250g mixed dried fruit
- grated zest and juice 1 medium orange
- 175g softened butter
- 175g golden caster sugar
- 3 eggs , beaten
- 300g self-raising flour
- 1 tsp mixed spice

- ½ tsp freshly grated nutmeg
- 5 tbsp milk
- 175g marzipan
- 200g icing sugar
- 2 tbsp orange juice for mixing
- mini eggs

Method

STEP 1

Tip the fruit into a bowl, add the zest and juice and microwave on medium for 2 minutes (or leave to soak for 1 hour). Line 12 deep muffin tins with paper muffin cases.

STEP 2

Preheat the oven to fan 180C/ 160C/gas 4. Beat together the butter, sugar, eggs, flour, spices and milk until light and fluffy (about 3-5 minutes) – use a wooden spoon or hand held mixer. Stir the fruit in well.

STEP 3

Half fill the muffin cases with the mixture. Divide the marzipan into 12 equal pieces, roll into balls, then flatten with your thumb to the size of the muffin cases. Put one into each muffin case and spoon the rest of the mixture over it. Bake for 25-30 minutes, until risen, golden and firm to the touch. Leave to cool.

STEP 4

Beat together the icing sugar and orange juice to make icing thick enough to coat the back of a wooden spoon. Drizzle over the muffins and top with a cluster of eggs. Leave to set. Best eaten within a day of making.

Choco-dipped tangerines

Prep: 10 mins

Serves 1

Ingredients

- 1 tangerine , peeled and segmented
- 10g dark chocolate , melted

Method

STEP 1

Dip half of each tangerine segment in the melted chocolate, then put on a baking sheet lined with parchment. Keep in the fridge for 1 hr to set completely, or overnight if you prefer.

Chicken schnitzel strips with tomato spaghetti

Prep: 30 mins **Cook:** 20 mins

Serves 4

Ingredients

- 2 large eggs , beaten
- 3 tbsp plain flour
- 2 tbsp grated parmesan
- zest 1 lemon
- 150g fresh white breadcrumbs
- 4 small chicken breasts
- 350g spaghetti
- 3 tbsp sunflower oil
- rocket leaf or green salad, to serve

For the tomato sauce

- 400g can chopped tomatoes with olive oil and garlic
- 1 tbsp tomato purée
- handful basil leaves , torn

Method

STEP 1

First, make the tomato sauce. Tip the tomatoes into a medium saucepan and add 1 /2 a can of water. Stir in the tomato purée, season and simmer for 15 mins. Keep warm while you make the chicken.

STEP 2

Put the eggs in a shallow dish. Lightly season the flour and tip it into another shallow dish. Mix the Parmesan, lemon zest and breadcrumbs together and tip onto a plate.

STEP 3

Place each chicken breast between two sheets of cling film on a chopping board. Ask your child to help bash them gently with a rolling pin until they are about 2cm thick. Cut each flattened chicken breast into five or six strips.

STEP 4

Cook the spaghetti in a pan of boiling salted water for 10-12 mins or following pack instructions. Get your child to help you coat the chicken strips in the flour and shake off any excess. Dip them in the beaten egg, letting any excess drip off, then finally coat them well in the breadcrumbs and put on a plate. Once all the chicken strips are coated, heat the oil in a large frying pan until hot.

STEP 5

Add the chicken strips to the pan in batches and fry for 2-3 mins each side until cooked through – you may need to wipe out the pan in between batches. Lift out and drain on kitchen paper.

STEP 6

Drain the spaghetti, then mix with the tomato sauce. Serve alongside the chicken strips and some rocket leaves or a crisp green salad.

Chocolate crunch bars

Cook: 5 mins

Prep: 20 mins plus chilling

Cuts into 12

Ingredients

- 100g butter , roughly chopped
- 300g dark chocolate (such as Bournville), broken into squares
- 3 tbsp golden syrup
- 140g rich tea biscuit , roughly crushed
- 12 pink marshmallows , quartered (use scissors)
- 2 x 55g bars Turkish delight , halved and sliced (or use Maltesers, Milky Way or Crunchie bars)

Method

STEP 1

Gently melt the butter, chocolate and syrup in a pan over a low heat, stirring frequently until smooth, then cool for about 10 mins.

STEP 2

Stir the biscuits and sweets into the pan until well mixed, then pour into a 17cm square tin lined with foil and spread the mixture to roughly level it. Chill until hard, then cut into fingers.

Eerie eyeball pops

Prep:30 mins **Cook:**5 mins

Makes 10

Ingredients

- 100g/4oz madeira cake
- 100g Oreo cookie
- 100g bar milk chocolate, melted

You will also need

- 10 wooden skewers

- 200g bar white chocolate, melted
- few Smarties and icing pens, to decorate

- ½ small pumpkin or butternut squash , deseeded, to stand pops in

Method

STEP 1

Break the Madeira cake and cookies into the bowl of a food processor, pour in the melted milk chocolate and whizz to combine.

STEP 2

Tip the mixture into a bowl, then use your hands to roll into about 10 walnut-sized balls. Chill for 2 hrs until really firm.

STEP 3

Push a skewer into each ball, then carefully spoon the white chocolate over the cake balls to completely cover. Stand the cake pops in the pumpkin, then press a Smartie onto the surface while wet. Chill again until the chocolate has set. Before serving, using the icing pens, add a pupil to each Smartie and wiggly red veins to the eyeballs.

Fruity Neapolitan lolly loaf

Prep:25 mins

25 mins plus 8 hours freezing time

Serves 8

Ingredients

- 200g peaches nectarines or apricots (or a mixture), stoned
- 200g strawberries or raspberries (or a mixture), hulled
- 450ml double cream
- ½ x 397g can condensed milk
- 2 tsp vanilla extract
- orange and pink food colouring (optional)
- 8 wooden lolly sticks

Method

STEP 1

Put the peaches, nectarines or apricots in a food processor and pulse until they're chopped and juicy but still with some texture. Scrape into a bowl. Repeat with the berries and scrape into another bowl.

STEP 2

Pour the cream, condensed milk and vanilla into a third bowl and whip until just holding soft peaks. Add roughly a third of the mixture to the peaches and another third to the berries, and mix both until well combined. Add a drop of orange food colouring to the peach mixture and a drop of pink food colouring to the berry mixture if you want a really vibrant colour. Line a 900g loaf tin or terrine mould with cling film (look for a long thin one, ours was 23 x 7 x 8cm), then pour in the berry mixture. Freeze for 2 hrs and chill the remaining mixtures in the fridge.

STEP 3

Once the bottom layer is frozen, remove the vanilla mixture from the fridge and pour over the berry layer. The bottom layer should now be firm enough to support your lolly sticks, so place these, evenly spaced, along the length of the loaf tin, pushing down gently until they stand up straight. Return to the freezer for another 2 hrs.

STEP 4

4 Once the vanilla layer is frozen, pour over the peach mixture, easing it around the lolly sticks. Return to the freezer for a further 4 hrs or until completely frozen. Remove from the freezer 10 mins before serving. Use the cling film to help you remove the loaf from the tin. Take to the table

on a board and slice off individual lollies for your guests. Any leftovers can be kept in the freezer for up to 2 weeks.

Easy tuna pasta bake

Prep: 10 mins

Cook: 20 mins

Serves 4

Ingredients

- 400g fusilli pasta
- 100g frozen pea
- 50g butter
- 50g plain flour
- 600ml milk

- 1 tsp Dijon mustard
- 2 x 195g cans tuna , drained
- 4 spring onions , sliced
- 198g can sweetcorn , drained
- 100g cheddar , grated

Method

STEP 1

Bring a pan of water to the boil. Add the pasta and cook, following pack instructions, until tender. Add the peas for the final 3 mins cooking time.

STEP 2

Meanwhile, melt the butter in a pan over a medium heat. Stir in the flour and cook for 2 mins. Add the milk, whisking constantly, then slowly bring to the boil, stirring often, until sauce thickens. Remove from the heat, add the mustard and season well.

STEP 3

Heat the grill to medium. Drain the pasta and peas, then return to the pan and stir in the tuna, spring onions, sweetcorn and sauce. Tip into a shallow baking dish, top with the cheddar and cook under the grill for 5 mins or until golden and bubbling.

Crisp chicken bites

Prep: 10 mins **Cook:** 15 mins

Serve 12 for lunch

Ingredients

- 4 boneless chicken breast fillets
- 6 tbsp red pesto

- 3 large handfuls breadcrumbs , frsh or dried (about 300g/10oz)
- olive oil

Method

STEP 1

Cut the chicken breasts into small chunks, each about the size of a marble (you should get roughly 15 pieces per breast). Put the pesto in a bowl and mix together with the chicken until coated all over. Tip the breadcrumbs into a large freezer bag.

STEP 2

Add the chicken pieces in batches to the bag and give it a good shake to coat. Place a piece of greaseproof paper on a baking sheet, then lay the chicken pieces on the sheet, making sure none of them are touching. Put in the freezer and, when frozen solid, take off the baking sheet and store in a container or freezer bag.

STEP 3

To cook, heat oven to 220C/fan 200C/ gas 7. Pour a little oil onto a shallow baking tray, just enough to cover it. Put the tray in the oven and let it heat up for 5 mins. Tip the chicken onto the sheet and return to the oven for 10-15 mins until crisp and cooked through.

Mulled apple juice

Prep: 5 mins **Cook:** 10 mins

Serves 8

Ingredients

- 1l apple juice
- strips of orange peel

- 1 cinnamon stick , plus extra to garnish, if you like
- 3 cloves

- sugar or honey, to taste

Method

STEP 1

Simmer the apple juice with the strips of orange peel, cinnamon stick and cloves for about 5-10 mins until all the flavours have infused. Sweeten to taste.

STEP 2

Serve each drink with a little orange peel and a piece of cinnamon stick, if you like.

Stuffed jacket potatoes

Prep:20 mins **Cook:**1 hr and 15 mins

Serves 4

Ingredients

- 4 medium potatoes
- 100g strong cheddar, grated, plus extra for topping
- 100g sweetcorn
- 100g mixed pepper, diced
- small handful fresh herbs, such as oregano, basil, coriander, dill or thyme

Method

STEP 1

Equipment you will need: medium mixing bowl, small mixing bowl, dessertspoon, fork, baking tray, grater, oven gloves.

STEP 2

Get an adult to heat the oven to 200C/180C fan/gas 6 and bake the potatoes for about 1 hr until cooked and the skins are crispy. Leave to cool completely. This can be done up to 2 days ahead.

STEP 3

To stuff the jacket potatoes, heat the oven to 200C/180C fan/gas 6. Ask an adult to cut the potatoes in half. Using a spoon, carefully scoop out the middle of the potato, leaving the skin unbroken (like a boat). Place the scooped potato into a mixing bowl.

STEP 4

Using the fork, mash the potato until there are no lumps. Add the cheese, sweetcorn and peppers and mix well. Gently pick the leaves from the herbs. You can rip the larger leaves into smaller pieces. Stir the herbs into the cheesy potato mixture.

STEP 5

Using the spoon, carefully scoop the mixture back into the potato boats. Make sure that you use all the mixture up. Sprinkle with a little extra grated cheese and place on a baking tray. Using oven gloves, place the tray in the oven and bake for 10-15 mins until golden.

Creamy linguine with ham, lemon & basil

Prep:10 mins **Cook:**15 mins

Serves 6

Ingredients

- 400g linguine or spaghetti
- 90g pack prosciutto
- 1 tbsp olive oil
- juice 1 lemon
- 2 egg yolks

- 3 tbsp crème fraîche
- large handful basil leaves
- large handful grated parmesan , plus extra to serve, if you like

Method

STEP 1

Cook the linguine. Meanwhile, tear the ham into small pieces and fry in the olive oil until golden and crisp.

STEP 2

Drain the pasta, reserving a little of the cooking water, then return to the pan. Tip in the cooked ham. Mix together the lemon juice, egg yolks and crème fraîche, then add this to the pan along with the basil and Parmesan. Mix in with tongs, adding a little of the cooking water, if needed, to make a creamy sauce that coats the pasta. Serve with extra Parmesan grated over the top, if you like.

Millionaire's chocolate tart

Prep: 30 mins **Cook:** 55 mins

Serves 10

Ingredients

- 375g pack dessert shortcrust pastry
- 1 tsp vanilla paste or extract
- flour , for dusting
- 250g/9oz caramel (we used Carnation caramel from a can)
- 100g 70% plain chocolate , broken into pieces

- 100g white chocolate , broken into pieces
- 6 tbsp melted butter
- 2 eggs , plus 3 egg yolks
- 4 tbsp golden caster sugar
- icing sugar and single cream, to serve (optional)

Method

STEP 1

Break the pastry into chunks and drop into a food processor. Drizzle over the vanilla paste and pulse until the vanilla is speckled through the pastry (the extract should be completely absorbed). Tip out onto a floured surface, bring together into a ball, then roll out to line a 23cm tart tin (leave any overhanging pastry as you will trim this away when the tart is baked). Chill for 30 mins.

STEP 2

Heat oven to 200C/180C fan/gas 6. Line the pastry with greaseproof paper. Fill with baking beans, bake blind for 15-20 mins, then remove the paper and beans and bake for 5-10 mins more until pale golden. Carefully spread caramel over the base and set aside while you make the filling. Lower oven to 180C/160C fan/gas 4.

STEP 3

Melt the chocolates in a bowl over a pan of barely simmering water, then stir in the melted butter. Whisk the eggs, yolks and sugar together with an electric whisk in a large mixing bowl for 10 mins, until pale and thick enough to leave a trail when the beaters are lifted up. Fold in the melted chocolate with a large metal spoon, then scrape into the tin.

STEP 4

Bake for 20-25 mins – the surface should be set and puffed but still with a slight wobble. Cool, then chill for at least 3 hrs or overnight, before dusting with icing sugar and serving.

Celebration piñata cake

Prep: 3 hrs **Cook:** 2 hrs

plus 4 hrs chilling

Serves 20

Ingredients

For the bottom-tier cake

- 500g butter , softened
- 500g golden caster sugar
- 8 large eggs , beaten
- 500g self-raising flour
- 2 tsp lemon extract
- zest 2 lemons

For the bottom-tier icing

- 175g butter , softened
- 500g icing sugar , sifted
- 2 tbsp whole milk
- zest 1 lemon and juice of 2 (from the lemons above)
- 200g lemon curd

For the top-tier cake

- 200g butter , softened
- 200g golden caster sugar
- 4 large eggs , beaten
- 200g self-raising flour
- 1 tsp vanilla extract

For the top-tier icing

- 100g butter , softened
- 300g icing sugar
- 3 tbsp whole milk
- 1 ½ tbsp freeze-dried strawberry or raspberry powder (see tip)

To decorate

- 100g icing sugar , mixed with a drop of water to make a runny icing for glue, plus extra icing sugar for dusting
- 2kg ready-made fondant icing
- selection of food colouring pastes (we used blue, pink, orange, lilac, mint green and yellow)
- sweets, such as Smarties (about 12 tubes), to fill the cake
- 4 cake dowels
- white pearlescent balls or silver balls
- candles

Method

STEP 1

To make the bottom-tier cake, heat oven to 180C/160C fan/gas 4. Grease and line a 23cm cake tin with baking parchment. Put 250g of the butter and 250g sugar in a large bowl and, using an electric hand whisk, cream until light and fluffy. Add 4 eggs, one at a time, beating well after each addition. Fold in 250g of the flour, 1 tsp lemon extract, and the zest of 1 lemon until you have a smooth batter. Spoon into the tin and smooth the surface. Bake for 40 mins or until a skewer poked into the centre comes out clean. Leave to cool in the tin for 10 mins, then turn out onto a wire rack, remove the parchment and cool completely. Repeat with the remaining half of the ingredients, so that you have 2 large cakes.

STEP 2

Meanwhile, make the icing for the bottom tier. In a large bowl, beat the butter with a quarter of the icing sugar. When fully combined, add the rest in 3 additions, beating between each. When the icing is smooth, add the milk, zest and juice, and curd, then whisk until fluffy. Set aside until needed, or chill, but bring to room temperature before using.

STEP 3

Now make the top tier. Heat oven to 180C/160C fan/gas 4 (if not already on). Grease and line a 15cm cake tin with baking parchment. Cream together the butter and sugar until light and fluffy. Add the eggs, one at a time, beating well after each addition. Fold in the flour and extract until you have a smooth batter. Transfer to the tin, smooth the surface and bake for 20 mins, then reduce the oven to 160C/140C fan/gas 3 and cook for a further 25 mins. Remove from the oven and allow to cool in the tin for 10 mins, then turn out onto a wire rack, remove the parchment and cool completely.

STEP 4

To make the icing for the top tier, cream the butter and 100g icing sugar together until smooth, then gradually incorporate the rest. Add the milk and strawberry powder, then whisk thoroughly until light and fluffy.

STEP 5

When the larger cakes are completely cool, slice each in half horizontally so that you have 4 sponge layers. Using a 10cm cutter, cut a hole in the centre of each of the lemon sponges for the bottom tier. Sandwich the 4 sponges together on a cake stand, using the lemon buttercream, then cover the whole cake in a thin layer of the remaining lemon icing. Put in the fridge for a minimum of 2 hrs to firm up.

STEP 6

When completely cool, slice the small top tier cake horizontally so that you have 3 sponge layers. Use the strawberry buttercream to sandwich them together on a chopping board, then use the remaining strawberry icing to cover the outside. Leave in the fridge for a minimum of 2 hrs to firm up while you ice the bottom tier.

STEP 7

Now start to make the pale blue icing. Dust your work surface with a little icing sugar. Knead a little blue food colouring into 1.5kg fondant icing until it's an even colour. Remove 500g, wrap in cling film and set aside for the top tier. Roll out the remaining 1kg to a circle wide enough to cover the bottom tier – you can check this with a piece of string. Gently roll up your fondant onto your rolling pin and unfold onto your cake. Smooth the icing on the outside with your hands, then trim off the excess at the bottom. Cut a small cross in the centre of the fondant where the hole sits and push the remaining fondant carefully onto the inside of the hole, trimming any excess. Fill the centre with sweets of your choice. Place the 4 dowels into the cake at 3, 6 and 9 and 12 o'clock, just next to the hole in the middle, then trim so they are flush with the cake.

STEP 8

Cover the top tier cake in the remaining blue fondant in the same way, then mount onto the bottom cake, enclosing the sweets. Transfer the icing glue to a small piping bag and snip off the end. Use to pipe a drizzle of icing around the base of each tier. Place pearlescent or silver balls around the base of each cake to cover any rough edges.

STEP 9

To make the balloon decorations, divide the remaining 500g of fondant into the number of colours you are using. Use different food colourings to colour each piece of fondant. Roll out on a surface dusted with icing sugar and, using small cookie cutters, cut out circles of fondant. Use the icing glue to stick the balloons onto the cake. Decorate with colourful candles. Will keep for up to 3 days.

Eyeball & hand fruit punch

Prep: 10 mins

Serves 14-15

Ingredients

- 425g can lychees
- 225g jar cocktail cherries
- 15 raisins
- 1 litre carton blueberry, blackberry or purple grape juice , chilled

You'll also need

- 1 litre carton cherry or cranberry juice , chilled
- 1litre sparkling water , chilled

- 2 pairs powder-free disposable gloves

Method

STEP 1

Rinse the disposable gloves and fill each with water. Tie a knot in the top of each as you would a balloon, or use a tight bag clip to hold the opening closed. Freeze overnight.

STEP 2

Drain the lychees and cocktail cherries, reserving the juices in a jug. Push a raisin into one end of each cherry, then push the cherries into the lychees to make 'eyeballs'.

STEP 3

Tip all of the juices, plus the reserved lychee and cherry juices, into a large bowl with the 'eyeballs'. Carefully peel the gloves from the ice hands, add to the punch, then top up with the sparkling water.

Chicken nacho grills

Prep:5 mins **Cook:**20 mins

Serves 4

Ingredients

- 40g bag tortilla chip
- 4 skinless chicken breasts
- 200g tub spicy tomato salsa

- 142ml pot soured cream
- handful grated mature cheddar

Method

STEP 1

Heat oven to 200C/fan 180C/gas 6. Crush the tortilla chips. Put the chicken breasts on a non-stick baking tray, season, then slash each 3 times with a knife. Spoon 1 tbsp of salsa on top of each, then 1 tbsp soured cream.

STEP 2

Sprinkle the chips over the chicken, then the cheese. Roast for 15-20 mins until the topping is golden and melting.

RECIPE TIPS

USING TACOS

Spicy chicken tacos: Cube the chicken, then fry for 5 mins until golden. Toss with salsa and stuff into warmed taco shells. Dollop on soured cream and sprinkle with cheese and shredded lettuce.

SLASHING THE CHICKEN

Slashing the chicken helps the topping to stay on and also allows the heat to penetrate the chicken more quickly.

Rudolph cupcakes

Prep: 35 mins **Cook:** 30 mins

Makes 12

Ingredients

- 200g butter , cubed
- 200g plain chocolate , broken into squares
- 200g light soft brown sugar

- 2 large eggs , beaten
- 1 tsp vanilla extract
- 250g self-raising flour

For the icing

- 200g plain chocolate , broken into squares
- 100ml double cream , not fridge-cold

- 50g icing sugar

For the reindeers

- 12 large milk chocolate buttons (we used Cadbury Dairy Milk Giant Buttons)
- 24 white chocolate buttons
- 12 red Smarties

- black icing pens
- mini pretzels , carefully cut in half horizontally

Method

STEP 1

Get started: Heat oven to 160C/140C fan/gas 3. Line a 12-hole muffin tin with paper cases. Gently melt the butter, chocolate, sugar and 100ml hot water together in a large saucepan, stirring occasionally. Set aside to cool a little while you weigh the other ingredients.

STEP 2

Make your cakes: Stir the eggs and vanilla into the chocolate mixture. Put the flour in a large mixing bowl, and stir in the chocolate mixture until smooth. Spoon into the cases until just over three-quarters full. Bake on a low shelf in the oven for 20-22 mins. Leave to cool.

STEP 3

Ice the tops: To make the icing, melt the chocolate in a heatproof bowl over a pan of barely simmering water. Once melted, turn off the heat, stir in the double cream, sift in the icing sugar and mix well. When spreadable, top each cake with some icing.

STEP 4

Have fun decorating: Position a milk chocolate button on top of each cake, then 2 white chocolate buttons above it. Use a little icing as glue to stick a red Smartie onto the milk chocolate button for a nose. Then use your icing pens to draw black dots on the white buttons for eyes. Stick 2 pretzel top halves into the top of each cake for antlers, and stick the bottom half of a pretzel under the Smartie for a mouth. These cakes will keep in a sealed container for up to 3 days, but we doubt they'll last that long!

Unicorn poo meringues

Prep: 20 mins **Cook:** 1 hr and 20 mins

Makes 44

Ingredients

- 4 large egg whites , at room temperature
- 100g caster sugar
- 100g icing sugar , sifted

- 4 food colouring gels or pastes (we used pink, yellow, blue and green)
- small amount of white and black ready-to-roll fondant icing for the eyes and mouth

You will also need

- 4cm round cutter or circle to drawn around

- 1 large piping bag fitted with a large open star nozzle (1cm)
- 4 small paintbrushes

Method

STEP 1

Heat oven to 120C/100C fan/gas ½. Line 2 baking sheets with parchment. Using a 4cm round cutter as a guide, draw 22 circles on each piece of parchment in pencil. Turn the parchment over.

STEP 2

Whip up the egg whites in a stand mixer or with an electric hand whisk until they form stiff peaks. Gradually add the caster sugar in, a spoonful at a time, whisking in completely between each addition. Repeat with the icing sugar until the mixture is glossy and stiff.

STEP 3

Put the piping bag nozzle down in a tall glass or jug. Roll down the top of the bag a little, over the rim, then paint a thin stripe of each coloured food gel from the nozzle all the way up to the top of the bag. Spoon in the meringue mixture.

STEP 4

Pipe swirls of meringue onto the trays using the circles as a guide. Bake for 20 mins then turn down to 100C/80C fan/gas ¼ and cook for a further hour, or until they are completely cooked through and sound hollow when tapped on the base. Leave to cool in the oven.

STEP 5

Mould small pieces of white and black fondant icing to create eyes and mouths. Stick these on the cooled meringues with a small dab of royal icing (if they don't stick by themselves).

Gingerbread stained glass biscuits

Prep: 40 mins **Cook:** 5 mins - 6 mins

Makes 30

Ingredients

- 175g dark soft brown sugar
- 85g golden syrup
- 100g unsalted butter
- 2-3 tsp ground ginger
- 350g plain flour, plus extra to dust

- 1 tsp bicarbonate of soda
- 1 large egg, lightly beaten
- clear fruit-flavoured boiled sweets (don't use anything with a soft centre)
- white icing, to decorate

You will need

- star or snowflake cutters

Method

STEP 1

Heat the sugar, golden syrup and butter in a pan until melted. Mix the ginger and flour in a large bowl and make a well in the centre. Add the bicarbonate of soda to the melted mixture and stir – it will fizz a little – then pour into the flour mixture with the egg. Stir to combine. The mix will be soft but will firm up as it cools.

STEP 2

Scoop the mixture into a box or fridge bag and chill for at least 1 hr until firm enough to roll out. The dough can be kept in the fridge for up to a week or frozen for three months.

STEP 3

Heat oven to 190C/170C fan/gas 5. Turn the dough out onto a lightly floured surface and cut in half. Briefly knead the first piece, then roll it on a lightly floured surface to 2mm thick. Cut into shapes with snowflake or star cutters about 12cm across, then transfer to lined baking sheets, leaving a little room for them to spread. Cut a window out of each biscuit using another cutter about about 6cm across, then add a sweet to the centre.

STEP 4

If the sweets are large, chop them up first – you'll have to judge by the size of the hole. (Don't be tempted to add too much or it will spill over the edge.) If you plan to hang the biscuits, make a small hole in the top of each one using the end of a piping nozzle (the hole will close up a little so make sure it's big enough). Repeat with remaining dough.

STEP 5

Bake in batches for 5-6 mins or until they darken slightly and the sweets have melted. If the holes have closed up, remake them while the biscuits are warm. Leave to cool and harden up completely before moving them. Don't forget to bake the parts you've cut out, too! You can decorate the biscuits further by using white piped icing, if you like.

Loaded open sandwiches

Prep: 20 mins

Makes 20-24 small sandwiches

Ingredients

- 12 small slices rye bread or 6 slices thin, firm bread
- softened butter , for spreading
- 6 tbsp mayonnaise
- 2 tsp cucumber relish or piccalilli
- 2 slices ham , shredded
- 2 tbsp cream cheese
- ¼ cucumber , halved, peeled and thinly sliced
- 2 boiled eggs , halved and sliced
- 100g frozen north Atlantic prawns , defrosted
- sliced radishes , dill sprigs and cress, to garnish

Method

STEP 1

Trim the crusts from the bread if you like and cut each slice into smaller pieces. Spread each slice with butter and lay out on a board.

STEP 2

Mix 2 tbsp mayonnaise with the cucumber relish and spread over a quarter of the buttered bread slices. Arrange the ham and the radishes over the top. Spread the cream cheese over another quarter and arrange the cucumber and dill on top. Mash the egg with 2 tbsp mayonnaise and spread over another quarter, then top with the cress. Mix the prawns with the remaining mayonnaise and spoon over the remaining bread slices, then grind over a little black pepper. Add a garnish of dill, if you like.

Easy classic lasagne

Prep:15 mins **Cook:**1 hr

Serves 4 - 6

Ingredients

- 1 tbsp olive oil
- 2 rashers smoked streaky bacon
- 1 onion , finely chopped
- 1 celery stick, finely chopped
- 1 medium carrot , grated
- 2 garlic cloves , finely chopped
- 500g beef mince
- 1 tbsp tomato purée

- 2 x 400g cans chopped tomatoes
- 1 tbsp clear honey
- 500g pack fresh egg lasagne sheets
- 400ml crème fraîche
- 125g ball mozzarella , roughly torn
- 50g freshly grated parmesan
- large handful basil leaves , torn (optional)

Method

STEP 1

Heat the oil in a large saucepan. Use kitchen scissors to snip the bacon into small pieces, or use a sharp knife to chop it on a chopping board. Add the bacon to the pan and cook for just a few mins until starting to turn golden. Add the onion, celery and carrot, and cook over a medium heat for 5 mins, stirring occasionally, until softened.

STEP 2

Add the garlic and cook for 1 min, then tip in the mince and cook, stirring and breaking it up with a wooden spoon, for about 6 mins until browned all over.

STEP 3

Stir in the tomato purée and cook for 1 min, mixing in well with the beef and vegetables. Tip in the chopped tomatoes. Fill each can half full with water to rinse out any tomatoes left in the can, and add to the pan. Add the honey and season to taste. Simmer for 20 mins.

STEP 4

Heat oven to 200C/180C fan/gas 6. To assemble the lasagne, ladle a little of the ragu sauce into the bottom of the roasting tin or casserole dish, spreading the sauce all over the base.

Place 2 sheets of lasagne on top of the sauce overlapping to make it fit, then repeat with more sauce and another layer of pasta. Repeat with a further 2 layers of sauce and pasta, finishing with a layer of pasta.

STEP 5

Put the crème fraîche in a bowl and mix with 2 tbsp water to loosen it and make a smooth pourable sauce. Pour this over the top of the pasta, then top with the mozzarella. Sprinkle Parmesan over the top and bake for 25–30 mins until golden and bubbling. Serve scattered with basil, if you like.

Chicken skewers with tzatziki

Prep:10 mins **Cook:**15 mins

Serves 8

Ingredients

- 4 skinless chicken breasts
- 1 lemon
- 2 tsp oregano
- 1 garlic clove
- 1 small yellow pepper

- 1 small red pepper
- wholemeal tortilla wraps, to serve
- baby spinach leaves, to serve
- few sprigs flat-leaf parsley , to serve

For the tzatziki

- ½ cucumber
- ¼ garlic clove

- 4 tbsp Greek yogurt
- 1 tbsp extra virgin olive oil

You will need

- eight bamboo skewers

Method

STEP 1

Soak eight bamboo skewers in water. Using sharp kitchen scissors, chop the chicken into small pieces. Pop into a plastic box with a lid. Pare strips of lemon zest from the lemon using a vegetable peeler, then juice the lemon as well. Add both the peel and the juice to the chicken in the box along with the oregano and the garlic, crushed in. Season generously, mix and put in the fridge for 15 mins with the lid on. Deseed and chop the peppers into similar-sized pieces to those of the chicken.

STEP 2

Heat a griddle pan to high while you get the chicken out. Discard the lemon zest and thread the chicken onto the skewers, alternating every few bits of chicken with a piece of red pepper followed by a piece of yellow pepper. Griddle for 10 mins, turning halfway.

STEP 3

While the skewers are cooking, make the tzatziki. Get a box grater and a bowl. Cut the cucumber into long lengths, discarding the watery seedy core. Grate into the bowl, then grate the ¼ garlic clove. Season generously and stir in the Greek yogurt. Drizzle with a little extra virgin olive oil.

STEP 4

Serve the skewers hot off the griddle with the dip, or take the chicken and peppers off the skewers, leave to cool and pack into wholemeal wraps spread with a little tzatziki and rolled up with baby spinach and a few picked leaves of parsley.

Vegan nuggets

Prep: 20 mins **Cook:** 40 mins

plus 1 hr chilling

MAKES 30

Ingredients

- 300g cauliflower florets (or 3/4 small cauliflower)
- 2 carrots , chopped (about 165g)
- ½ medium onion , chopped
- 1 tbsp olive oil
- 1 garlic clove , crushed

For the coating

- 2 tbsp nutritional yeast
- 2 tsp yeast extract
- 400g can cannellini beans , drained
- 50g gram (chickpea) flour
- olive oil , for the baking tray

- 100g gram flour , plus a little extra
- 100g breadcrumbs (use gluten-free if necessary)

Method

STEP 1

Pulse the cauliflower, carrots and onion in a food processor until very finely chopped, like rice. Heat the oil in a large frying pan and gently fry the mix for 12-15 mins until softened. Add the garlic and fry for a further 1 min, then take off the heat and stir in the nutritional yeast and yeast extract. Set aside.

STEP 2

Blend the beans into a mushy purée in a food processor, then add to the veggie mix and combine well. Stir in the flour and season. Put in the fridge to firm up for 1 hr.

STEP 3

Heat the oven to 220C/200C fan/gas 7. Line a large baking tray with baking parchment and coat with a little olive oil. To make the coating, mix the gram flour with 150ml water using a fork so it resembles beaten egg, then season. Scatter the extra gram flour on a plate and fill a second with the breadcrumbs.

STEP 4

Roll the bean mixture into walnut-sized pieces, then flatten to form nugget shapes. Dip the pieces first in the gram flour, then in the gram batter, and finally roll in the breadcrumbs – handle carefully as they will be a little soft. When the nuggets are fully coated, lay them out on the prepared tray.

STEP 5

Bake for 20 mins, then use tongs to turn each nugget over and bake for a further 15 mins until they are dark golden and crisp. Leave to cool for 20 mins before serving with your choice of dipping sauces.

Egg-less mayo sandwiches

Prep:5 mins plus 30 mins draining

Makes 16-20 sandwiches

Ingredients

- 400g block of medium-firm tofu in water
- 6 tbsp vegan mayo
- ½ tsp Dijon mustard
- ¼ tsp ground turmeric
- 1 tbsp nutritional yeast

- 2 tsp finely chopped chives
- 1 large white sandwich or wholemeal loaf (10-12 slices), or 12 mini rolls (use gluten-free bread if necessary)
- 1 punnet cress (optional)

Method

STEP 1

Remove the tofu from the pack and press out the excess water, either between sheets of kitchen paper or a clean tea towel, weighed down with a plate for about 30 mins.

STEP 2

Mix the mayo, mustard, turmeric and nutritional yeast together with a little salt and pepper.

STEP 3

Crumble the tofu into a bowl, leaving large chunks to create a chopped egg texture. Gently stir in the chives. If you want it looser you can add more mayo.

STEP 4

Spread the mixture on the bread to make four or five rounds of sandwiches (depending on how much filling you want), then add cress, if you like. Use a sharp knife to cut into triangles.

Salmon tacos with lime dressing

Prep: 15 mins **Cook:** 10 mins

Serves 4

Ingredients

- olive oil , for the foil
- 500g piece salmon fillet
- 8 soft corn tacos
- 2 limes , zested and juiced
- 200g natural yogurt
- 2 ripe avocados , peeled and cubed
- 10 cherry tomatoes , halved
- 1 small red chilli , deseeded and sliced (optional)

Method

STEP 1

Cut a piece of foil big enough to wrap the salmon in and brush with oil. Put the salmon on top, season and sprinkle with some of the lime zest and juice. Fold up the foil around the salmon so it all meets at the top and makes a handle to lift the parcel with.

STEP 2

Heat a barbecue until the coals are glowing white hot. Make sure the grill is set high above the coals and put the foil parcel on. Cook for 10 mins and then open it and have a look. The salmon should be opaque – if it isn't, wrap it up and continue cooking.

STEP 3

Wrap the tacos in foil and warm them at the side of the barbecue. Mix the remaining lime zest and juice with the yogurt and season. When the salmon is cooked, open out the foil and flake it into pieces. Serve the tacos with the salmon, tomato, avocado, chilli and sauce so people can stuff their own. Napkins are necessary.

Mexican-style stuffed peppers

Prep:15 mins **Cook:**35 mins

Serves 2 adults, 2 children

Ingredients

- 3 large mixed peppers , halved
- oil , for drizzling
- 2 x 250g pouches lime & coriander rice , cooked
- 400g can black beans , drained and rinsed

- 6 Mexican-style chilli cheese slices (use regular cheddar or monterey jack, if you like)
- 150g fresh guacamole

Method

STEP 1

Heat the oven to 220C/200C fan/gas 7. Remove the seeds and any white pith from the peppers and arrange, cut-side up, in a roasting tin. Drizzle with oil and season, then bake for 20 mins.

STEP 2

Combine the rice and beans. Remove the peppers from the oven and fill with the rice mixture. Top each with a slice of cheese and bake for 10-15 mins more, until the rice has melted and the filling is hot. Top with spoonfuls of guacamole.

Chocolate brownie cake

Prep:15 mins

Serves 6 - 8

Ingredients

- 100g butter
- 125g caster sugar
- 75g light brown or muscovado sugar
- 125g plain chocolate (plain or milk)

- 1 tbsp golden syrup
- 2 eggs
- 1 tsp vanilla extract/essence
- 100g plain flour

- ½ tsp baking powder
- 2 tbsp cocoa powder

Method

STEP 1

Heat oven to 180C/fan 160C/gas 4. Grease and line a 20cm cake tin.

STEP 2

Place the butter, caster sugar, brown sugar, chocolate and golden syrup in the pan and melt gently on a low heat until it is smooth and lump-free.

STEP 3

Remove the pan from the heat.

STEP 4

Break the eggs into the bowl and whisk with the fork until light and frothy. 5 Add the eggs, vanilla extract or essence, flour, baking powder and cocoa powder to the chocolate mixture and mix thoroughly.

STEP 5

Put the mixture into the greased and lined cake tin and place on the middle shelf of the oven. Bake for 25-30 mins.

STEP 6

Remove and allow to cool for 20-30 mins before cutting into wedges and serving.

STEP 7

Serve with cream or ice cream and plenty of fresh fruit.

Chicken fajitas

Prep: 20 mins **Cook:** 25 mins

Serves 8

Ingredients

- 24 flour tortillas

For the chicken

- 6 chicken breasts
- 4 tbsp olive oil
- 2 garlic cloves , crushed
- 2 limes , juiced

For the pepper mix

- 2 tbsp olive oil
- 1 large red onion , cut into thin wedges

- 300g soured cream

- 1 tsp chilli powder
- 1 tsp ground cumin
- small pack coriander , finely chopped

- 2 red and 2 yellow peppers , cut into thin strips
- 200g cherry tomatoes , halved

Method

STEP 1

Slice the chicken breasts in half horizontally, then cut them into thin strips. Put them in a bowl, add the remaining ingredients and rub into the chicken with your hands.

STEP 2

Heat the oil for the pepper mix in a large frying pan and fry the onion wedges for 6 mins or until softened. Turn the heat up high so the wedges char slightly at the edges, season well and, using a slotted spoon, lift them onto a baking tray and keep warm.

STEP 3

Add the peppers in batches, cook them the same way, then transfer to the baking tray with the onions. Cook the tomatoes in the same way and add them to the peppers.

STEP 4

Heat a griddle pan or use the same frying pan and cook the chicken in batches over a high heat – allow them to catch a little on the edges but don't overcook them. Add them to the baking tray to keep warm.

STEP 5

Heat the tortillas on the griddle, then wrap in foil and keep warm in the oven, or heat in the microwave following pack instructions.

Omelette in a bun

Prep:5 mins **Cook:**20 mins

Serves 3

Ingredients

- 1 tbsp olive oil
- 1 medium potato , cut into cubes
- 1 spring onion , finely sliced
- handful baby spinach leaves

- 4 eggs
- 9 small cherry tomatoes , halved
- handful crumbled feta or grated cheddar
- 3 rolls

Method

STEP 1

Heat the oil in a small non-stick frying pan and fry the potato over a low heat until it is browned and tender, this will probably take about 10 mins in all. Add the spring onion and fry for a minute then stir in the spinach.

STEP 2

Whisk the eggs lightly with a little seasoning and then pour them into the pan and cook until set on the base. Dot on the tomatoes, sprinkle on the cheese and grill until the top browns. Cool a little then slide out of the pan and cut into thirds.

STEP 3

Split the rolls and stuff them with a piece of omelette, sandwich together and halve.

Chicken & sweet potato curry

Prep:10 mins **Cook:**45 mins

Serves 4

Ingredients

- 1 tbsp sunflower oil
- 1 onion, chopped
- 450g boneless, skinless chicken thigh, cut into bite-sized pieces
- 165g jar korma paste

- 2 garlic cloves, crushed
- 500g sweet potato, cut into small chunks
- 400g can chopped tomato
- 100g baby spinach
- basmati rice, to serve

Method

STEP 1

Heat the oil in a pan, add the onion and cook over a low heat for about 5 mins until softened. Increase the heat slightly, add the chicken pieces and brown.

STEP 2

Stir in the curry paste and garlic, cooking for 2 mins before adding 100ml water, the sweet potatoes and chopped tomatoes. Simmer for 20-30 mins until the chicken is cooked through and the sweet potato is tender – add a splash more water if it starts to look dry. Season to taste and add the spinach, removing the pan from the heat and stirring until the spinach has wilted. Serve with basmati rice.

Unicorn biscuits

Prep:15 mins **Cook:**30 mins

around 20

Ingredients

- 250g plain flour
- 150g butter
- 100g caster sugar

- 1 egg
- ½ tsp vanilla extract
- pink food colouring

- 50g icing sugar
- 1 lemon , juice only
- your choice of coloured sprinkles (we used hundreds and thousands, pink and yellow sugar and some white chocolate stars)

Method

STEP 1

Rub the flour and butter together with your fingertips until it looks and feels like fresh breadcrumbs then add a pinch of salt. In another bowl, mix together the sugar, egg and vanilla extract then pour it over the butter and flour mixture. Gently knead it together then separate the dough into 2 equal blocks. Knead some pink food colouring into one of them and keep the other plain. Wrap both types of dough in sheets of cling film and chill in the fridge for 20-30 mins.

STEP 2

Roll the plain dough out onto a lightly floured surface until it's about 25cm long and 20cm wide. Do the same with the pink dough and lay one on top of the other. Lightly roll over the surface once or twice with your rolling pin just to press them together. Trim off all the edges so they're straight then carefully roll them up from one of the short edges to make a tight spiral. Wrap tightly in cling film and chill for 1hr or overnight.

STEP 3

Heat oven to 180C/160C fan/gas 4 and line 2 trays with baking parchment. Unwrap the dough, trim the end and cut the rest into 20 slices and lay them cut side down on your prepared baking tray. Bake for 15-17 mins or until ever so slightly golden at the very edges. Allow them to cool on the tray before transferring them to a wire rack to cool completely.

STEP 4

Mix the icing sugar with enough lemon juice to make it the consistency of smooth peanut butter and pour the sprinkles into a shallow bowl or plate. Dip the outside edges of the biscuits into the icing (or spread it onto the edges using the back of a teaspoon) and then into the sprinkles, turning to coat. Leave to set before serving.

Hedgehog rolls

Prep: 20 mins **Cook:** 15 mins

makes 6

Ingredients

- 500g pack brown bread mix
- 25g butter
- plain flour , for dusting

- 12 raisins
- 6 flaked almonds

Method

STEP 1

Make the bread mixture with the butter following pack instructions. It's easiest to use a stand mixer but not difficult to do by hand. Leave the dough to rest for 5 mins, then knead for 5 mins.

STEP 2

Cut the dough into six pieces. Dust the surface with a little flour and shape each piece into a ball by rolling it between your hand. Now make it hedgehog-shaped by pulling one side out a little and squeezing it gently into a snout. Be quite firm or it will bounce back.

STEP 3

Put the hedgehogs on a baking sheet, cover with a damp tea towel and leave to rise for 1 hr.

STEP 4

Heat oven to 200C/180C fan/gas 6. Using kitchen scissors (supervise younger children), carefully snip into the dough to make the spikes on the backs of the hedgehogs. Press raisins in for the eyes and push a flaked almond into the end of each snout.

STEP 5

Bake for 15 mins or until the rolls are risen and golden. Will keep for two days in an airtight container.

Rainbow pizzas

Prep:20 mins **Cook:**20 mins

Serves 4

Ingredients

- 2 plain pizza bases
- 6 tbsp passata
- 400g mixed red and yellow tomatoes , sliced
- 75g sprouting broccoli , stems finely sliced
- handful fresh basil leaves, to serve

- 8 green olives , pitted and halved (optional)
- 150g mozzarella cherries (bocconcini)
- 2 tbsp fresh pesto

Method

STEP 1

Heat the oven to 180C/160C fan/gas 4. Put each pizza base on a baking sheet and spread each with half of the passata. Arrange the tomatoes on the top in rings or wedges of colour and add the broccoli and the olives, if using. Squish the mozzarella cherries (bocconcini) a little before dotting them over the pizzas, then drizzle 1 tbsp pesto over each.

STEP 2

Bake for 15-20 mins or until the top is bubbling and just starting to brown a little. Scatter over the basil leaves before serving.

Teriyaki salmon parcels

Prep:15 mins **Cook:**20 mins

Serves 4

Ingredients

- 2 tbsp low-salt soy sauce
- 1 tbsp clear honey

- 1 garlic clove, finely chopped
- 1 tbsp mirin (optional)

- a little sunflower oil
- 300g Tenderstem broccoli
- 4 x 100g salmon fillets
- 1 small piece of ginger, cut into matchsticks

- a little sesame oil (optional)
- sliced spring onions, toasted sesame seeds and cooked rice, to serve

Method

STEP 1

KIDS: The writing in bold is for you. ADULTS: The rest is for you. **Make the sauce and marinade.** In a small bowl, whisk together the soy, honey, garlic and mirin and set aside.

STEP 2

Cut out some squares of foil. Using scissors, cut out 4 squares of foil, each about 30cm square. Brush each piece of foil with a little oil and bring the edges of the foil up a little.

STEP 3

Fill your parcels. Place a couple of broccoli stems on each one, then sit a salmon fillet on top and scatter over the ginger.

STEP 4

Spoon over the sauce. Spoon the sauce over each salmon fillet and drizzle with a little sesame oil, if you like.

STEP 5

Close the parcels. Fold over the edges of the foil together to seal and place the parcels on a baking sheet. Can be prepared up to 1 day ahead.

STEP 6

Cook the parcels. Heat oven to 200C/180C fan/gas 6. Get your child to place the parcels in the oven for 15-20 mins, but ensure an adult removes them, then leave to stand for a few mins. Serve each parcel on a plate and let each person open it themselves. Serve with spring onions and sesame seeds for scattering over, and some rice on the side.

Healthy veg patch hummus

Prep: 20 mins

Serves 6

Ingredients

- 1 x 400g can chickpeas , drained and rinsed
- ½ lemon , juiced
- 1 garlic clove , crushed
- 2 tbsp olive oil
- 2 tbsp tahini
- 250g baby carrots
- 1 pot of parsley

Method

STEP 1

Put the chickpeas, lemon juice, garlic, olive oil and tahini into a food processor and blitz to a smooth consistency. Loosen with 1–2 tbsp water if it seems a little thick.

STEP 2

Make a hole in the top of each carrot with a skewer or by cutting a small hole with the tip of a sharp knife. Dab a small amount of hummus into the hole and push in a small sprig of parsley.

STEP 3

Spoon the hummus into thoroughly cleaned small, plant pots or bowls and push in the carrots. Let the children dunk into the hummus with the carrots.

Healthy Halloween nachos

Prep: 40 mins **Cook:** 5 mins

Serves 4 - 6

Ingredients

For the guacamole

- 2 limes , juiced
- 2 small avocados , peeled and chopped

- 1 bunch coriander , finely chopped

For the sweetcorn salsa

- ½ a 160g can sweetcorn
- 200g cherry tomatoes , quartered
- 1 red pepper , finely chopped
- 2 spring onions , thinly sliced
- 3 sundried tomatoes , finely chopped

- 400g can black beans
- ½ tsp cumin
- ½ tsp coriander
- ½ tsp smoked paprika

For the bat-shaped nachos

- 4 wholewheat tortillas
- 1 ½ tsp oil

- 4 purple carrots , cut into sticks

Method

STEP 1

Start by making the guacamole. Pour the lime juice into a bowl and add the avocado. Mash well with a potato masher or the back of a fork until it's the consistency you like – we served ours fairly chunky. Add half of the chopped coriander, season to taste and spoon into a shallow bowl or serving dish.

STEP 2

Now mix all of the salsa ingredients together, along with the remaining chopped coriander. Season with salt and pepper. Arrange clumps of the salsa on top of the guacamole – this will allow guests to get a bit of everything with each scoop. Cover and chill for up to 30 mins while you make the bat nachos.

STEP 3

Lay a tortilla wrap out on your chopping board and brush with a little of the oil. Cut out bats (or other spooky shapes) using a cookie cutter, scissors or both. Cut them as close together as possible to minimise waste. You should be able to get about 8-10 from each wrap, depending on the size of your cutter.

STEP 4

Heat oven to 200C/180C fan/gas 6. Put all the tortilla shapes on 2 or 3 large baking sheets and bake for about 4-5 mins or until golden and crisp, then serve with the carrot sticks, guacamole and salsa plate.

Sausage & squash risotto

Prep:15 mins **Cook:**25 mins

Serves 4

Ingredients

- 350g pack ready-chopped butternut squash , or half a medium squash, peeled and chopped
- 2 low-sodium chicken stock cubes
- 2 tsp olive oil
- 6 good-quality sausages , meat squeezed from the skins and rolled into mini meatballs

- 1 large onion , finely chopped
- 2 garlic cloves , crushed
- 6-8 thyme sprigs , leaves picked and chopped
- ½ tsp turmeric
- 200g risotto rice
- 25g parmesan , grated, plus a little to serve

Method

STEP 1

Boil the kettle. Put the squash in a heatproof bowl, add a splash of water and cover with cling film. Microwave on High for 8-10 mins or until the squash is tender. Meanwhile, crumble the stock cubes into a pan, add 1.2 litres hot water from the kettle and set over a low heat to simmer gently.

STEP 2

Heat the oil in a large, high-sided frying pan. Add the sausage meatballs and roll them around in the pan for 5-10 mins until browned all over and cooked through. Remove from the pan and set aside. Add the onion and sizzle gently for 5 mins, then add the garlic and cook for 1 min more, stirring to prevent it from burning. Stir in the thyme, turmeric and risotto rice for 1 min, coating the rice in the oil from the pan. Start adding the stock, a ladleful at a time, stirring well every 1-2 mins until the liquid is absorbed and the rice is cooked.

STEP 3

Mash half the squash and add to the pan along with the sausage meatballs and Parmesan. Stir, then top with the remaining squash, cover with a lid and leave for 2 mins. Serve with extra Parmesan.

Christmas rocky road

Prep: 20 mins **Cook:** 5 mins

plus at least 3 hrs chilling

20 squares

Ingredients

- 100g butter , cut into cubes, plus extra for the tin
- 250g Christmas biscuits , such as shortbread or chocolate biscuits
- 75g shelled nuts (use up a bag of whole nuts, or bits and bobs from the baking cupboard)

- 100g mixed dried fruit (such as raisins, cherries or glacé ginger)
- 75g Christmas sweets (candy canes, marshmallows or jelly sweets)
- 400g milk or plain chocolate (or a mixture of both), chopped
- 140g golden syrup (weigh this straight into the pan you will use for melting)

- 2 tbsp sprinkles , or more sweets, to decorate

Method

STEP 1

Butter and line a 20cm square tin, or use a 20cm square silicone mould. Break the biscuits into pieces – they need to be no smaller than a pea, but not too chunky or your rocky road won't hold together.

STEP 2

Halve any larger nuts either by snapping them or carefully cutting with a knife, then combine them with the biscuits. Halve any large pieces of dried fruit and chop or snap sweets into smaller pieces, then add these to the bowl.

STEP 3

Melt 300g of the chocolate, the butter and the golden syrup carefully in a pan set over a low heat, stirring occasionally, then pour this over the biscuit and nut mixture and mix together so the chocolate covers everything.

STEP 4

Tip the mixture into the tin, then level the top – it doesn't need to be completely smooth. Melt the remaining chocolate in the microwave in short blasts, or in a heatproof bowl over a small pan of simmering water, then drizzle this over the top and sprinkle with the decorations. Chill for at least 3 hrs or overnight before cutting into squares. Will keep in the fridge for three to four days.

Gravity-defying sweetie cake

Prep: 1 hr **Cook:** 35 mins

Serves 12

Ingredients

For the chocolate sponges

- 150ml vegetable oil, plus extra for greasing
- 200g plain flour
- 8 tbsp cocoa powder
- 2 tsp baking powder
- 1 tsp bicarbonate of soda

- 280g light brown soft sugar
- 200ml buttermilk
- 100ml strong coffee or espresso
- 2 tsp vanilla extract
- 2 large eggs

To decorate

- 2½ x 114g packs milk chocolate fingers

- 8 tubes of Smarties, or other sweets

For the chocolate fudge icing

- 100g milk chocolate, chopped into small pieces, plus 50g/2oz for decorating
- 200g slightly salted butter, softened

- 400g icing sugar, seived
- 4 tbsp cocoa powder
- 2 tbsp milk

You'll also need

- 1 bendy straw

- 2 wooden skewers

- 1 paper bag or sweet packet (see tip)
- sticky tape

Method

STEP 1

Heat oven to 180C/160C fan/gas 4. Grease and line two 20cm cake tins with baking parchment – if your cake tins are quite shallow, line the sides to a depth of at least 5cm. Put the flour, cocoa powder, baking powder, bicarbonate of soda, sugar and 1 tsp salt in a bowl and mix well. If there are any lumps in the sugar, squeeze these through your fingers to break them up.

STEP 2

Measure the buttermilk, coffee, oil and vanilla in a jug. Add the egg and whisk until smooth. Pour the wet ingredients into the dry and whisk until well combined. Pour the cake mixture evenly into the two tins, and bake for 25-30 mins until risen and a skewer inserted into the centre comes out clean. Cool in the tins for 10 mins, then turn out onto a wire rack, peel off the baking parchment and leave to cool. These sponges can be made up to three days ahead and will stay moist if wrapped in cling film, or you can wrap well and freeze for up to two months.

STEP 3

To make the chocolate fudge icing, put the chocolate in a heatproof bowl, suspended over a pan of barely simmering water. Stir every now and then until melted. (Alternatively, melt in the microwave, stirring the chocolate every 20 secs so it doesn't burn.) Remove the bowl from the heat and leave to cool a little. Meanwhile, put the butter and icing sugar in another large bowl and mash with a spatula to combine (this will prevent you covering the work surface in icing sugar), then whisk with a hand mixer until smooth. Sift in the cocoa and pour in the melted chocolate and milk, then mix again until smooth.

STEP 4

Use roughly half the icing to sandwich the cakes together on a cake stand or board. Use a palette knife to cover the entire cake with the remaining icing – don't worry about being too neat. Use the chocolate fingers to cover the sides of the cakes – do this straight after icing as the icing will set after a while, and the chocolate fingers won't stick.

STEP 5

Melt the remaining 50g chocolate in the microwave or in a small bowl suspended over a pan of gently simmering water. Leave to cool until the chocolate is a spreadable consistency. You can speed this up by putting it in the fridge – just stir it every 5 mins or so to prevent the chocolate from setting.

STEP 6

Push a skewer into the centre of the cake and slip the straw over the top – this will give it more stability. Push 1-2cm of the straw into the cake. Use a cutlery knife to spread a blob of chocolate onto a Smartie and, starting at the base, stick the Smarties to the straw. You will have to do this in stages to allow the chocolate to set a little before adding another layer of Smarties. Work your way up the straw until it's completely covered. If the chocolate in your bowl becomes too firm, simply heat again until it is at the correct consistency. Stop when you reach the bend in the straw.

STEP 7

Stick the remaining skewer into the top of the straw so that it pokes out at an angle. Place the paper bag on top – you may have to use a little sticky tape to hold it in place. If any of the straw is exposed, cover it with more Smarties.

STEP 8

Tip the remaining Smarties on top of the cake to flood the surface. Will keep well stored in an airtight tin for 2 days.

Green spaghetti & meatballs

Prep:15 mins **Cook:**25 mins

Serves 3 - 6

Ingredients

- 500g lean pork mince
- 1 apple , grated
- 1 tsp fennel seeds
- 1 tbsp oil

- 250g-300g wholemeal spaghetti (for children, use white spaghetti as wholemeal can be too filling)
- 200g baby spinach , plus extra to serve

- 1 ripe avocado , stoned and peeled, plus extra to serve
- small bunch basil
- 100g frozen peas
- 25g parmesan , grated, plus extra to serve

Method

STEP 1

Mix the mince, apple and fennel seeds in a bowl. Divide and roll into 24 cherry tomato-sized balls. Heat the oil in a large frying pan. Cook the meatballs until golden brown and cooked through. Heat a large pan of water and cook the pasta following pack instructions.

STEP 2

Meanwhile, make the sauce. Set aside a handful of spinach, 4 tbsp peas and half the avocado for later. Pour hot water over the rest of the peas to defrost them, then drain well. Whizz the defrosted peas, spinach, avocado, basil and parmesan in a blender with 100ml pasta water, adding more if needed, to make sauce. Season well.

STEP 3

Add the reserved frozen peas to the pasta for the last min of cooking. Drain, saving some of the water, and tip the pasta into the meatball pan. Add the sauce and cook for a minute or 2 until hot, adding more seasoning or pasta water if you need to. Serve a salad of spinach and avocado on the side and top the pasta with extra parmesan for adults, if you like.

Black cat cake

Prep: 50 mins **Cook:** 1 hr and 40 mins

Serves 16

Ingredients

- icing sugar , for dusting
- 100g each black and yellow or orange fondant icing
- 200g butter , cubed, plus extra for the tin
- 200g dark chocolate , chopped
- 1 tbsp instant coffee granules
- 170g plain flour
- ½ tsp bicarbonate of soda
- 400g golden caster sugar
- 30g cocoa powder
- 3 medium eggs

- 75ml milk
- 1 heart-shaped jelly sweet , plus Pocky sticks, Matchmakers or liquorice sticks

For the frosting

- 150g butter , very soft
- 330g icing sugar
- 60g cocoa powder
- 4 tbsp milk
- 100g dark chocolate

Method

STEP 1

Lightly dust your work surface with icing sugar, then roll out a quarter of the black fondant icing to the thickness of a £1 coin. Cut out two triangles for the ears and leave to dry overnight.

STEP 2

Heat oven to 160C/140C fan/gas 3. Butter and line a 20cm round cake tin (about 7.5cm deep). Put the dark chocolate in a medium pan with the butter. Mix 1 tbsp coffee granules into 125ml cold water and add to the pan. Warm over a low heat until just melted – don't let it boil. Alternatively, melt in the microwave for about 5 mins, stirring halfway through.

STEP 3

Mix the flour, bicarb and sugar with the cocoa powder. Beat the eggs with the milk. Pour the melted chocolate mixture and the egg mixture into the flour mixture and stir everything together to make a smooth batter.

STEP 4

Pour the batter into the tin and bake for 1 hr 25-1 hr 35 mins until a skewer inserted into the centre of the cake comes out clean and the top feels firm (don't worry if it cracks a bit). Leave to cool in the tin for 30 mins – the top may sink a little as it cools – then turn out onto a rack to cool completely. Cut the cake horizontally into three.

STEP 5

To make the frosting, put the butter in a bowl and beat until light and fluffy. Gradually beat in the icing sugar and cocoa powder, then stir in enough milk to make the icing fluffy and spreadable. Sandwich the layers of the cake together using a small amount of frosting. Melt the chocolate in a microwave or small bowl set over a pan of simmering water, then stir it into the remaining frosting. Use the mixture to cover the sides and the top of the cake.

STEP 6

Stick the black fondant ears into the top of the cake. Cut out two yellow or orange fondant circles to make the eyes and use the black fondant to make the pupils. Stick these onto the cake and add a heart-shaped jelly sweet for the nose. Use Pocky sticks, Matchmakers or liquorice cut into lengths for the whiskers.

Pea-camole

Prep: 10 mins

Serves 8

Ingredients

- 200g frozen peas
- 2 ripe avocados , halved, stoned and peeled

- 2 limes , juiced
- small bunch coriander

Method

STEP 1

Boil the kettle. Tip the peas into a mixing bowl and cover with about 2.5cm of boiling water. Leave for 5 mins to defrost, then drain well and tip back into the bowl.

STEP 2

Add the avocados with the lime juice and some salt, and mash everything together. Roughly chop the coriander and briefly mash through before serving.

Vegetable cheese dip

Prep: 10 mins

Serves 6 - 8

Ingredients

- 180g light cream cheese
- 30g mild cheddar , finely grated
- 1 small red pepper , very finely chopped
- 1 small celery stick , finely chopped
- pitta bread or mini breadsticks, carrot sticks and baby cucumbers, to serve

Method

STEP 1

Tip the cream cheese, cheddar, pepper and celery into a mixing bowl and stir together until well combined. Spoon the dip in to a bowl and serve with raw vegetables and strips of wholemeal pitta bread or breadsticks to scoop it up with.

Slow cooker meatballs

Prep:1 hr Cook:5 hrs

Serves 4 - 5

Ingredients

- 1 tbsp rapeseed oil
- 1 onion, finely chopped
- 2 carrots, finely diced
- 2 celery sticks, finely diced
- 2 garlic cloves, thinly sliced
- 500g carton tomato passata
- 2 tbsp chopped parsley
- For the meatballs
- 400g lean mince turkey
- 4 tbsp porridge oats
- pinch paprika
- 1 garlic clove, crushed
- spray of oil

Method

STEP 1

Heat the slow cooker if necessary. Heat the oil in a non-stick frying pan and add the onion, carrots, celery and garlic and fry gently for a minute. Pour in the passata, add the parsley and stir, then transfer the lot to the slow cooker.

STEP 2

To make the meatballs, tip the mince into a large bowl. Add the oats, paprika, garlic and plenty of black pepper, and mix everything together with your hands. Divide the mixture into 20 lumps about the size of a walnut and roll each piece into a meatball. Spray or run a non-stick pan with a little oil and gently cook the meatballs until they start to brown. Add them to the tomato base and cook on Low for 5 hours. Serve over rice or pasta if you like, or with a green salad.

Fairy cakes

Prep:25 mins **Cook:**12 mins

makes 20-24

Ingredients

- 75g butter , softened
- 50ml vegetable oil
- 125g caster sugar
- 2 large eggs

- 125g self-raising flour
- 2 tbsp milk
- 1 tsp vanilla extract

To decorate

- 250g icing sugar
- Your choice of sprinkles such as hundreds and thousands, sugar stars, berries or small sweets

- food colouring (optional)

Method

STEP 1

Heat oven to 180C/160C fan/gas 4. Line 2 x 12 hole bun tins or mini muffin tins with paper cake cases. Put all the fairy cake ingredients into a large bowl and whisk together with electric hand beaters until smooth. If you don't have these you can use a wooden spoon or balloon whisk (see tip).

STEP 2

Dollop the mixture into the prepared cases until it's all used up. Bake for 10-12 mins or until golden and springy. To be sure they're cooked through, poke a cocktail stick into the centre of one of the cakes in a middle row – if it comes out cleanly, it's cooked. Leave to cool in the tin for 5-10mins then transfer to a wire rack to cool completely before decorating.

STEP 3

Mix the icing sugar with enough water to make it the consistency of thick cream. Colour some or all of the icing with a few drops of your chosen food colouring(s) then drizzle over the top of the cooled fairy cakes. Sprinkle with your chosen toppings while the icing is still wet. Leave to set firm before serving. Will keep for 2 days in an airtight container.

Bunny cupcakes

Prep:40 mins **Cook:**25 mins

12

Ingredients

- 185g self-raising flour
- 120g golden caster sugar
- 120g butter , softened
- 100g pot natural yogurt

for the frosting

- 85g unsalted butter , softened
- few drops vanilla extract

- 1 lemon , zested
- 2 eggs
- 250g pack fondant icing

- 200g icing sugar
- few drops green food colouring

Method

STEP 1

Heat oven to 190C/170 fan/gas 5 and line a 12-hole bun tin with paper cases. Put the flour, sugar, butter, yogurt, lemon zest and eggs in a bowl and mix with electric beaters until smooth. Spoon a large tablespoon of the mixture into each of the cases, making them as even as possible. Bake for 20-25 mins until the cakes are risen and golden, and a skewer poked into the centre of one comes out clean. Set aside to cool on a wire rack.

STEP 2

For the frosting, beat the butter, vanilla extract and icing sugar until the mixture is pale and creamy, and completely combined. Add a few drops of green colouring and beat it in. If piping, scoop the frosting into a piping bag fitted with a star nozzle, then pipe stars of green icing all over the tops of the cakes like tufts of grass. If not piping, spread the icing over the cakes and run a fork across to make it resemble grass.

STEP 3

Roll the fondant icing into small balls no bigger than a walnut (these are the bunnies' bottoms). Roll smaller balls to make tails and stick them on top of the bigger balls. Put one rabbit on each cake. Now make the feet by rolling two more small balls for each bunny and shape them into ovals. Rest these at one end of the ball so they look like feet.

BLT pasta salad

Prep:10 mins **Cook:**10 mins

Serves 1

Ingredients

- 25g pasta bows
- 2 cooked crispy bacon rashers , broken into pieces
- 15g spinach , chopped

- 6 cherry tomatoes , halved
- ½ tbsp crème fraîche
- ¼ tsp wholegrain mustard

Method

STEP 1

The night before school, cook the pasta following pack instructions and run under cold water to cool quickly. Mix in the bacon, spinach, tomatoes, crème fraîche and mustard, and season with a little salt. Spoon into an airtight container and keep overnight in the fridge.

Funfetti cake

Prep:30 mins **Cook:**25 mins - 30 mins

Serves 20 - 25

Ingredients

- 300g golden caster sugar
- 450g butter, softened
- 1 tbsp vanilla bean paste
- 8 eggs, beaten
- 450g self-raising flour

For the icing

- 150g softened butter
- 450g icing sugar, sifted

- 1 tsp baking powder
- 4 tbsp whole milk
- 200g rainbow sprinkles, plus extra to decorate

- 180g tub full-fat cream cheese
- 1 tbsp vanilla paste

Method

STEP 1

Preheat the oven to 180C/160 fan/ gas 4 and grease and line 4 x 20cm cake tins. If you don't have 4, halve the sponge recipe and bake in 2 batches.

STEP 2

Put the sugar, butter and vanilla paste in a large bowl and beat with an electric whisk (or in a table top mixer) until pale and fluffy. Add the eggs gradually, beating between each addition until fully incorporated. Add a tbsp or 2 of flour if the mixture looks like it's curdling.

STEP 3

Sift in the flour and baking powder with a tsp of salt and fold into the cake batter. Pour in the milk and beat to loosen the mixture. Scatter over the sprinkles and ripple through the cake batter before dividing between each cake tin. Bake for 25-30 mins until golden and the sponge springs back when you press it lightly. Swap the tins around in the oven after 15 mins to ensure they cook evenly. Cool on wire racks completely before icing.

STEP 4

Meanwhile, make the icing by beating the butter with half of the icing sugar until combined and fluffy. Add the cream cheese and the rest of the icing sugar, beating again until fully combined. Drizzle over the vanilla paste and beat until incorporated. Put a large round nozzle into a piping bag and spoon in the icing.

STEP 5

When the cakes have cooled put a blob of icing onto a cake board and sit 1 of the sponges on top. Pipe blobs of vanilla icing in a circle covering the whole base of the sponge, then top with the next sponge. Repeat with all 3 layers, scattering over some extra sprinkles on the top. Serve in slices.

Cloud meringues

Prep:30 mins **Cook:**1 hr and 20 mins

Serves 6 - 8

Ingredients

- 4 egg whites (choose large eggs)
- 200g white caster sugar
- black food colouring gel

- 200g stiff white royal icing (made according to packet instructions)
- coloured sprinkles

You will also need

- lolly sticks

- cloud template (10cm x 8cm)

Method

STEP 1

Heat oven to 120C/100C fan/gas 1. Line 2 baking sheets with parchment paper. Using a pencil, draw 6-8 clouds on each piece of parchment measuring about 10cm across by 8cm in height. Use a template as the left half of the cloud needs to be a mirror image of the right (or they won't match when they are sandwiched together). Then, turn the parchment over so the pencil marks don't come into contact with the meringue.

STEP 2

Whisk the egg whites until stiff, then gradually whisk in the sugar, a tablespoon at a time, until stiff and glossy. Add in the black food colouring to make a light grey.

STEP 3

Place the meringue mix in a large piping bag and pipe over the templates. Bake for 20 mins then reduce the heat to 100C/80C fan/gas ¼ and cook for a further hour or until completely dry. Leave to cool thoroughly in the oven.

STEP 4

To create the storm cloud lollies, pipe stiff royal icing on the meringue, just around the edge, then add a little more to secure the stick. Fill the inside of the piped area with coloured sprinkles of your choice. Add the lolly stick to the cloud, over the icing, then sandwich the other meringue over the top to enclose the sprinkles and the top of the lolly stick. Leave to dry completely for about 3 hours or overnight.

Honey & spice cookies

Prep:30 mins **Cook:**12 mins

Makes approx 35

Ingredients

- 400g plain flour
- 200g butter
- 1 beaten egg
- 2 tbsp festive spice

- 100g golden caster sugar
- 2 tbsp honey
- ½ tsp cream of tartar
- melted dark chocolate

Method

STEP 1

Rub the butter into the flour in a large bowl until you have fine crumbs. Stir in the beaten egg, our festive spice, golden caster sugar, honey and cream of tartar. Stir unil a soft dough forms, then wrap in cling film and chill for 20-30 mins.

STEP 2

Heat oven to 180C/160C fan/gas 4. Roll out the dough, cut into festive shapes and bake for 10-12 mins on lined baking trays. Dip in melted dark chocolate, if you like.

Chicken & sweetcorn ramen

Prep:5 mins **Cook:**10 mins

Serves 2

Ingredients

- 1 pack instant ramen noodles
- 600ml chicken stock
- ½ cooked chicken breast , sliced

- 4 tbsp sweetcorn , peas or chopped beans
- 1 egg
- sesame oil , to serve (optional)

Method

STEP 1

Put the noodles in a pan (don't add the flavour sachet). Pour over the stock, bring to the boil, then simmer until cooked (follow pack instructions for cooking time).

STEP 2

Lift the noodles out of the pan and transfer to two bowls. Bring the stock in the pan back to a simmer, then add the chicken and cook until heated through. Scoop the chicken out with a slotted spoon, then transfer to the bowls. Warm the sweetcorn or cook the peas or beans in the stock, bringing back to the boil if you need to, then transfer to the bowl.

STEP 3

Meanwhile, cook the egg in a pan of boiling water for 6 mins. Remove carefully and cool under the cold tap, then peel and halve. Add an egg half to each bowl, then bring the stock back to a simmer and pour it over the noodles. Add a few drops of sesame oil, if you like.

Ghoulish Halloween cupcakes

Prep: 1 hr **Cook:** 25 mins

Serves 12

Ingredients

- 100g butter , cubed
- 100g plain chocolate
- 100g golden caster sugar
- 1 egg

- ½ tsp vanilla extract
- 125g self-raising flour
- 250g white fondant icing
- 500g mixed pack coloured fondant

You will need

- paper cases
- icing pens

- icing eyes

Method

STEP 1

Heat oven to 160C/140C fan/gas 3. Line a 12-hole cupcake tin with paper cases. Gently melt the butter, chocolate, sugar and 100ml hot water together in a large saucepan, stirring occasionally. Set aside to cool a little.

STEP 2

Stir the egg and vanilla into the chocolate mixture. Put the flour in a large mixing bowl, then add the chocolate mixture and stir until smooth. Divide the mixture evenly between the paper cases; they should be about three-quarters full. Bake on a low shelf in the oven for 20-22 mins. Press on the cupcakes to check if they're cooked; the tops should spring back. Remove from the oven and leave to cool.

STEP 3

Use the image above as a guide to decorating the cupcakes. Packet fondant can often be quite sticky; if yours is, pat walnut-sized lumps of fondant over the surface of each cake, rather than trying to roll it all out. Knead yellow and red fondant together to make orange icing. Make extra decorations, like hair and mouths, out of fondant and stick them on using a little water. Use the icing pens to draw lines in the fondant. Add icing eyes wherever you like.

Cheese & chorizo or prosciutto skewers

Prep: 20 mins **Cook:** 5 mins

Serves 6

Ingredients

- 150g manchego
- 12 slices chorizo
- 6 red grapes , halved

- 12 mini mozzarella balls
- 12 small basil leaves (optional)
- 6 slices prosciutto , halved

Method

STEP 1

Heat oven to 180C/160C fan/gas 4. Cut the manchego into 12 cubes or oblongs. Fold a slice of chorizo around each piece of cheese and push a cocktail stick through the middle to secure it. Push half a grape on to one side, then transfer skewers to a baking tray and cook for 5 mins. Cool.

STEP 2

Wrap each mozzarella ball in basil, top with half a slice of prosciutto and push a skewer through. To serve young children, slide everything off the skewers.

Super-versatile meatballs

Prep: 15 mins **Cook:** 30 mins

Serves 4

Ingredients

- ½ medium onion , roughly chopped
- 85g fresh white breadcrumbs
- 1 tbsp chopped parsley
- 200g lean pork mince
- 200g turkey mince
- grating of nutmeg

- 1 tbsp plain flour plus more for dusting
- rapeseed oil for frying
- 1 tbsp butter
- 400ml hot beef stock
- 2 tbsp single cream

Method

STEP 1

Whizz the onion, breadcrumbs and parsley in a food processor until finely chopped. Add the mince, nutmeg and seasoning. Use the pulse button to mix but don't overdo it or you'll make a paste. Form into 20 walnut-sized meatballs and dust with flour.

STEP 2

Heat the oil in a large frying pan and fry the meatballs in batches until they are browned all over, then carefully lift them out with a slotted spoon and drain them on kitchen paper.

STEP 3

Melt the butter in the pan, then sprinkle over the flour and stir well. Cook for 2 mins, then slowly whisk in the stock. Keep whisking until it is a thick gravy, then return the meatballs to the pan and cook them for 5 mins. Stir in the cream. Before serving, check one to see if they are cooked all the way through to the centre.

BBQ sausages with smoky tomato sauce

Prep:5 mins **Cook:**30 mins

Serves 6

Ingredients

- 24 chipolata sausages

For the smoky tomato sauce

- 100g low-sugar ketchup
- 100g passata
- 100ml cider vinegar
- 100g light brown soft sugar

- 1 garlic clove , crushed
- 1 tsp chipotle paste
- 2 tbsp butter

You will need

- 8 wooden or metal skewers (if using wooden, soak in water for at least 15 mins first)

Method

STEP 1

To make the sauce, combine the ingredients in a saucepan, then season. Bring to the boil and bubble for 3-4 mins until the sugar has completely dissolved and the sauce is glossy. Leave to cool. The sauce will keep in the fridge for up to two weeks or freeze for up to two months.

STEP 2

Heat a barbecue until the coals are glowing white hot. Lay six of the sausages next to each other and push one stick through one end of all the sausages and the other stick through the other ends so the sausages look like a ladder (leave a gap between each sausage). Repeat with the other sausages in batches of six.

STEP 3

Barbecue the sausages on each side until they are browned and cooked through, then brush with sauce and cook for a minute on each side until sticky-looking. Brush once more with the sauce before serving, and serve the rest of the sauce on the side.

Polar bear peppermint creams

Prep: 30 mins

makes 15-20

Ingredients

- 250g icing sugar
- 1 egg white , beaten
- few drops of peppermint essence

- 15 chocolate sweets (we used Waitrose blue and green chocolate beans)

Method

STEP 1

Sieve the icing sugar into a large bowl. Mix in the egg white, a little at a time – stop adding it when you have a soft dough that feels like plasticine.

STEP 2

Add 3 drops of the peppermint essence, mix well and taste. Add another drop if it isn't minty enough.

STEP 3

Roll half the mixture into 15 balls, about the size of cherry tomatoes, then flatten them with your hand to make the bear heads.

STEP 4

Place on sheets of baking parchment on a large board or tray. Using half the remaining mixture, make blueberry-sized balls and flatten them out onto the heads to make snouts. Add chocolate sweets for the noses.

STEP 5

Use the rest of the mixture to make the ears. Shape them into tiny balls and press them gently into the top of the heads with your fingertips. Use a cocktail stick to shape the eyes.

STEP 6

Leave the polar bears to dry for 3-4 hrs, or overnight. Eat within 1 month.

Unbelievably easy mince pies

Prep:30 mins - 40 mins **Cook:**20 mins

Makes 18 pies

Ingredients

- 225g cold butter, diced
- 350g plain flour
- 100g golden caster sugar

- 280g mincemeat
- 1 small egg, beaten
- icing sugar, to dust

Method

STEP 1

To make the pastry, rub the butter into the flour, then mix in the golden caster sugar and a pinch of salt.

STEP 2

Combine the pastry into a ball – don't add liquid – and knead it briefly. The dough will be fairly firm, like shortbread dough. You can use the dough immediately, or chill for later.

STEP 3

Heat the oven to 200C/180C fan/gas 6. Line 18 holes of two 12-hole patty tins, by pressing small walnut-sized balls of pastry into each hole.

STEP 4

Spoon the mincemeat into the pies. Take slightly smaller balls of pastry than before and pat them out between your hands to make round lids, big enough to cover the pies.

STEP 5

Top the pies with their lids, pressing the edges gently together to seal – you don't need to seal them with milk or egg as they will stick on their own. Will keep frozen for up to one month.

STEP 6

Brush the tops of the pies with the beaten egg. Bake for 20 mins until golden. Leave to cool in the tin for 5 mins, then remove to a wire rack. To serve, lightly dust with the icing sugar. Will keep for three to four days in an airtight container.

Weaning recipe: Chicken meatballs

Prep:15 mins **Cook:**10 mins

serves family of 4 (makes 16-20 meatballs)

Ingredients

- ½ celery stick , cut into small chunks
- 1 small carrot , cut into small chunks
- 500g boneless skinless chicken thighs, cut into chunks

- a few chives , snipped
- oil , for greasing

To serve

- boiled rice

- steamed broccoli

Method

STEP 1

Heat oven to 200C/180C fan/gas 6. Blitz the celery, carrot, chicken and chives in a food processor until finely chopped. You may need to use a spatula to scrape the sides of the bowl a few times.

STEP 2

Shape into small meatballs. If freezing, space out on a tray and put in the freezer. Once frozen, transfer to a freezer bag and take them out when needed. Defrost thoroughly in the fridge before cooking.

STEP 3

To cook, put on a baking tray lined with greased foil and bake for 10 mins or until browned and cooked through.

STEP 4

Served with boiled rice and steamed broccoli.

Smoky black bean chilli

Prep: 15 mins **Cook:** 2 hrs and 55 mins

Serves 4

Ingredients

- 1-2 tsp chipotle paste
- 400g black beans or kidney beans, drained
- small bunch coriander , chopped
- 4 (or more) tortilla bowls (we used Old El Paso Stand 'n' Stuff)

- 1 avocado , sliced
- 1 lime , juiced
- soured cream , to serve
- grated cheddar , to serve

For the mince base

- 1 tbsp olive oil
- 1 small onion , finely chopped
- 1 garlic clove , crushed
- ½ celery stick, finely sliced
- 1 small carrot , finely chopped

- 500g beef mince , 10% fat
- 3 tbsp tomato & vegetable purée
- 200ml passata
- 50ml milk

Method

STEP 1

Heat half of the oil in a pan, add the onion and fry until it starts to soften, then add the garlic, celery and carrot and cook until soft. Meanwhile, heat the remaining oil in a separate frying pan and fry the mince in batches, scooping each batch out with a slotted spoon and leave any excess oil behind.

STEP 2

Add the mince to the veg, then stir in the tomato purée and cook for 1 min. Stir in the passata and bring to a simmer. Cover and cook over a very low heat for 1½-2 hrs, then add the milk and cook for 30 mins. If you're making the base ahead of time, you can leave it to cool at this stage then freeze for up to a month. (Defrost fully before using in the next step.)

STEP 3

Put the mince base in a pan and add 1 tsp chipotle paste, bring to a simmer and taste it – add the other tsp if you need to. Stir in the black beans and cook for 5 mins, then stir in the coriander.

STEP 4

Warm the tortilla bowls in a low oven. Serve the bowls filled with chilli and add the avocado, a squeeze of lime, soured cream and cheese.

Layered rainbow salad pots

Prep:25 mins **Cook:**12 mins

Serves 4

Ingredients

- 350g pasta shapes (De Cecco is a good brand that stays nice and firm)
- 200g green beans , trimmed and chopped into short lengths
- 160g can tuna in olive oil, drained
- 4 tbsp mayonnaise
- 4 tbsp natural yogurt
- ½ small pack chives , snipped (optional)
- 200g cherry tomatoes , quartered

- 1 orange pepper , cut into little cubes   195g can sweetcorn, drained

Method

STEP 1

Cook the pasta until it is still a little al dente (2 mins less than the pack instructions) and drain well. Cook the green beans in simmering water for 2 mins, then rinse in cold water and drain well. Mix the tuna with the mayonnaise and yogurt. Add the chives, if using.

STEP 2

Tip the pasta into a large glass bowl or four small ones, or four wide-necked jars (useful for taking on picnics). Spoon the tuna dressing over the top of the pasta. Add a layer of green beans, followed by a layer of cherry tomatoes, then the pepper and sweetcorn. Cover and chill until you're ready to eat.

Mince & pea pies

Prep:20 mins **Cook:**55 mins

Serves 4

Ingredients

- 500g lean minced beef
- 1 tbsp olive oil
- 1 onion , finely chopped
- 2 large carrots (about 200g), finely chopped
- 2 celery sticks (about 200g), finely chopped

- 1 tbsp tomato purée
- 1 beef stock cube
- 200g frozen peas
- 1 egg , lightly beaten
- 375g ready-rolled shortcrust pastry
- Tenderstem broccoli or other greens, to serve

Method

STEP 1

Fry the mince in a little oil over a high heat, stirring to break up any lumps, until it's well browned all over. Transfer the mince to a plate, then fry the onion, carrots and celery in the rest of the oil over a low heat until softened. Stir in the tomato purée and crumble in the stock cube, then return the mince to the pan and give everything a good stir. Fry for a minute, then add 300ml water. Cover with a lid and simmer for 20 mins, then remove the lid and simmer until the sauce has thickened slightly. Stir in the peas, then turn off the heat and leave to cool for 10 mins

STEP 2

Heat oven to 200C/180C fan/gas 6. Divide the mince mixture between four individual pie dishes (or use one large dish). Brush the dish rims with egg. Unroll the pastry and cut it into four pieces for the individual pies – roll the pieces out a little more to fit the pie dishes if you need to. Top each pie with some pastry, press down against the rim and trim any excess. Seal the edges with a fork, or crimp if you like, then brush the pastry with egg.

STEP 3

Poke a little hole in the top, decorate with any offcuts if you like (brushed with a little egg), then cook for 25-30 mins or until the pastry is golden and risen. Cool for 5-10 minutes before serving.

Caramelised honey carrots

Cook: 35 mins

Serves 4

Ingredients

- 500g pack Chantenay carrots , trimmed
- 1 tbsp honey
- 2 tsp butter
- 1 tsp thyme leaves

Method

STEP 1

Put the carrots in a large frying pan with a lid. Cover with cold water, put the lid on and bring to a boil. Once boiling, take the lid off and cook over a medium heat for about 25-30 mins until all the water has evaporated.

STEP 2

Reduce the heat, add the honey, butter and thyme leaves and gently cook for about 5 mins until the carrots are caramelised and golden.

Pick & mix omelette with crunchy croutons

Prep:5 mins **Cook:**5 mins

Serves 1

Ingredients

- 1 thick slice bread , cut into small cubes
- 1 tbsp olive oil
- 2 eggs
- 2 tbsp grated cheese
- your choice of 1 slice ham , 1 slice chicken, 2 slices salami, 2 slices chorizo, or a handful prawns
- your choice of a handful quartered cherry tomatoes , 2 tbsp drained sweetcorn, 2 tbsp defrosted frozen peas, or a handful rocket
- salad , to serve

Method

STEP 1

Heat ½ tbsp oil in a small non-stick frying pan. Add the bread, toss it around and fry over a medium heat until it starts to brown and crisp all over. Tip the croutons onto a plate, then carefully wipe out the pan. Shred the meat you have chosen to use or roughly chop the prawns.

STEP 2

Beat the eggs lightly with a fork and season if you want. Heat ½ tbsp oil in the frying pan, then pour in the egg. Tip the pan from side to side until the base is covered and starting to set. Add the meat and veg to the side of the omelette nearest you. Cover the pan with a lid for a minute, then add the cheese and cover for another minute. Finally add the croutons and flip the far side of the omelette towards you so that it covers the filling. Slide onto a plate and serve with whatever kind of salad you can get away with.

Homemade cocoa pops

Prep:10 mins **Cook:**16 mins

Serves 20

Ingredients

- 100g coconut oil
- 200g honey
- 100g cocoa powder
- 850g buckwheat

- 150g pack cacao nibs (if you're cooking with kids, you can substitute with chopped dark chocolate)

Method

STEP 1

Heat oven to 180C/160C fan/gas 4. Line two large baking trays with baking parchment. In a large microwaveable bowl, melt the coconut oil with the honey, cocoa powder and a pinch of sea salt. Stir in the buckwheat, covering well in the chocolate mixture.

STEP 2

Spread the mixture onto the baking trays and bake for 15 mins, stirring halfway, then mix in the cacao nibs. Allow to cool before storing in a Kilner jar or airtight container. Best eaten within 1 month.

Child-friendly Thai chicken noodles

Prep:10 mins **Cook:**15 mins - 20 mins

Serves 2 adults + 2 children

Ingredients

- 100g sugar snap peas
- 1 tbsp oil
- 2 spring onions , finely chopped
- 2 garlic cloves , crushed
- 1 tsp grated ginger

- 3 x chicken breasts, cut into chunks
- ½ tbsp Thai curry paste (we used Thai Taste)
- 400ml can coconut milk
- limes , juice of one, other quartered
- 50g frozen peas
- nests egg noodles

- handful chopped coriander , to serve

Method

STEP 1

Blanch the sugar snap peas in a bowl of boiling water for 2 mins, then drain. Heat the oil in a large frying pan. Add the spring onions, garlic, ginger and chicken. Gently fry for 2-3 mins. Stir in the curry paste and cook for 1 minute more. Add the coconut milk to the pan, along with a splash of water, the lime juice, peas and sugar snap peas. Gently bubble for around 5 mins until the chicken is cooked through.

STEP 2

Meanwhile, cook the noodles according to the pack instructions. Drain. Stir the noodles through the sauce, scatter with coriander and serve with a wedge of lime for squeezing over.

Caramel & coffee ice cream sandwich

Prep:5 mins

Serves 2

Ingredients

- 1 tbsp chocolate-coated coffee beans , roughly chopped
- 2 scoops coffee ice cream , softened
- 4 caramel wafers

Method

STEP 1

Mix the chocolate coffee beans into the softened ice cream until combined, then transfer to a small loaf tin and freeze for a few hours or until solid.

STEP 2

Use cookie cutters to cut the ice cream to the same size as the waffles, then sandwich between two waffles.

Creamy salmon, prawn & almond curry

Prep:15 mins **Cook:**25 mins

Serves 3 (or 2 adults and 2 children)

Ingredients

- 2 tbsp oil
- 1 onion , chopped
- 2 garlic cloves , crushed
- 2 red peppers , sliced
- ½ tsp ground turmeric
- 2 tsp ground cumin
- 2 tsp ground coriander
- 1 tbsp tomato purée
- 70g ground almonds

- 1 low-salt vegetable or chicken stock cube
- 1½ tbsp double cream
- 300g green beans
- 2 salmon fillets (around 300g-350g), skin removed and cut into chunks
- 150g raw king prawns
- handful of coriander , leaves picked
- 150g brown rice , cooked, to serve
- ½ lime , cut into wedges to serve

Method

STEP 1

Heat the oil in a pan and cook the onion for 8-10 mins until starting to soften, then stir in the garlic and cook for 1 min. Add the peppers, spices, tomato purée and a splash of water. Cook for 1-2 mins until the peppers soften.

STEP 2

Add the almonds, stock cube and 500ml water to the pan, season and simmer for 10 mins. Stir in the cream. Cook the beans in a small pan of boiling water for 2 mins until just tender, then drain.

STEP 3

When you're ready to eat, add the salmon to the sauce, simmer gently for 2-3 mins until the fish turns opaque, then add the prawns and cook for a further 1 min until they turn pink. Check the salmon is cooked through (it should easily flake when gently pressed with a knife). Remove from the heat and add a little lime juice. Serve scattered with the coriander, the beans with the rice and the lime wedges for squeezing over.

Watermelon doughnuts

Prep:20 mins **Cook:**10 mins

Makes 12 large doughnuts

Ingredients

For the batter

- 200g plain flour
- 180g golden caster sugar
- 2 tsp baking powder
- ½ tsp ground cinnamon

- 250g buttermilk
- 2 medium eggs , lightly beaten
- 30g butter , melted
- 1 tsp vanilla extract

To decorate

- 300g pink candy melts
- 200g green candy melts

- 2 tbsp vegetable oil
- 30g dark chocolate chips

You will need

- 12-hole doughnut tin

Method

STEP 1

Heat oven to 220C/200C fan/gas 7. Put all the dry ingredients together in a bowl and mix well with a whisk to distribute the cinnamon and baking powder. Add the wet ingredients and mix until just combined. Pour the batter into a piping bag and fill the doughnut pan until each hole is approximately three quarters full. Do this in batches if needed.

STEP 2

Bake for 9–10 minutes until risen, golden brown and the tops are springy to the touch. Allow to cool for a couple of mins then turn out onto a wire rack to cool completely. If the doughnuts have lost their holes during baking use a small cutter or piping nozzle to recut them.

STEP 3

Put your pink candy melts in a microwaveable bowl with 1 tbsp vegetable oil. Melt at 30 second intervals at a medium heat until silky and completely melted. Spoon the pink candy melt over the top of each doughnut wiping off any drips that fall down the edge. Leave on a wire rack until set (about 5-10 mins). Do not throw away the excess pink!

STEP 4

Meanwhile melt the green candy melts in the same way. Hold your doughnuts on the edge and roll them through the green candy melts only covering the outside not the pink. Leave to set.

STEP 5

Cut the chocolate chips in half to create watermelon seed shapes. Dip a cocktail stick into the pink candy melt and mark out the spots to place your seeds then stick on the chocolate chips.

Pea & pesto soup with fish finger croûtons

Prep:5 mins **Cook:**15 mins

Serves 4

Ingredients

- 500g frozen pea
- 4 medium potatoes, peeled and cut into cubes
- 1l hot vegetable stock
- 300g pack fish finger (about 10)
- 3 tbsp green pesto

Method

STEP 1

Tip the peas and potatoes into a large saucepan, then pour in the stock. Bring to the boil and simmer for 10 mins, until the potato chunks are tender. Meanwhile, grill the fish fingers as per pack instructions until cooked through and golden. Cut into bitesize cubes and keep warm.

STEP 2

Take a third of the peas and potatoes out of the pan with a slotted spoon and set aside. Blend the rest of the soup until smooth, then stir in the pesto with the reserved vegetables. Heat through and serve in warm bowls with the fish finger croûtons on top.

Cherry ripple, chocolate & rose ice cream

Prep: 15 mins

Plus 4 hrs freezing

Serves 8

Ingredients

- 425g can pitted cherries in syrup, drained (reserve the syrup)
- ½ tsp rose water
- 600ml double cream
- ½ a 397g can condensed milk
- 100g bar of dark chocolate , chopped (you want a nice mixture of chunks and smaller bits)
- shortbread biscuits , cones and extra cherries, to serve (optional)

Method

STEP 1

Line a 900g loaf tin with parchment or cling film. Tip the cherries into a food processor with 2 tbsp syrup from the tin, add the rose water and blend to a purée.

STEP 2

Whip the cream until it holds soft peaks, then stir in the condensed milk and half the cherry purée. Pour roughly a third of the mixture into the loaf tin, swirl through some of the purée and scatter with chocolate, then repeat the layers until you've used all the ingredients up. Freeze for at least 4 hrs. Turn out the ice cream, slice and serve with biscuits and extra cherries, or use a scoop for balls to fill ice cream cones.

Weaning recipe: Fish pie bites

Prep: 20 mins **Cook:** 1 hr and 45 mins

Makes 8-9 bites

Ingredients

- 1 medium baking potato
- 1 small salmon fillet , about 120g
- 1 tbsp frozen sweetcorn and peas, defrosted

- 1 tsp fresh chives , snipped into little strands
- 25g mild cheddar , grated
- ½ small egg , beaten
- oil , for greasing

Method

STEP 1

Heat the oven to 200C/ 180 fan/ gas 6. Wrap the potato in foil, place on a baking tray and roast in the oven for 1 hour 15 mins. Wrap the fish in foil, put on the same tray and continue cooking for around 10- 12 mins until opaque and cooked through.

STEP 2

Once cooked, halve the potato and scoop out the filling. Flake the fish, removing any bones and discarding the skin.

STEP 3

Grease a baking tray with a little oil. Mash the potato, then mix through the flaked fish, veg, chives, cheese and egg. Allow to cool a little, then take golf-ball sized dollops of mixture and form into little croquette shapes. Arrange on a foil-lined tray and chill in the fridge for 30 mins. If freezing, put the tray in the freezer instead. Once frozen, transfer to a freezer bag and take them out when needed. Thoroughly defrost in the fridge before cooking.

STEP 4

To cook, heat the oven to 200C/ 180 fan/ gas 6. Arrange as many as you need on a baking tray and cook for around 15 mins or until golden and cooked through. The inside will be very hot so make sure it's sufficiently cooled before serving to your little one.

Halloween toffee apples

Prep:20 mins **Cook:**10 mins

Serves 8

Ingredients

- 8 red apples
- 400g caster sugar
- 1 tsp lemon juice
- 4 tbsp golden syrup

- red or black food colouring
- red or black food glitter (optional)

You will need

- 8 sturdy, clean twigs or lolly sticks

Method

STEP 1

Pull any stalks off the twigs and push the sharpest end of each stick (or the lolly sticks) into the stalk-end of each apple, making sure it is firmly wedged in. Put a large piece of baking parchment onto a wooden board.

STEP 2

Tip the sugar into a large saucepan and add the lemon juice and 100ml water. Bring to a simmer and cook until the sugar has dissolved. Swirl the pan gently to move the sugar around, but don't stir. Add the golden syrup and bubble the mixture (be careful it doesn't boil over) until it reaches 'hard crack' stage or 150C on a sugar thermometer. If you don't have a thermometer, test the toffee by dropping a small amount into cold water. It should harden instantly and, when removed, be brittle. If it's soft, continue to boil. When it's ready, drip in some food colouring and swirl to combine. Add the glitter, if using, and turn off the heat.

STEP 3

Working quickly, dip each apple into the toffee, tipping the pan to cover all the skin. Lift out and allow any excess to drip off before putting on the baking parchment. Repeat with the remaining apples. Gently heat the toffee again if you need to. Best eaten on the same day.

Malted milk melting snowman cake

Prep:1 hr **Cook:**1 hr and 25 mins

Serves 25 - 30

Ingredients

For the sponges

- 500g unsalted butter , softened, plus extra for greasing
- 500g golden caster sugar
- 10 eggs

194

- 200g plain flour
- 200g full-fat natural yogurt
- 460g self-raising flour

- 4 tbsp malt extract (or 2 tbsp vanilla paste)
- 1 tbsp full-fat milk (or 2 tbsp if using vanilla paste)

For the buttercream

- 400g unsalted butter , softened
- 700g icing sugar

- 2 tbsp malt extract (or 1 tbsp vanilla paste)
- 1 tbsp full-fat milk

For the drippy ganache

- 100g white chocolate

- ½ tsp vegetable oil

To decorate

- 30g black fondant
- 30g bright orange fondant
- 1 wooden dowel , cut the same length as the nose

- 2-3 giant chocolate buttons
- 2 white chocolate Mikado sticks , for the arms

You will need

- 2 x 20cm cake tins
- 16cm hemisphere cake tin
- 23cm cake board

- 16cm cake board
- squeezy bottle

Method

STEP 1

Heat oven to 160C/140C fan/gas 3. Grease two 20cm round cake tins and line with baking parchment. Heavily grease a 16cm hemisphere cake tin and stand on a ramekin on a baking sheet to hold it steady.

STEP 2

First, make the sponges. Using electric beaters or a tabletop mixer, beat the butter and sugar together until pale and fluffy. Pour the eggs in, one at a time, giving the mix a thorough beating before adding the next. If the mix starts to look curdled, add 2 tbsp of the plain flour. Beat in the yogurt.

STEP 3

Mix both the flours together, adding ½ tsp salt, and slowly beat into the batter, followed by the malt extract (or vanilla paste) and milk. Spoon half the mixture into one of the 20cm tins, and split the remaining half between the other 20cm tin and the 16cm hemisphere. Bake the smaller amount of cake batter in the 20cm tin and the 16cm tin for 1 hr, and the larger amount for 1 hr 20 mins or until a skewer comes out clean when inserted into the middle of the cakes. Cool in the tin for 10 mins before turning out onto a wire rack to cool completely. Can be frozen at this stage for up to three months.

STEP 4

Meanwhile, make the buttercream by beating all the butter and half the icing sugar together using an electric whisk or tabletop mixer. Add the rest of the icing sugar once incorporated, followed by the malt extract (or vanilla paste) and milk. Set aside until ready to use.

STEP 5

To assemble, halve the largest 20cm cake horizontally so you are left with two equal-sized sponges the same size as the remaining 20cm cake. Put a blob of buttercream onto a 23cm cake board (or cake stand) and spread using a palette knife. Stick one of the sponges to the board. Spread a thick layer of buttercream on top of the cake and sandwich another sponge on top. Spread over another thick layer and sit the final sponge on top. Using a palette knife, coat the entire cake in a thin layer of buttercream and smooth the sides and top carefully, working around the whole cake, scraping off any excess icing. Chill in the freezer for 10 mins or in the fridge for 1 hr until set.

STEP 6

Meanwhile, put the hemisphere sponge on the smaller cake board and halve horizontally. Fill the middle with some buttercream, sandwich with the top and coat the entire cake in a thin layer of buttercream. Chill in the freezer for 5 mins or in the fridge for 30 mins.

STEP 7

Take the larger cake out of the fridge/ freezer and coat in another layer of buttercream. Take care when covering this time, as you want a smooth finish to the cake. Running the palette knife under hot water helps smooth over the sides once it is coated completely. Chill again for 5 mins in the freezer.

STEP 8

Cover the hemisphere sponge with buttercream and smooth over with the palette knife. Carefully lift the hemisphere onto the centre of the cake (as the sponge has been frozen you shouldn't leave finger marks). Press down lightly to set on the buttercream. If there is a gap around the rim, use a small palette knife to fill in with any remaining buttercream. Chill for 10-15 mins.

STEP 9

Meanwhile, make the eyes and nose using coloured fondant. Roll the black fondant into two balls for the eyes, and five smaller balls for the mouth. Roll the orange fondant into a carrot shape. Leave to set and harden slightly while you make the drippy ganache.

STEP 10

Make the drippy ganache by mixing the chocolate and oil and microwaving for 30 secs, stirring and then giving it another 30 secs until melted. Transfer to a squeezy bottle, then pour down the edges of the round cake to create the melting snow effect.

STEP 11

To finish the cake, stick the eyes to the head using a little remaining buttercream. Poke the wooden dowel into the carrot nose, leaving some poking out to stick it to the face. Stick the five small black fondant balls for the mouth and the chocolate buttons down the front of the cake for buttons. Insert the Mikado sticks on either side for the arms. Bring the cake to room temperature before serving.

Chicken schnitzel with coleslaw

Prep:30 mins **Cook:**10 mins

Serves 4

Ingredients

For the schnitzel

- 4 small chicken breasts
- 3 tbsp grated parmesan
- 100g flour
- 1 large egg , beaten

- 75g dried breadcrumbs (we used panko)
- 75ml vegetable oil

For the coleslaw

- 300g white cabbage , shredded
- 1 large carrot , peeled and grated
- 6 spring onions , sliced diagonally
- 1 red-skinned apple , grated
- 150g pot natural yogurt
- juice 0.5 lemon
- 2 tsp English mustard

Method

STEP 1

For the coleslaw, get your child to mix all the ingredients in a large bowl. Season a little and set aside.

STEP 2

Place a layer of cling film on your work surface and pop the chicken fillets on top. Cover with another piece of cling film and, using a rolling pin, ask your child to bash the chicken until it is 2-3mm thick.

STEP 3

Put the flour on a plate and season, then put the egg on another plate. Get your child to dip the chicken in the flour to coat, then into the egg.

STEP 4

Mix together the breadcrumbs and Parmesan in a shallow bowl, then ask your child to toss the chicken in the mixture to completely coat in the crumbs. Put the chicken on a plate and chill in the fridge until ready to eat if you're not cooking them straight away.

STEP 5

Heat the oil in a large frying pan over a fairly high heat and cook the chicken schnitzels two at a time. Sizzle them for 2-3 mins each side until completely golden, then lift out onto kitchen paper to drain. You can keep them warm in a low oven while you cook the rest. Serve with the coleslaw.

Orange and raspberry Hey Duggee cake

Prep: 1 hr and 30 mins **Cook:** 1 hr and 40 mins

Serves 16

Ingredients

For the cake

- 300g unsalted butter , room temperature
- 300g caster sugar
- 2 tsp vanilla extract
- 6 large eggs
- 400g self-raising flour
- 130g natural yogurt
- 2 tbsp milk (if needed)

For the syrup

- 50g caster sugar
- 1 tsp vanilla extract

For the orange buttercream & jam filling

- 250g unsalted butter , softened
- 550g icing sugar
- 75g orange curd
- 3 tbsp raspberry jam

For the decoration

- 500g red sugarpaste
- 250g yellow sugarpaste
- 140g blue sugarpaste
- 100g brown sugarpaste
- 25g black sugarpaste
- 80cm length of yellow ribbon (optional)

Method

STEP 1

Start by making the cake. Heat oven to 180C/160C fan/gas 4 and lightly grease a 23cm deep round cake pan, lining the base with parchment paper.

STEP 2

Cream the butter and sugar together in a large bowl using an electric hand whisk until light and fluffy – this should take about 10 mins. Add the vanilla and whisk again to combine. Beat the eggs a little with a fork, and with the beaters still running, add the eggs a little bit at a time. Wait until each addition has been fully combined before adding more.

STEP 3

Once all of the eggs have been added, fold in the flour with a spatula in three additions, alternating with the yogurt. If the finished batter feels a little stiff, mix in a couple tbsp of milk to loosen it. Transfer the batter into the prepared cake pan and level out with a spatula.

STEP 4

Bake in the preheated oven for about 1 hr 30 – 1 hr 40 mins or until a skewer inserted into the middle of the cake comes out clean. If the cake is browning too quickly, cover loosely with baking parchment for the last 15 mins of cooking. Allow the cake to cool in the tin for 20 mins.

STEP 5

While the cake is cooling in the tin make the syrup. Place the sugar, 50ml water and vanilla extract into a small saucepan over a medium heat and bring to a simmer, cooking for a few mins until the sugar has dissolved. Transfer the cake onto a wire rack to cool completely then use a skewer to poke holes all over the top of the cake. Use a pastry brush to spread the syrup over the top of the cake, allowing it to soak into the sponge before adding more.

STEP 6

To make the buttercream, beat the butter and icing sugar together with an electric hand whisk until light and fluffy, then add the orange curd and whisk again to combine. If the cake is domed on the top, use a large serrated knife to level it off then cut the cake through the middle, into two layers. Place the bottom layer of cake onto a 23cm round cake board and spread a thin layer of buttercream on the cake and top with the raspberry jam. Place the second layer of cake on top and spread the remaining buttercream over the top and sides of the cake.

STEP 7

On a work surface lightly dusted with icing sugar, knead the red sugarpaste until soft and pliable. Roll it out until about 3-4mm thick and wide enough to cover the cake. Roll the sugarpaste onto the rolling pin and carefully drape over the cake. Gently smooth the sugarpaste down the sides of the cake and trim off the excess with a small sharp knife. Reserve the trimmings for the details later on.

STEP 8

Repeat the rolling process with the yellow sugarpaste but this time cutting into thin strips. Cut 30 strips approx 1.5cm x 10cm and stick to the sides of the cake all the way around, dipping your finger in water to brush onto the back of each one, which will act as glue (the strips should cover the entire height of the cake but only reach a couple of centimetres over the top of cake).

STEP 9

Next roll out the blue sugarpaste to the same thickness as the red and yellow but this time cut out a 20cm circle and stick it in place in the middle of the cake using a little water. Roll out the brown sugarpaste as well and use a thin sharp knife to cut out Duggee's face and attach to the blue circle.

STEP 10

For Duggee's clothes knead a little yellow into the remaining brown sugarpaste until it is a light brown colour and use this to cut out his shirt and lip area, sticking with a little water as before. Use the black sugarpaste to roll his eyes and nose, using your hands rather than rolling on the work surface. Use the remaining sugarpaste to shape the decorations for his outfit and mouth and stick as before with a little water. Wrap the ribbon around the bottom edge of the cake and secure with tape or a pin but remember to remove before serving. This cake will keep in a sealed container for up to 4 days.

Mini Egg cake

Prep: 1 hr and 15 mins **Cook:** 45 mins

Serves 16

Ingredients

- 250g butter , softened, plus a little extra, melted, for the tin
- 250g self-raising flour , plus extra for dusting

For the drizzle

- 2 oranges , juiced (use the ones you've zested)

- 225g golden caster sugar
- 2 oranges , zested
- 5 large eggs
- 1 tsp baking powder

- 2 tbsp golden caster sugar

For the icing

- 150g butter , softened
- 500g icing sugar

- 1 tsp vanilla extract
- 180g tub full-fat cream cheese

For the decoration

- 4 x 90g bags Cadbury's Mini Eggs

Method

STEP 1

Heat oven to 180C/160C fan/gas 4. Butter a bundt tin or fluted cake ring (at least 2.5-litre capacity), then dust the tin with a little flour, shaking off the excess. Beat all the cake ingredients with a pinch of salt using an electric whisk until you have a smooth batter. Spoon into the prepared tin, smoothing the top with a palette knife, then bake for 35 mins until a skewer inserted into the centre comes out mostly clean with a few dry crumbs attached.

STEP 2

For the drizzle, combine the sugar with the orange juice in a saucepan, then reduce over a medium heat to a loose syrupy consistency. Prick the base of the cake all over with a skewer, then pour over half the syrup, adding the rest once it has been absorbed, Leave the cake to cool in the tin for 15 mins, then turn out onto a wire rack to cool completely.

STEP 3

While the cake is cooling, make the icing. Beat the butter with half the icing sugar and the vanilla extract until smooth and fluffy. Add the remaining icing sugar and the cream cheese and beat again until well combined – don't overbeat or the icing will become runny.

STEP 4

Spread a thin layer of the icing over the entire cake, taking care to get into all the crevices, then pop in the fridge for 20 mins to set. If you are short of time, you can always put it in the freezer. Spread the remaining icing onto the cake in an even layer. Once iced, the cake will keep in the fridge for three days. Bring to room temperature before decorating and serving.

STEP 5

Sort the Mini Eggs into different colours (a possibly therapeutic exercise, depending on your organisational tendencies). Stick the Mini Eggs all over the top of the cake.

Lunchbox pasta salad

Prep:15 mins **Cook:**11 mins

Serves 4

Ingredients

- 400g pasta
- 4-5 tbsp fresh pesto
- 1 tbsp mayonnaise
- 2 tbsp Greek yogurt
- ½ lemon , juiced

- 200g mixed cooked veg such as peas, green beans, courgette (chop the beans and courgette into pea-sized pieces)
- 100g cherry tomatoes , quartered
- 200g cooked chicken , ham, prawns, hard-boiled egg or cheese

Method

STEP 1

Cook the pasta in boiling water until it is al dente, so about 11 mins, but refer to the pack instructions. Drain and tip into a bowl. Stir in the pesto and leave to cool.

STEP 2

When the pasta is cool, stir through the mayo, yogurt, lemon juice and veg. Spoon into lunchboxes or on to pasta plates and put the cooked chicken or protein of your choice on top. Chill until ready to eat if intended for a packed lunch.

BBQ chicken with corn rice

Prep:10 mins **Cook:**40 mins

Serves 4

Ingredients

- 4 chicken leg portions, cut into thighs and drumsticks, skin removed

- 2 onions , 1 chopped, 1 cut into wedges

- 1 red and 1 green pepper , deseeded and thickly sliced
- 2 tbsp olive oil
- 200ml bottled barbecue sauce
- 2 tsp thyme leaves

- 250g long grain rice , rinsed
- 600ml chicken stock
- 340g can sweetcorn , rinsed and drained
- ½ red chilli , finely chopped (optional)

Method

STEP 1

Heat oven to 200C/180C fan/gas 6. Slash each piece of chicken 2-3 times. Put the chicken, onion wedges and peppers in a roasting tin or ovenproof pan, then toss with 1 tbsp oil and the barbecue sauce. Roast for 40 mins, turning halfway, until sticky and tender. Add a splash of water if the sauce dries up a little at the edges.

STEP 2

Meanwhile, heat 1 tbsp oil in a medium pan, then soften the chopped onion for 5 mins. Stir in the thyme, rice, stock and seasoning. Bring to the boil, cover and simmer for 12 mins. Turn off the heat, tip in the corn, add chilli if using, put the lid back on and let the rice steam for 10 mins more. Fluff up the rice, then serve with the chicken, vegetables and pan juices.

Stripy hummus salad jars

Prep:15 mins

6 jars

Ingredients

- 140g frozen soya beans or peas
- 200g tub hummus (reserve 2 tbsp for the dressing)
- 2 red peppers (or a mixture of colours) finely chopped
- Half cucumber , finely chopped

- 200g cherry tomatoes , quartered
- 2 large carrots
- small pack basil
- 2 large carrots , peeled and grated
- 4 tbsp pumpkin seeds (optional)

For the dressing

- zest and juice 1 lemon
- 1 tbsp clear honey

- 2 tbsp hummus (from the tub, above)

Method

STEP 1

First make the dressing. Put the ingredients in a jam jar with 1 tbsp water. Screw on the lid and shake well. Set aside.

STEP 2

Bring a small pan of water to the boil, add the beans or peas and cook for 1 min until tender. Drain and run under cold water until cool. Divide the remaining hummus between 6 large jam jars. Top with the drained soya beans or peas, peppers, cucumber, tomatoes, basil leaves, carrots and pumpkin seeds, if using. Screw on the lids and chill until needed. Will keep in the fridge for 24 hrs.

STEP 3

When ready to serve, pass around the jars and let everyone pour over a little dressing.

Mini elf doughnuts

Prep: 45 mins **Cook:** 8 mins - 10 mins

Makes 24

Ingredients

- 2 tbsp melted butter , plus an extra 1 tbsp for greasing
- 100g plain flour
- ½ tsp baking powder
- 1 tsp ground cinnamon
- ¼ tsp ground nutmeg

- 3 tbsp golden caster sugar
- 1 large egg
- 1 tsp vanilla extract
- 2 tbsp maple syrup
- 4 tbsp buttermilk

For the icing

- 250g icing sugar
- 50ml milk
- red and green food colouring

- red, green & white sprinkles
- red and green writing icing tubes (optional)

Method

STEP 1

Heat oven to 180C/160C fan/gas 4. Brush some melted butter in the holes of a 24-hole mini muffin tin.

STEP 2

Put the flour, baking powder, cinnamon, nutmeg and sugar in a big bowl and mix together with your hands.

STEP 3

Pour the melted butter into a jug with the egg, vanilla, maple syrup and buttermilk, and mix together with a fork.

STEP 4

Pour the wet ingredients over the dry ones and use a big wooden spoon to mix until there are no lumps.

STEP 5

Use teaspoons to divide the mixture between the holes in the tin. Bake in the oven for 8-10 mins, then cool in the tin.

STEP 6

Now it's time to turn them into doughnuts. Once cool, carefully tip the cakes out. Sit each on a chopping board and push an apple corer into the centre to cut the middle out so you have a ring.

STEP 7

Put the icing sugar and milk in a saucepan over a low heat. Whisk until runny and smooth. Divide the icing between three bowls, and mix a little green food colouring into one bowl, and a little red colouring into another.

STEP 8

Sit the doughnuts on a wire rack (so the drips can fall off), then spoon a little icing onto each. Decorate with sprinkles and writing icing, if you like. As this glaze dries quickly, finish decorating one colour, then start the next colour. If the icing is not runny enough, put in the microwave for 10 secs and stir well. Will keep for 2 days.

Toffee popcorn bark

Prep:10 mins **Cook:**5 mins

Serves 8

Ingredients

- 200g milk chocolate

- 200g white chocolate

- x bags toffee popcorn

Method

STEP 1

Line a 20 x 30cm baking tray with baking parchment. Melt the milk chocolate and white chocolate separately, then allow to cool slightly.

STEP 2

Pour most of the chocolate onto the tray, roughly swirling together. Sprinkle over the toffee popcorn, then drizzle over the remaining milk and white chocolate, and chill until set. Break into big chunks before serving.

Chocolate-chip cookie ice-cream sandwiches

Prep:20 mins **Cook:**20 mins

Makes 12 sandwiches or 24 cookies

Ingredients

- 280g light soft brown sugar
- 225g granulated sugar
- 250g butter
- 2 large eggs
- 1 tbsp vanilla extract

- 450g plain flour
- 2 tsp baking powder
- 300g good-quality milk chocolate , roughly chopped into chunks
- vanilla ice cream , to serve

Method

STEP 1

To make the cookies, tip the sugars and butter into a large bowl. Get a grown-up to help you use an electric hand mixer to blend them together until the mixture looks smooth and creamy, and a little paler in colour.

STEP 2

Carefully break in the eggs, one at a time, mixing well between each egg and pausing to scrape down the sides with a spatula. Mix in the vanilla. (To avoid unwanted crunchy bits, get your helper to crack the eggs into a separate bowl first, then it's easy to pick out any shell before tipping into the mixture.)

STEP 3

Sift in the flour and baking powder, then mix well with a wooden spoon.

STEP 4

Stir through the chocolate chunks. Use your hands to squeeze the dough together in 1 big lump, then split into 2 even pieces. Put each piece on a sheet of cling film.

STEP 5

Roll each piece of dough in the cling film so that they form thick sausage shapes, then seal the ends. Put them in the fridge and chill for at least 3 hrs or overnight – can be frozen at this point.

STEP 6

Heat oven to 180C/160C fan/ gas 4. Take the dough rolls out of the fridge, unwrap and use a small knife to slice each one into 12 pieces, so you have 24 in total.

STEP 7

Place the slices on a baking tray lined with baking parchment. Ask a grown-up to put this in the oven to bake for 20 mins or until the cookies are golden brown on the edges, but still pale in the centre.

STEP 8

Allow to cool slightly before lifting them onto a wire rack to cool completely. Sandwich the cookies together with ice cream and dig in!

Rigatoni sausage bake

Prep:20 mins **Cook:**45 mins - 50 mins

Serves 6

Ingredients

- 400g good quality pork sausage
- 1 tbsp olive oil
- 1 onion, chopped
- 1 large carrot, grated

For the sauce

- 50g butter
- 50g plain flour
- 600ml milk

- 150ml red wine
- 300ml vegetable stock
- 3 tbsp tomato purée

- freshly grated nutmeg
- 500g rigatoni or penne
- 200g fresh spinach

- 140g mature cheddar, grated

Method

STEP 1

Slit the sausages and remove them from their skins, then chop them into small pieces. Heat the oil in a pan, add the onion and fry for 5 minutes, until softened and lightly browned. Stir in the sausages and fry until lightly coloured. Add the carrot, then stir in the wine, stock, tomato purée, and season.

STEP 2

Bring to the boil, then simmer uncovered for about 15 minutes until thickened. Taste and season. Set aside.

STEP 3

Put the butter, flour and milk in a pan. Gently heat, whisking, until thickened and smooth. Add a sprinkle of freshly grated nutmeg, season, then simmer for 2 minutes.

STEP 4

Preheat the oven to 190C/Gas 5/fan 170C. Bring a large pan of salted water to the boil. Add the pasta, stir well, then cook, uncovered, for 10-12 minutes, until tender. Remove from the heat, stir in the spinach and, when just wilted, drain well.

STEP 5

Tip half the pasta into a shallow ovenproof dish, about 2.2 litre/4 pint, and level. Spoon over the sausage sauce, then cover with the remaining pasta. Pour the white sauce evenly over the top and sprinkle with the cheddar. Bake for 20-25 minutes until golden brown. Leave for 5 minutes before serving.

Chicken pesto wrap

Prep: 10 mins

Serves 2

Ingredients

- 1 cooked chicken breast , shredded
- 2 tbsp soured cream , plain yogurt or mayo
- 2 tsp pesto
- 2 thin slices mild cheese , such as Edam
- 2 flour tortillas

- handful chopped red pepper or sweetcorn kernels
- lettuce leaves

Method

STEP 1

Mix together the shredded chicken, soured cream, yogurt or mayonnaise with the pesto. Season.

STEP 2

Lay a slice of cheese on each wrap, then divide the chicken mixture between them. Sprinkle with red pepper or sweetcorn, then top with the lettuce leaves. Be careful not to overfill or it will be tricky to contain all the filling. Wrap and roll each one, then pack in a lunchbox or tightly wrap in foil.

Holiday pizzas

Prep:30 mins **Cook:**15 mins

Makes 6 x 20cm, or 10-12 smaller pizzas

Ingredients

For the dough

- 500g strong white bread flour , plus extra for dusting
- small pinch of sugar
- 7g sachet fast-action dried yeast
- 2 tbsp olive oil , plus extra for greasing
- 300ml warm water

For the sauce

- 1 garlic clove
- 400ml chunky passata
- 1 tbsp tomato purée
- 1 tsp dried oregano
- handful basil leaves , snipped
- small pinch of sugar
- 1 tsp red wine vinegar

For the toppings

- ham, red peppers, black olives, salami, mozzarella , cherry tomatoes, cheddar, tuna, sweetcorn
- houmous and green salad, to serve

Method

STEP 1

KIDS: The writing in bold is for you. GROWN-UPS: The rest is for you. **Mix a sticky dough.** Put the flour, sugar and yeast in a bowl and get the child to make a hole in the middle. Measure 300ml water – that isn't cold and isn't hot but just right (like the little bear's porridge in Goldie Locks). Add the oil and water; point out that the two don't mix well. Stir with a wooden spoon until you have a sticky dough. Add a splash more water if needed.

STEP 2

Now you need to do something called kneading. Scatter a bit more flour over the surface and tip the dough onto it. You now want to 'stretch' the dough and bring it back into a ball shape. This will need to be done for about 10 mins. I usually give children a few minutes bashing the dough about, then take over to make sure that the dough is smooth and elastic enough.

STEP 3

Leave the dough to grow. Brush a clean bowl with a little olive oil, put the dough in it and cover with cling film. Leave it somewhere warm for it to grow until doubled in size. Now is a good time to tidy up and wipe down surfaces a little before you start again.

STEP 4

Make a tasty tomato sauce. Crush the garlic by using a garlic crusher or by grating it on the fine edge of a box grater. Tip into a bowl and mix with the other sauce ingredients. Stir well until everything is combined, then set aside.

STEP 5

Roll out the dough. Heat oven to 220C/200C fan/gas 8. Show your child how the dough has grown, then divide into the amount of pizzas you want to make. Brush the baking trays with extra oil. Divide the dough and roll out, then lift onto the baking trays.

STEP 6

Spoon on the tomato sauce. You need to be a bit more careful with this task than you think. If the dough is thin, a child can easily tear it, so make sure that they use the back of the spoon to spread the sauce over. You can now freeze the pizzas – see tip, below.

STEP 7

Build your own pizza. Put all the toppings out in different bowls and let the child 'build' their own pizza. Little ones will need to be handed the ingredients as they will try to just pile up as much as they can or not be able to scatter things evenly.

STEP 8

Get cooking. You can get older kids to carefully place the tray in the oven using oven gloves (see safety first, opposite). Bake pizzas for 12-15 mins until puffed up and golden around the edges, then carefully lift out of the oven. Leave to cool slightly, then slip onto a board or plate. Serve cut into pieces with houmous and a simple green salad.

RECIPE TIPS

FREEZE YOUR PIZZAS

If you want to freeze any pizza bases for later, roll to your desired size, spread with tomato sauce (see Step 5) and layer up between sheets of baking parchment. Wrap in foil and freeze for up to 1 month or until needed.

THROW A KIDS PIZZA PARTY

Have the dough already made then let the kids get on with the rolling and topping. Have the topping ingredients out in bowls and get the kids to taste things they might normally shy away from, like red pepper or olives. Serve the pizzas with something to dip the crusts in, like houmous, so nothing goes to waste.

WHAT SKILLS CAN KIDS LEARN FROM PIZZA MAKING?

MIXING AND KNEADING DOUGH to make and shape basic breads. **ROLLING** to later use when making pastry and biscuits. **MAKING TOMATO SAUCE** to use as a pasta sauce for a weeknight family meal.

Gooey brownies

Prep:10 mins **Cook:**35 mins

Makes 16-20

Ingredients

- 100g unsalted butter , softened
- 175g caster sugar
- 2 large eggs , beaten
- 75g plain flour
- 50g cocoa powder
- 1 tsp baking powder

- 3 tbsp milk
- 4 tbsp mixed white and milk chocolate chips
- 100g milk chocolate
- 75g full-fat soft cheese

Method

STEP 1

Heat oven to 180C/160C fan/gas 4 and line a 20cm square brownie tin with baking parchment. Beat the butter and sugar together with an electric whisk, then add the eggs one by one.

STEP 2

Sift in the flour, cocoa powder and baking powder, and add the milk. Mix everything together, then stir in the chocolate chips. Spoon into the tin and level the top. Bake for 30 mins, or until the top is set, then cool completely.

STEP 3

Meanwhile, make the topping, melt the milk chocolate, cool a little, then mix it with the soft cheese until fully combined and silky.

STEP 4

Spread the topping over the cooled brownies and cut into small squares – these are very rich.

Shimmering forest cake

Prep:30 mins

Ingredients

To cover the cake

- 20cm/8inch round fruitcake
- 3 tbsp apricot jam , warmed
- icing sugar , for dusting

- 750g natural-coloured marzipan
- 750g white ready-to-roll icing

To decorate

- 500g white ready-to-roll icing
- green food colouring paste
- 200g icing sugar , plus extra for dusting
- 2Christmas tree cutters , about 5cm and 10cm tall

- 1 egg white
- edible sparkles , available from cookshops
- green Smarties and silver chocolate buttons (optional)

Method

STEP 1

Cover the cake with marzipan and white icing. (See step 5 for more information).

STEP 2

Knead the ready-to-roll icing, then split into three balls. Leave one ball white, and knead a little green colouring into the other two to give two different shades of green. Roll out each ball to about 5mm thick on a work surface lightly dusted with icing sugar. Stamp out about 15 tree shapes using tree cutters, then leave to dry for a few hours or overnight.

STEP 3

Once firm, lift half of the trees onto a cooling rack. Combine the 200g icing sugar and egg white to make an icing, then drizzle it over the trees with a teaspoon. Scatter with edible sparkles and leave to dry again until solid.

STEP 4

Put a little icing on the back of each tree and press the trees around the edge of the cake, overlapping some to give a 3-D effect. Scatter the sweets over the top of the cake to finish. Can be iced up to a week ahead.

STEP 5

To cover a cake with marzipan, first brush the cake all over with a thin layer of warmed apricot jam. Dust the work surface with icing sugar, then roll out the marzipan evenly until you have a 5mm-1cm thick round, about 40cm across for a 20cm cake. Lift over the cake, using a rolling pin to help, then smooth with your hands and trim off the excess. Leave to dry overnight or for a few hours. Lightly brush the marzipan all over with cooled, boiled water. Roll the icing out as you did the marzipan, then smooth with your hands, trim off the excess and leave to dry.

Christmas cake cupcakes

Prep:40 mins **Cook:**45 mins

Makes 12

Ingredients

For the batter

- 200g dark muscovado sugar
- 175g butter , chopped
- 700g luxury mixed dried fruit
- 50g glacé cherries
- 2 tsp grated fresh root ginger
- zest and juice 1 orange
- 100ml dark rum , brandy or orange juice
- 85g/3oz pecan nuts, roughly chopped
- 3large eggs , beaten
- 85g ground almond
- 200g plain flour
- ½ tsp baking powder
- 1 tsp mixed spice
- 1 tsp cinnamon

For the icing

- 400g pack ready-rolled marzipan (we used Dr Oetker)
- 4 tbsp warm apricot jam or shredless marmalade

- 500g pack fondant icing sugar
- icing sugar , for dusting

You will also need

- 6 gold and 6 silver muffin cases
- 6 gold and 6 silver sugared almonds

- snowflake sprinkles

Method

STEP 1

Tip the sugar, butter, dried fruit, whole cherries, ginger, orange zest and juice into a large pan. Pour over the rum, brandy or juice, then put on the heat and slowly bring to the boil, stirring frequently to melt the butter. Reduce the heat and bubble gently, uncovered for 10 mins, stirring every now and again to make sure the mixture doesn't catch on the bottom of the pan. Set aside for 30 mins to cool.

STEP 2

Stir the nuts, eggs and ground almonds into the fruit, then sift in the flour, baking powder and spices. Stir everything together gently but thoroughly. Your batter is ready.

STEP 3

Heat oven to 150C/130C fan/gas 2. Scoop the cake mix into 12 deep muffin cases (an ice-cream scoop works well), then level tops with a spoon dipped in hot water. Bake for 35-45 mins until golden and just firm to touch. A skewer inserted should come out clean. Cool on a wire rack.

STEP 4

Unravel the marzipan onto a work surface lightly dusted with icing sugar. Stamp out 12 rounds, 6cm across. Brush the cake tops with apricot jam, top with a marzipan round and press down lightly.

STEP 5

Make up the fondant icing to a spreading consistency, then swirl on top of each cupcake. Decorate with sugared almonds and snowflakes, then leave to set. Will keep in a tin for 3 weeks.

Asian chicken salad

Prep: 10 mins **Cook:** 10 mins

Serves 2

Ingredients

- 1 boneless, skinless chicken breast
- 1 tbsp fish sauce
- zest and juice ½ lime (about 1 tbsp)
- 1 tsp caster sugar
- 100g bag mixed salad leaves
- large handful coriander , roughly chopped
- ¼ red onion , thinly sliced
- ½ chilli , deseeded and thinly sliced
- ¼ cucumber , halved lengthways, sliced

Method

STEP 1

Cover the chicken with cold water, bring to the boil, then cook for 10 mins. Remove from the pan and tear into shreds. Stir together the fish sauce, lime zest, juice and sugar until sugar dissolves.

STEP 2

Place the leaves and coriander in a container, then top with the chicken, onion, chilli and cucumber. Place the dressing in a separate container and toss through the salad when ready to eat.

RECIPE TIPS

DRESS IT UP

Ginger chicken lettuce cups - Finely chop 2 chicken breasts. Heat 1 tbsp oil in a pan, cook chicken until golden, then stir in 1 finely chopped lemongrass, 1 tbsp minced ginger and 2 crushed garlic cloves. Cook 1 min more, stir in 2 tbsp fish sauce, juice ½ lime and 2 tsp caster sugar. Cool. Separate the leaves from 2 Little Gem lettuces, then spoon chicken mix into these, scattered with coriander and chopped red chilli.

MAKE IT FOR KIDS

Shred 1 roast chicken breast, toss with 100g salad leaves and chopped cucumber. Mix 2 tbsp sweet chilli sauce with a squeeze lime juice and drizzle over.

Fruity ice-lolly pens

Prep:10 mins **Cook:**15 mins - 20 mins

Makes 6

Ingredients

- 50ml sugar-free blackcurrant cordial
- 50ml sugar-free orange cordial
- 5 tsp each red and orange natural food colouring , plus extra for painting

- 50g blueberry
- 50g strawberry , chopped
- a few red grapes , halved

Method

STEP 1

Pour each cordial into a separate jug, and add the corresponding food colouring. Stir in 100ml water. Put the blueberries, strawberries and grapes into the ice-lolly moulds and pour the blackcurrant mixture up to the brim of 3 moulds. Pour the orange cordial into the remaining 3 moulds. Freeze for 4 hrs.

STEP 2

Remove the lollies from the moulds and dot extra food colouring onto a dish. Dip the lollies into the colouring and use to draw on clean paper – while enjoying the lolly at the same time.

Cheeseburgers

Prep:15 mins **Cook:**20 mins

Makes 12

Ingredients

- 1kg minced beef
- 300g breadcrumbs
- 140g extra-mature or mature cheddar , grated

- 4 tbsp Worcestershire sauce
- 1 small bunch parsley , finely chopped
- 2 eggs , beaten

To serve

- split burger buns
- sliced tomatoes
- red onion slices

- lettuce , tomato sauce, coleslaw, wedges or fries

Method

STEP 1

Crumble the mince in a large bowl, then tip in the breadcrumbs, cheese, Worcestershire sauce, parsley and eggs with 1 tsp ground pepper and 1-2 tsp salt. Mix with your hands to combine everything thoroughly.

STEP 2

Shape the mix into 12 burgers. Chill until ready to cook for up to 24 hrs. Or freeze for up to 3 months. Just stack between squares of baking parchment to stop the burgers sticking together, then wrap well. Defrost overnight in the fridge before cooking.

STEP 3

To cook the burgers, heat grill to high. Grill burgers for 6-8 mins on each side until cooked through. Meanwhile, warm as many buns as you need in a foil-covered tray below the grilling burgers. Let everyone assemble their own, served with their favourite accompaniments.

Chocolate & raspberry pots

Prep:15 mins **Cook:**10 mins

Serves 6

Ingredients

- 200g plain chocolate (not too bitter, 50% or less)
- 100g frozen raspberry , defrosted or fresh raspberries
- 500g Greek yogurt
- 3 tbsp honey
- chocolate curls or sprinkles, for serving

Method

STEP 1

Break the chocolate into small pieces and place in a heatproof bowl. Bring a little water to the boil in a small saucepan, then place the bowl of chocolate on top, making sure the bottom of the bowl does not touch the water. Leave the chocolate to melt slowly over a low heat.

STEP 2

Remove the chocolate from the heat and leave to cool for 10 mins. Meanwhile, divide the raspberries between 6 small ramekins or glasses.

STEP 3

When the chocolate has cooled slightly, quickly mix in the yogurt and honey. Spoon the chocolate mixture over the raspberries. Place in the fridge to cool, then finish the pots with a few chocolate shavings before serving.

Fish cake fingers

Prep: 30 mins **Cook:** 40 mins

Makes 8

Ingredients

- 800g floury potato
- 2 skinless salmon fillets (about 250g), cut into chunks
- 3 smoked mackerel fillets (about 140g)
- zest 1 lemon , saving juice to serve

To serve

- 6 tbsp mayonnaise
- lemon juice , from above
- 1 small garlic clove , chopped (optional)

- plain flour , for dusting
- 3 eggs
- 100g dried breadcrumb
- 3 tbsp sunflower oil , plus more if needed

- 200g frozen pea , cooked
- few handfuls watercress

Method

STEP 1

KIDS: The writing in bold is for you GROWN-UPS: The rest is for you. **Make some mash.** Tip the potatoes into a pan of cold water and bring to the boil. Boil for 10 mins then lower the heat and drop in the salmon. Turn down the heat and simmer for about 3-5 mins more until the fish is cooked. Lift the fish onto a plate with a slotted spoon. Continue cooking the potatoes until soft, then drain. Tip the potatoes into a bowl and get your child to mash them.

STEP 2

Flake the fish. While the potatoes cook, peel away the skin from the mackerel fillets and get your child to flake the meat into a small bowl – they can taste some at this point, if they like.

STEP 3

Mix it all up. Add the lemon zest to the potato, and mash some more. Then add all the flaked fish and mix together well – don't worry about breaking up the fish. If you want, divide the mix in half and add any grown-up ingredients at this stage. Leave until cool enough to handle.

STEP 4

Roll out into long sausages. Lightly flour a surface and crack the eggs into a dish. Get your child to whisk them while you tip the breadcrumbs into another dish. Then ask them to divide the mash into eight and roll them on the flour into long, fat cylinders.

STEP 5

Dip them in egg. Working methodically, roll the sausages carefully in the egg.

STEP 6

Coat in crunchy breadcrumbs. Once the sausages are completely coated in egg, roll them in the breadcrumbs, making sure that they are well coated. The fingers can now be kept in the fridge for 2-3 days, or frozen for 1 month. To cook from frozen, Heat oven to 180C/160C fan/gas 4. Drizzle some olive oil over the Fish cake fingers and bake for 25-30 mins, until cooked through and golden.

STEP 7

Get a grown-up to cook them. Heat the oil in a frying pan and cook the fingers in batches. Sizzle them for 8-10 mins, turning regularly until completely golden, then lift them out onto kitchen paper to drain. Keep them warm in a low oven while you cook the rest.

STEP 8

Make a tasty sauce. While you are cooking the fingers, your child can mix the mayonnaise with the lemon juice and garlic – then get them to tip it into a small dish. Serve the fish cake fingers on a plate with the peas, watercress and some of the mayonnaise dip on the side.

RECIPE TIPS

GIVE YOUR FISH CAKES EXTRA CRUNCH

For really well-coated fish cakes, dip them twice in egg and breadcrumbs. However, this does make for a thicker coating that will absorb more oil while cooking.

ADDING OTHER FLAVOURS

You can gauge how adventurous your kids are and what you can add to your fish cakes; lots of flavours like different herbs, chopped capers, mild curry powder or mustard can be added as well.

COOKING FROM FROZEN

Heat oven to 180C/160C fan/gas 4. Drizzle some olive oil over the fish cake fingers and bake for 25-30 mins, until cooked through and golden.

Veggie noodle pot

Prep:10 mins **Cook:**10 mins

Serves 2

Ingredients

- 100g noodles (rice, soba or egg)
- 3 tbsp frozen peas
- handful sugar snap peas or mangetout, halved lengthways

- handful baby corn , halved lengthways
- 1 spring onion , sliced
- ½ red pepper , deseeded and chopped

For the dressing

- 1 tbsp reduced-salt soy sauce
- 1 tsp clear honey
- ½ garlic clove , crushed

- juice 1/2 lemon
- grating of fresh ginger (optional)

For the omelette

- 1 tbsp olive oil
- splash of milk

- 2 eggs , beaten

Method

STEP 1

To make the omelette, heat the olive oil in a small non-stick frying pan. Add a splash of milk to the beaten eggs, then tip into the pan. Stir once and allow to cook over a gentle heat until almost set. Flip (using a plate if necessary) and cook on the other side until cooked through. Tip onto a board and cut into strips. (You can roll the omelette up and cut slices to give you spirals, if you like.)

STEP 2

Cook the noodles following pack instructions. Drain and rinse under cold water, then set aside. Meanwhile, mix the dressing ingredients together. Blanch the peas and sugar snap peas, then drain and run under cold water to stop them cooking any further.

STEP 3

To assemble the salad, mix the noodles with the baby corn, spring onion, red pepper and green veg, then toss with the dressing and top with strips of omelette.

Cauliflower cheese pasta bake

Prep: 20 mins **Cook:** 1 hr

Serves 4

Ingredients

- 1 cauliflower , broken down into florets, core sliced, leaves removed and reserved, thick stems sliced
- 2 tbsp olive oil
- 6 shallots , sliced
- 1 tsp caster sugar
- 1 thyme sprig
- 2 tbsp white wine
- 100g large pasta shapes, such as conchiglioni

- 20g butter
- 1 bay leaf
- 2 tbsp plain flour
- 600ml milk
- 100g mature cheddar
- 50g parmesan (or vegetarian alternative), plus extra to top
- nutmeg , grated
- 50g gruyère or comté
- 1 tsp white wine vinegar or lemon juice

Method

STEP 1

Heat oven to 220C/200 fan/gas 9. Toss the cauliflower florets, leaves and sliced core with 1 tbsp olive oil in a roasting tin and season. Roast in the oven for 30-40 mins, or until the cauliflower is turning golden and smelling nutty. While it's roasting, heat 1 tbsp of olive oil in a non-stick frying pan and add the shallots, sugar and thyme. Cook for 10-15 mins until soft, sweet and caramelised. Add the wine and cook for a few more mins until evaporated. Meanwhile, cook the pasta in salty boiling water until just cooked. Drain and set aside.

STEP 2

For the cheese sauce, melt the butter in a non-stick saucepan over a medium heat with the bay leaf. Add the flour and cook, stirring, for 2 mins or so, until the roux is starting to bubble. Pour in the milk, little by little, stirring with a whisk, until fully incorporated and you have a smooth, lump-free sauce. Cook for about 10 mins until thickened, and then season with nutmeg and black pepper. Next, add the cheese and stir over the heat until it's melted and smooth. Taste the sauce and adjust the seasoning, adding the vinegar or lemon juice to taste.

STEP 3

Tip the pasta and shallots into the cauliflower roasting dish, then pour over the cheese sauce and stir so everything is well coated. Sprinkle over the remaining parmesan, reduce the oven to 180C/160C fan/gas 4 and bake for 20 mins, or until golden. Remove from the oven and allow to settle for about 10 mins, then serve with a crisp chicory salad.

Mango crunch cookies

Prep: 15 mins **Cook:** 15 mins

Makes about 14 large or 28 small cookies

Ingredients

- 140g butter , at room temperature
- 50g golden caster sugar
- 1 egg yolk
- 1 tsp vanilla extract

- 1 tbsp maple syrup
- 100g dried mango , roughly chopped
- 175g plain flour , plus extra for dusting

To decorate (optional)

- 200g icing sugar , sifted
- 3 tbsp mango juice

- sprinkles

Method

STEP 1

Heat the oven to 180C/160C fan/gas 4. Place the butter and sugar in a food processor and blitz until smooth and creamy. Add the egg yolk, vanilla, maple syrup and mango. Whizz to blend in and chop the mango a little more finely. Add the flour and briefly blitz to form a soft dough. Turn out onto a floured surface and shape into a ball. Chill for 20 mins.

STEP 2

Using a rolling pin, roll the cookie dough to the thickness of a £1 coin on a lightly floured surface, then cut out biscuit shapes with a 10cm cutter for large, or a 5cm cutter for smaller cookies.

STEP 3

Transfer to a baking tray lined with baking parchment, and cook for 12-15 mins or until lightly golden and firm. Remove and leave to cool on a wire rack.

STEP 4

If decorating, mix the icing sugar with the mango juice to make a runny icing. Drizzle or spoon the icing over the biscuits, then add the sprinkles if using, and leave to set. Will keep in a biscuit tin for up to 1 week.

Chocolate gingerbread Advent calendar

Prep:1 hr **Cook:**1 hr and 15 mins

Makes a few more than 24 biscuits

Ingredients

- 300g plain flour
- 50g cocoa
- 1 tbsp ground ginger
- 120g butter , cubed
- 120g brown sugar
- 140g golden syrup
- You will need

- baking parchment
- cookie cutters or cardboard to make templates
- a few plastic straws
- icing and sprinkles , to decorate
- string or ribbon for hanging

Method

STEP 1

Heat oven to 180C/160C fan/gas 4. Put the flour, cocoa, ginger, butter and sugar in a processor, and whizz until you can't see any lumps of butter. Dribble in the syrup and pulse to a smooth dough.

STEP 2

Take about a quarter of the dough at a time and roll out between 2 sheets of baking parchment to the thickness of a £1 coin. Peel away the top layer of parchment and use cookie cutters to make shapes – leaving about 2cm between each shape as they will spread as they cook. Peel away the dough trimmings and lift the parchment with the shapes onto a baking tray. Bake for 12-15 mins until firm. Remove from the oven and use a plastic straw to make a hole for hanging. Work quickly – if the biscuits cool and harden too much, the holes won't be as neat – then pop the tray back in the oven for 1 min to re-warm.

STEP 3

Continue rolling and shaping all the remaining dough and trimmings while you bake a tray at a time, until all the dough is used up and you have at least 24 biscuits. Cool completely, then decorate and string up as you wish.

STEP 4

To make number bunting: Cut your biscuits into triangles using a template – ours was 7cm on each side. After baking, cut two hanging holes in the middle of one side. Use number cutters (or cut out with a small sharp knife like we did) to stamp out 1 to 24 from a sheet of ready-rolled icing.

Make runny icing by mixing some sifted icing sugar with a dribble of water. Use small paintbrushes to paint the tops of the icing numbers with some runny icing before dunking in their favourite coloured sprinkles and edible glitters. Leave the numbers to dry for 10 mins, then use more runny icing painted on the bottom of the numbers to stick them to the biscuits.

STEP 5

To make sparkly snowflakes: Stamp your biscuits out using different snowflake cutters – cakescookiesandcraftsshop.co.uk have pretty ones. Decorate each biscuit differently by painting some with runny icing (see instructions above), then dunking into edible glitters and sprinkles – it's easiest if you tip them onto a small, flat saucer first. Add more icing sugar to your runny icing to make a stiffer consistency, spoon into a piping bag and pipe on pretty details. You can pipe a number onto each with this icing too, if you want.

STEP 6

To make biscuit baubles: Make a stiff-ish icing using fondant icing sugar this time (this results in a shinier finish). Then thinly pipe around the outsides and holes of each biscuit. You're making a 'wall' to hold in the other icing, so make sure you don't leave any gaps. Leave to set for 30 mins until hard. Make more icing of a slightly runnier consistency. Pipe or spoon the icing onto the biscuits, 'flooding' the area inside your icing 'walls'. Shake a little to evenly spread the runny icing, then immediately use the remaining stiffer icing to pipe on a number. These biscuits will need at least a day to harden before hanging. For step-by-step instructions on 'flooding' icing, see Edd Kimber's Fancy iced biscuits (see 'goes well with')

RECIPE TIPS

MAKING A CHOCOLATE GINGERBREAD ADVENT CALENDAR

However you decide to hang your Advent biscuits, remember you'll be untying them every day. So if you go for a bunting style, you might want to hang them individually from a main string or ribbon. We've baked grown-up sized biscuits, but if you're making for little ones, scale down the size, then one batch of dough should make enough for two or three children. If you haven't got enough room to hang three Advent calendars, just make sure the biscuits are thoroughly dry, then hang each day's treats off the same string.

CREATE A BOARD FOR YOUR CHOCOLATE GINGERBREAD ADVENT CALENDAR

We painted a sheet of plywood with chalkboard paint (both from Homebase), then used white chalk to draw our Christmas tree, and hung our biscuits on it using drawing pins. If you put up your real tree early enough, you could hang them from there, or tie the biscuits on a long string and hang along a wall.

Vegan gingerbread

Prep:20 mins **Cook:**12 mins

Serves 10

Ingredients

- 1tbsp ground flaxseed
- 140g dairy-free margarine
- 100g dark muscovado sugar
- 3tbsp golden syrup
- 350g plain flour, plus extra for dusting
- 1tsp bicarbonate of soda
- 1tbsp ground ginger
- 2tsp ground cinnamon

Method

STEP 1

Combine the flaxseed with 2½ tbsp water, and leave to thicken for 5 mins. Line two baking sheets with baking parchment. Melt the margarine, sugar and syrup in a pan over a low heat, then transfer to a medium bowl and leave to cool slightly. Stir in the flaxseed mix, then the flour, bicarb, spices and a pinch of salt until it comes together into a smooth dough. Chill for 30-45 mins until firm.

STEP 2

Heat the oven to 200C/180C fan/gas 6. Roll the dough out on a lightly floured surface to a 5mm thickness. Stamp out as many gingerbread people as you can, then re-roll the trimmings and continue until all the dough is used. Put on the sheets and bake for 12 mins until golden. Leave to cool on the sheets for 10 mins, then transfer to wire racks to cool completely. Will keep in an airtight container for two weeks.

Lemony Easter chicks

Prep:45 mins **Cook:**30 mins

Makes approx 25 chicks

Ingredients

- 2 medium egg whites
- 100g golden caster sugar
- ½ tsp cornflour
- grated zest 1/2 lemon , plus 1 tsp juice
- yellow food colouring paste
- orange, black and yellow icing pen , to decorate

Method

STEP 1

Heat oven to 140C/120C fan/gas 1. Line a baking sheet with baking parchment and put a medium-sized plain nozzle on a piping bag.

STEP 2

In a clean bowl, whisk the egg whites until they are very stiff. Add half the sugar and continue to whisk until the mixture is becoming firm and shiny.

STEP 3

Stir the cornflour into the remaining sugar and add to the meringue, along with the lemon zest and juice, and a smidge of yellow food colouring paste. Whisk again until you have a very thick, firm and glossy pale yellow meringue.

STEP 4

Carefully spoon the meringue into the piping bag. Push any air out of the top and tightly twist the opening to seal. Pipe about 25 thumb-sized dollops onto your baking sheet – if possible, try to make them wider at the base than the top, resembling a chick's body and head. Leave a gap between each chick to allow for expanding when cooking.

STEP 5

Cook in the oven for 30 mins until they are crisp, firm and come off the baking parchment easily. Leave to cool on a wire rack.

STEP 6

To decorate, use the orange icing pen to make a V-shaped beak, and a black icing pen for eyes and feet. The yellow icing pen can be used to decorate fluffy hair on the chick's head and/or wings. Will keep for up to 1 week in an airtight container.

Cheese & ham pancake roll-ups

Prep:40 mins **Cook:**50 mins

Serves a family of 4 (makes 8 pancakes)

Ingredients

For the pancakes

- 140g plain flour

- 2 eggs

- 25g butter , melted plus extra for buttering
- 350ml semi-skimmed milk
- sunflower or vegetable oil , for frying

For the roll-ups

- 12 thin slices of ham (125g pack), torn
- 260g bag spinach , cooked - see tip, below
- 140g grated cheddar
- 100ml half-fat crème fraîche
- 3 spring onions , sliced (optional)
- handful dried breadcrumbs

Method

STEP 1

KIDS the writing in bold is for you ADULTS the rest is for you. FOR THE PANCAKES **Tip in the flour, make a well, crack the eggs in dishes – whisk together.** Tip the flour into a mixing bowl and make a well in the middle. Crack the eggs into separate dishes, remove any shell, and add to the flour. Tip in the butter, add a little milk and whisk until smooth.

STEP 2

Whisk in the rest of the milk. Whisk in the rest of the milk, in a steady stream, until you have a smooth batter that is similar to the consistency of double cream. Now carefully pour the batter into a jug.

STEP 3

Wipe the pan with oil and pour in the batter. Using kitchen paper, wipe the pan with a little oil. Place the pan on the stove and heat until hot. Remove from the heat and pour in enough batter to cover the base, swirling it around. Return to the heat for 3 mins until the underside is cooked.

STEP 4

Now flip the pancake. Take the pan off the heat and, using a spatula, loosen the pancake. Flip the pancake in the air (or simply turn it over with the spatula) and cook the other side. When cooked, put the pancake to one side, then repeat the procedure to cook 7 more pancakes.

STEP 5

FOR THE ROLL-UPS **Butter a baking dish, then scatter ham and cheese over pancakes.** Heat oven to 200C/180C fan/gas 6. Butter a large baking dish. Now lay a pancake in front of you and scatter over some ham, spinach and cheese (remembering to save 25g of the cheese).

STEP 6

Roll up the pancakes and put them into the dish. Carefully roll up the pancakes and put them into the buttered dish. Repeat with all the pancakes.

STEP 7

Make the topping. In a small bowl, mix together the crème fraîche with the remaining cheese and spring onions, if you like.

STEP 8

Spread the topping, then sprinkle over the breadcrumbs. Spread the topping over the pancakes, sprinkle with breadcrumbs and bake for about 30 mins until bubbling and golden. Serve with a salad or veg.

RECIPE TIPS

COOKING LEAF SPINACH

The easiest way to cook leaf spinach is to put it in a large colander, then sit the colander in a sink and slowly pour over a kettle of hot water. Leave the spinach to wilt and cool. When it's cooled, squeeze out the water well and chop it up.

CATERING FOR FUSSY EATERS

This is a blueprint recipe that you can vary to cater for fussy eaters. The additional ingredients you choose are as countless as pizza toppings, but here are some that work well: fried mushrooms; chopped cherry tomatoes; cooked leeks; smoked haddock, cooked and flaked; cooked chicken, shredded; tinned tuna or sweetcorn.

Mini chocolate cheesecakes

Prep:20 mins **Cook:**30 mins

Makes 12

Ingredients

- 14 milk chocolate digestive biscuits , finely crushed
- 100g butter , melted

For the filling

- 500g tub ricotta
- 3 eggs , beaten
- 1 tsp vanilla extract

- 200g cheap dark chocolate , broken into chunks and melted
- 125g icing sugar
- 36 mini chocolate eggs

Method

STEP 1

Heat oven to 150C/130C fan/gas 2. Line the holes of a muffin tin with 12 paper muffin cases. Put the biscuits in a food bag and bash to small crumbs with the end of a rolling pin. Tip into a bowl, stir in the melted butter until the crumbs are nicely coated, then spoon between the paper cases. Press down into the bottoms to make a firm base.

STEP 2

To make the filling, put the ricotta, eggs, vanilla and melted chocolate in a large mixing bowl. Sift in the icing sugar. Beat everything together with an electric whisk or a wooden spoon until very well combined. Spoon into the paper cases right up to the tops, then tap the whole tin on the bench to get rid of any air bubbles. Bake for 30 mins, then remove from the oven and gently push 3 mini eggs into the top of each cheesecake. Let the cheesecakes cool completely before serving. Can be kept in the fridge for up to 3 days.

Little jam tarts

Prep: 15 mins **Cook:** 15 mins

Makes 20

Ingredients

- 500g sweet shortcrust pastry
- 20 tsp jam (we used apricot, blackcurrant and strawberry)

Method

STEP 1

Roll out the shortcrust pastry on a lightly floured surface to just under the thickness of £1 coin. Stamp out 20 x 5cm circles using a pastry cutter and line 2 mini muffin tins (or make in 2 batches).

STEP 2

Prick with a fork and spoon 1 tsp jam into each (we used apricot, blackcurrant and strawberry). Stamp out shapes from the leftover pastry to decorate the tarts, if you like.

STEP 3

Bake at 200C/180C fan/gas 6 for 12-15 mins, until the pastry is golden.

Christmas pudding cake pops

Prep:1 hr and 30 mins - 1 hr and 50 mins **Cook:**20 mins

Makes 10 cake pops

Ingredients

- 200g madeira cake
- 140g-160g white chocolate (see Tip)

To decorate

- 300g dark chocolate , 60-70% cocoa solids, broken into chunks
- 50g white chocolate , broken into chunks

- 1 orange , zest finely grated

- sugar holly decorations or red and green writing icing

Method

STEP 1

Pulse the madeira cake in a food processor until you have fine crumbs. Melt the white chocolate in a bowl over just simmering water or in the microwave. Shop bought madeira cake can vary in texture so you may need to add a little extra melted white chocolate to make the mixture stick into balls. Stir the orange zest into the chocolate, then work the chocolate into the crumbs using your hands.

STEP 2

Form into 10 small truffle-sized balls, then roll gently in your palms to smooth the surface. Arrange the balls on a baking parchment-lined dinner plate. Refrigerate for 30 minutes to allow the mixture to set.

STEP 3

Melt the dark chocolate in a microwave or over a bowl of just simmering water. Dip a lolly stick into the melted chocolate about 1.5cm in and poke half way into a cake ball. Repeat with the remaining balls. Put them back on the plate. Return to the fridge for five minutes.

STEP 4

Dip the cake pops one at a time into the melted chocolate, allowing any excess chocolate to drip off and spin the pops to even out the surface. Poke the pops into a piece of polystyrene or cake pop holder if you have one, keeping the pops apart. Allow to set for about half an hour.

STEP 5

Heat the white chocolate in a microwave or over a pan of simmering water. Allow to cool for a few minutes until it has a thick, runny consistency. If the chocolate is too hot, it will melt the dark chocolate underneath so make sure you do not overheat it. Spoon a small amount on top of the cake pops and tip them back and forth so that it runs down the sides a little. If you have holly decorations, set one on each pop. If using writing icing, wait for another 20 minutes or so until the white chocolate has set. To avoid a bloom on the chocolate, cover the cake pops in chocolate on the day you want to eat them – or the day before at the earliest.

STEP 6

Pipe on holly leaves with the green icing and two little dots for berries using the red. Once finished, store them in a cool place, though not the fridge

Family meals: Easy fish cakes

Prep:15 mins **Cook:**30 mins

Serves a family of 4-6 or makes 6-8 toddler meals

Ingredients

- 1 x pack fish pie mix (cod, salmon, smoked haddock etc, weight around 320g-400g depending on pack size)
- 3 spring onions, finely chopped
- 100ml milk
- 450g potato, peeled, large ones cut in half
- 75g frozen sweetcorn, defrosted
- handful of grated cheddar cheese
- 1 large egg, beaten
- flour, for dusting
- olive oil, for frying

Method

STEP 1

Cook the potatoes in boiling water until just tender. Drain well and return to the pan on a low heat. Heat for another minute or two to evaporate excess liquid. Mash the potato with a small knob of butter. Allow to cool.

STEP 2

Put the fish spring onions and milk in a shallow dish, cover with cling film and cook in the microwave for 1 ½ - 2 mins until just cooked. If you don't have a microwave, put everything in a saucepan and gently cook until just opaque and cooked through.

STEP 3

Drain the fish and spring onions through a fine sieve. Gently mix through the potatoes, avoiding breaking up the fish too much, along with the sweetcorn, cheddar and a generous grind of black pepper. Form into 6 - 8 patties. The cooler the mash potato is when you do this, the easier it will be to form the patties as the mixture will be very soft when warm.

STEP 4

Pour the egg on one plate and scatter flour on the other. Dip the patties in egg and then flour and arrange on a sheet of baking paper on a tray. Put the patties in the fridge for at least half an hour to firm up if the patties feel very soft. At this point you can freeze the patties, wrapped individually. Defrost throughly before moving onto the next stage.

STEP 5

Heat a large frying pan with a generous glug of olive oil. When the oil is hot, carefully lower the fish cakes into the pan. Cook for 5 - 7 minutes or until golden brown underneath and then carefully flip them over. Fry for another 5 - 7 minutes or until golden on the bottom and heated all the way through.

Creamy veggie risotto

Prep:10 mins **Cook:**30 mins

Serves 2 adults and 2-3 children

Ingredients

- 1 tbsp olive oil
- 1 onion , chopped
- 1 parsnip , finely diced
- 2 medium carrots , finely diced
- 350g risotto rice , such as arborio

- 1 bay leaf
- 1.2l hot vegetable or chicken stock
- 140g frozen pea or petit pois
- 50g parmesan (or vegetarian alternative), grated

Method

STEP 1

Heat the oil in a large shallow pan. Tip in the onion, parsnip and carrots, cover and gently fry for 8 mins until the onion is very soft.

STEP 2

Stir in the rice and bay leaf, then gently fry for another 2-3 mins until the rice starts to turn see-through around the edges. Add 300ml of the stock and simmer over a gentle heat, stirring until it has all been absorbed. Carry on adding the hot stock, a ladleful at a time, letting it be absorbed before adding more. Continue until the rice is just cooked and all the stock has been used, adding a little more water or stock if needed. This will take 18-20 mins.

STEP 3

Remove the bay leaf from the cooked risotto and stir in the peas. Heat through for a few mins, then add most of the Parmesan and season to taste. Sprinkle with the remaining Parmesan and serve.

Omelette wedges

Prep:20 mins **Cook:**10 mins

Serves 6

Ingredients

- 3 spring onions
- 200g new potatoes
- 4 rashers smoked bacon
- 2 tbsp sunflower oil , plus 1 tsp
- 8 eggs

- 1 tsp English mustard (ready-made rather than powder)
- 85g mature cheddar
- 2 tomatoes

Method

STEP 1

Finely chop the spring onions and set aside. Thickly slice the potatoes (there is no need to peel them first), then boil in a pan of lightly salted water for 10 mins until just tender. Drain.

STEP 2

Meanwhile snip the bacon into pieces with scissors. Heat a frying pan with 1 tsp oil, then stir-fry the bacon until it turns pink. Add the spring onions to the pan, stir briefly for a couple of secs to slightly soften, then tip the bacon and onion into a bowl. Wash and dry the frying pan.

STEP 3

Break the eggs into a bowl, then whisk with the mustard and a little salt and pepper. Make sure you don't get any shell into the mix. If you are worried you might, you can break the eggs into a cup, one at a time, before adding to the bowl – or ask an adult to break them for you.

STEP 4

Grate the cheese and add half to the egg mixture with the cooked bacon, onions and potatoes. Gently stir to mix everything. Heat 2 tbsp oil in the pan; when it is hot, pour in the mixture, then stir a couple of times as it sets on the base of the pan to start it cooking.

STEP 5

Turn on the grill so it has time to heat up. Leave the omelette to cook, undisturbed, over a low heat for about 6 mins. Meanwhile, cut the tomatoes into wedges, scatter over the omelette and sprinkle with the grated cheese.

STEP 6

When the omelette seems set on the base, but is still a little eggy on top, put the frying pan under the grill to cook the last of the egg mixture and melt the cheese. Cool for 5 mins, then turn out of the pan. Cut into wedges and serve with ketchup, toast, tea and orange juice for a delicious family breakfast.

RECIPE TIPS

SMOKED SALMON WEDGES

To give this omelette a more elegant twist, omit the bacon and tomatoes, and stir 3 slices smoked salmon, cut into thin slices, and 1 tbsp chopped dill in with the eggs in step 4. Continue to cook as before and serve cut into wedges.

Pumpkin risotto

Prep: 30 mins **Cook:** 1 hr

Serves 4

Ingredients

- 1 small pumpkin or butternut squash- after peeling and scraping out the seeds, you need about 400g/14oz
- 1 tbsp olive oil, plus a drizzle for the pumpkin
- 2 garlic cloves
- 8 spring onions
- 25g butter

- 200g risotto rice
- 2 tsp ground cumin
- 1l hot vegetable stock, plus extra splash if needed
- 50g grated parmesan (or vegetarian alternative)
- small handful coriander, roughly chopped

Method

STEP 1

Heat oven to 180C/160C fan/ gas 4. Chop up the pumpkin or squash into 1.5cm cubes (kids- ask for help if it's slippery). Put it on a baking tray, drizzle over some oil, then roast for 30 mins.

STEP 2

While the pumpkin is roasting, you can make the risotto. Put the garlic in a sandwich bag, then bash lightly with a rolling pin until it's crushed.

STEP 3

Cut up the spring onions with your scissors.

STEP 4

Heat 1 tbsp oil with the butter in your pan over a medium heat – not too hot. Add the spring onions and garlic. Once the onions are soft but not getting brown, add the rice and cumin. Stir well to coat in the buttery mix for about 1 min.

STEP 5

Now add half a cup of the stock, and stir every now and then until it has all disappeared into the rice. Carry on adding and stirring in a large splash of stock at a time, until you have used up all the stock – this will take about 20 mins.

STEP 6

Check the rice is cooked. If it isn't, add a splash more stock, and carry on cooking for a bit. Once the rice is soft enough to eat, gently stir in the grated cheese, chopped coriander and roasted pumpkin.

Macadamia & cranberry American cookies

Prep:20 mins **Cook:**12 mins

Makes 55

Ingredients

- 3 x 200g/7oz white chocolate bars, chopped
- 200g butter
- 2 eggs
- 100g light muscovado sugar

- 175g golden caster sugar
- 2 tsp vanilla extract
- 350g plain flour
- 2 tsp baking powder
- 1 tsp cinnamon

- 100g dried cranberry
- 100g macadamia nut , chopped

Method

STEP 1

Heat oven to 180C/160C fan/gas 4. Melt 170g of the chocolate, then allow to cool. Beat in the butter, eggs, sugars and vanilla, preferably with an electric hand whisk, until creamy. Stir in the flour, baking powder, cinnamon and cranberries with two-thirds of the remaining chocolate and macadamias, to make a stiff dough.

STEP 2

Using a tablespoon measure or a small ice-cream scoop, drop small mounds onto a large baking dish, spacing them well apart, then poke in the reserved chocolate, nuts and berries. Bake in batches for 12 mins until pale golden, leave to harden for 1-2 mins, then cool on a wire rack.

STEP 3

To freeze, open-freeze the raw cookie dough scoops on baking trays; when solid, pack them into a freezer container, interleaving the layers with baking parchment. Use within 3 months. Bake from frozen for 15-20 mins.

RECIPE TIPS

HAZELNUT & RAISIN COOKIES

Make as above, with 280g flour, replacing the white chocolate for dark chocolate and the macadamias and cranberries for hazelnuts and raisins. Pour boiling water over the raisins and allow them to plump up a little, then dry thoroughly - this stops them being too hard and catching in the oven.

Spicy meatballs

Prep:15 mins **Cook:**25 mins

Serves 6

Ingredients

- 500g minced chicken , turkey, lamb, beef or pork
- 1 medium onion
- 2 garlic cloves , crushed or chopped
- 2 tsp mild or medium curry powder
- 2 tsp ground cumin
- 1 tsp garam masala
- ½ tsp paprika or cayenne pepper
- 2 tbsp fresh coriander , chopped
- 1 egg , beaten

237

- 50g fresh breadcrumb
- 1 tbsp olive oil

Method

STEP 1

Heat oven to 180C/fan 160C/gas 4.

STEP 2

Put the mince into the mixing bowl. Add the onions, garlic, curry powder, cumin, garam masala, paprika or cayenne pepper and coriander, then mix well. By adding these spices, you'll get a delicious flavour without having to add any salt.

STEP 3

Add the beaten egg and breadcrumbs, then mix again.

STEP 4

Divide the meat mixture into 15-18 evensized pieces and shape into balls (they should be about the size of a walnut). Always wash your hands thoroughly after handling raw meat so you don't transfer any germs that may be on the meat to other food or equipment.

STEP 5

Heat the oil in the frying pan over a medium heat and add the meatballs using a spoon. Cook them for 5 mins, turning until golden brown. Remove from the pan and place them on to the tray. Bake in the oven for 15-20 mins.

STEP 6

Remove from the oven. Remember to use oven gloves! Allow to cool slightly and serve with a fresh, crisp green salad, some pitta bread and tomato salsa.

RECIPE TIPS

MAKE IT SAUCY

Fry 2 sliced garlic cloves in a little olive oil and add a 400g tin of chopped tomatoes. Bring to the boil, then transfer to an ovenproof dish. Add your meatballs, cover them with sauce and bake in the oven for 40 mins-1 hr. Serve with rice or pasta.

Sweet snowballs

Prep: 20 mins **Cook:** 5 mins

Makes 16

Ingredients

- 400g white chocolate , broken into pieces
- 100g rich tea biscuit
- 50g white Malteser
- 50g mini marshmallow
- 50g dried cranberries
- 50g cake crumbs (we used shop-bought Madeira cake)
- 3 tbsp golden syrup
- 100g desiccated coconut
- edible glitter (optional)

Method

STEP 1

Melt the chocolate in a bowl over a pan of simmering water. Meanwhile, crush the biscuits and Maltesers in a large bowl with a rolling pin.

STEP 2

Add mini marshmallows, dried cranberries and cake crumbs, then the chocolate and golden syrup. Mix well. Tip desiccated coconut onto a plate. Drop large spoonfuls of mixture onto the plate, then roll them around, coating in coconut and shaping into balls. Place on a baking tray and chill for 30 mins before serving. Sprinkle with edible glitter if you like.

Vietnamese veggie hotpot

Prep: 5 mins **Cook:** 20 mins

Serves 4

Ingredients

- 2 tsp vegetable oil
- thumb-size piece fresh root ginger , shredded
- 2 garlic cloves , chopped
- ½ large butternut squash , peeled and cut into chunks
- 2 tsp soy sauce
- 2 tsp soft brown sugar
- 200ml vegetable stock
- 100g green bean , trimmed and sliced
- 4 spring onions , sliced
- coriander leaves and cooked basmati or jasmine rice, to serve

Method

STEP 1

Heat the oil in a medium-size, lidded saucepan. Add the ginger and garlic, then stir-fry for about 5 mins. Add the squash, soy sauce, sugar and stock. Cover, then simmer for 10 mins. Remove the lid, add the green beans, then cook for 3 mins more until the squash and beans are tender. Stir the spring onions through at the last minute, then sprinkle with coriander and serve with rice.

RECIPE TIPS

TRY IT WITH CHICKEN

Add 2 chicken breasts, sliced, to the ginger and garlic, then stir-fry for a few mins until browned. Stir in the squash, soy sauce, sugar, stock and 2 tbsp crunchy peanut butter, then cook as above. Remove the lid, cook for a few mins more until thickened, then scatter with coriander and serve spooned over bowls of rice.

Quick pitta pizzas

Prep: 10 mins **Cook:** 10 mins

Serves 2

Ingredients

- 4 wholewheat pitta breads
- 4 tsp sun-dried tomato purée
- 3 ripe plum tomatoes , diced
- 1 shallot , thinly sliced

- 85g chorizo , diced
- 50g mature cheddar , grated
- few basil leaves , if you like

Method

STEP 1

Heat oven to 200C/180C fan/gas 6 and put a baking sheet inside to heat up. Spread each pitta with 1 tsp purée. Top with the tomatoes, shallot, chorizo and cheddar.

STEP 2

Place on the hot sheet and bake for 10 mins until the pittas are crisp, the cheese has melted and the chorizo has frazzled edges. Scatter with basil, if you like, and serve with a green salad.

RECIPE TIPS

CHORIZO

For the best results, use a whole piece of chorizo and cut it yourself, rather than buying pre-sliced chorizo.

SWEETCORN & HAM PITTA PIZZAS

Spread the pittas with 4 tsp pesto in place of the sun-dried tomato purée, and replace the shallot and chorizo with a handful sweetcorn kernels and shredded ham. Cook as before.

Baileys banana trifles

Prep:10 mins

Serves 6

Ingredients

- 300g pot extra-thick double cream
- 7 tbsp Baileys
- 6 chocolate brownies (about 250g/9oz), broken up, or use crumbled chocolate biscuits or loaf cake
- 3 bananas , sliced
- 500g pot vanilla custard
- 6 tbsp toffee sauce
- 25g chocolate , grated

Method

STEP 1

Mix the cream with 1 tbsp Baileys, and set aside. Divide the brownie pieces between 6 glasses, then drizzle each with 1 tbsp Baileys. Top with the sliced bananas, custard and Baileys cream, dividing equally, then drizzle with toffee sauce and finish with grated chocolate. Can be made a few hours ahead.

Rainbow cookies

Prep:25 mins - 30 mins **Cook:**15 mins

Makes 22

Ingredients

- 175g softened butter
- 50g golden caster sugar
- 50g icing sugar
- 2 egg yolks
- 2 tsp vanilla extract
- 300g plain flour
- zest and juice 1 orange
- 140g icing sugar , sifted
- sprinkles , to decorate

Method

STEP 1

Heat oven to 200C/180C fan/gas 6. Mix the butter, sugars, egg yolks and vanilla with a wooden spoon until creamy, then mix in the flour in 2 batches. Stir in the orange zest. Roll the dough into about 22 walnut-size balls and sit on baking sheets. Bake for 15 mins until golden, then leave to cool.

STEP 2

Meanwhile, mix the icing sugar with enough orange juice to make a thick, runny icing. Dip each biscuit half into the icing, then straight into the sprinkles. Dry on a wire rack.

Christmas biscuits

Prep:40 mins **Cook:**15 mins

Makes 30-40 depending on size

Ingredients

- 175g dark muscovado sugar
- 85g golden syrup
- 100g butter
- 3 tsp ground ginger
- 1 tsp ground cinnamon
- 350g plain flour, plus extra for dusting
- 1 tsp bicarbonate of soda
- 1 egg, lightly beaten

To finish

- 100g white chocolate
- edible silver balls

Method

STEP 1

Heat the sugar, golden syrup and butter until melted. Mix the spices and flour in a large bowl. Dissolve the bicarbonate of soda in 1 tsp cold water. Make a well in the centre of the dry ingredients, add the melted sugar mix, egg and bicarbonate of soda. Mix well. At this stage the mix will be soft but will firm up on cooling.

STEP 2

Cover the surface of the biscuit mix with wrapping and leave to cool, then put in the fridge for at least 1 hr to become firm enough to roll out.

STEP 3

Heat oven to 190C/170C fan/gas 5. Turn the dough out onto a lightly floured surface and knead briefly. (At this stage the dough can be put into a food bag and kept in the fridge for up to a week.) Cut the dough in half. Thinly roll out one half on a lightly floured surface. Cut into shapes with cutters, such as gifts, trees and hearts, then transfer to baking sheets, leaving a little room for them to spread. If you plan to hang the biscuits up, make a small hole in the top of each one using a skewer. Repeat with remaining dough.

STEP 4

Bake for 12-15 mins until they darken slightly. If the holes you have made have closed up, remake them while the biscuits are warm and soft using a skewer. Cool for a few mins on the baking sheets, then transfer to a wire rack to cool and harden up completely.

STEP 5

Break up the chocolate and melt in the microwave on Medium for 1-2 mins, or in a small heatproof bowl over simmering water. Drizzle the chocolate over the biscuits, or pipe on shapes or names, then stick a few silver balls into the chocolate. If hung up on the tree, the biscuits will be edible for about a week, but will last a lot longer as decorations.

Apple 'doughnuts'

Prep: 20 mins

Makes 15

Ingredients

- 150g soft cheese
- 2 tsp honey
- 3 apples (use a crunchy eating variety)

- 3-4 tbsp almond or peanut butter (optional)
- coloured sprinkles , to decorate

Method

STEP 1

Mix the soft cheese with the honey and set aside. Peel the apples, then slice each through the core into five or six rings, about 1cm thick. Use an apple corer or small round biscuit cutter to stamp out a circle from the middle of each slice, removing the core and creating 'doughnut' shapes. Pat the slices dry using kitchen paper – they should be as dry as possible to help the toppings stick.

STEP 2

Spread some nut butter over the slices, if using, then top with the sweetened soft cheese. Decorate with the sprinkles and serve.

Cheese roll-ups

Prep:30 mins **Cook:**25 mins

Makes 6

Ingredients

- 200g self-raising flour , plus extra for dusting
- 50g butter , softened

- 1 tsp paprika
- 100-125ml/3½-4fl oz milk
- 50g ready-grated mature cheddar

Method

STEP 1

Heat oven to 220C/200C fan/gas 7. Put the flour and butter in a bowl and rub them together with your fingers. Rubbing in mixture with cold butter is hard and tiring on young fingers, so use slightly softened butter – but not so soft that it is oily. Now stir in the paprika and mix again.

STEP 2

Add 100ml milk and mix with a fork until you get a soft dough. Add a splash more milk if the dough is dry. This process will teach you how to feel the dough and decide if it needs more liquid. You can always add more milk if required.

STEP 3

On a lightly floured surface, roll out the dough like pastry to about 0.5cm thick. Try to keep a rectangular shape. Only roll in one direction, and roll and turn, roll and turn – by keeping the dough moving, you avoid finding it stuck at the end.

STEP 4

Sprinkle the grated cheese on top, then roll up like a sausage along the long side. Cut into 12 thick rings using a table knife. Get an adult to show you how to hold the dough with one hand and cut straight through with the other.

STEP 5

Line the baking tray with baking parchment. Place the roll-ups on the parchment, cut-side down, almost touching each other, making sure that you can see the spiral. Get an adult to put them in the oven for you and bake for 20-25 mins until golden and melty. Ask an adult to remove them from the oven, then leave to cool. The cheese roll-ups will keep for up to 3 days in an airtight container.

Cuddly egg men

Prep:20 mins **Cook:**20 mins

Makes 4

Ingredients

- 400g strong white flour
- ½ tsp salt
- pinch of sugar

- 7g sachet fast-action dried yeast
- 2 tbsp olive oil
- 4 large eggs , at room temperature

Method

STEP 1

Put the flour into a large bowl and stir in the salt, sugar and yeast. Pour in 250ml water and the oil and mix to a soft dough. Add a little extra water if necessary.

STEP 2

Knead the dough for a few minutes until smooth and then put into a bowl, cover and leave in a warm place for about 1 hour or until doubled in size.

STEP 3

Heat the oven to 200C/180C fan/gas 6. Turn the dough out onto a board, knead briefly and then cut into four. Take one piece and cut off a quarter and shape into a ball for the head. Shape the other piece into a sausage. Attach the head to the body using a little cold water.

STEP 4

Place the dough onto a non-stick baking sheet. Using a sharp knife cut the bottom half of the sausage to make two legs, then cut into the sides up to the shoulders to make two arms. Using scissors, snip at intervals around the top of the head to make hair and make one snip for the mouth. Use a wooden skewer to make two eyes.

STEP 5

Take one egg and place on the dough man's tummy. Fold the arms over the egg and secure with a little cold water. Make three more egg men with the remaining dough. Leave to prove for about 10 mins.

STEP 6

Bake in the oven for 20 mins until well risen and golden. Cool on a wire rack for a few mins before peeling the egg and eating with the warm bread.

Fright Night fancies

Prep:25 mins

Serves 12

Ingredients

- 12 ready-made vanilla cupcakes or fairy cakes , or make your own (see tip)
- 2 x 410g cans apricot halves in light syrup, drained (reserve the syrup)
- 100g raspberry jam

- a little icing sugar or cornflour, for dusting
- 500g pack ready-to-roll white fondant icing
- black icing pen

Method

STEP 1

Remove the cakes from their paper cases – if the tops are rounded, trim them with a serrated knife to make a flat surface. Flip the cakes over and arrange on a large board or cake stand. Brush the cakes all over with the syrup from the drained apricots, then place 1 tsp jam on top of each cake. Pu an apricot half on top of the jam, rounded- side facing up.

STEP 2

Clean your work surface, then dust with a little icing sugar or cornflour. Roll out the icing to the thickness of a 50p piece – it will be easier if you work with half at a time, keeping the remaining icing well wrapped so it doesn't dry out. Use a 12cm fluted cookie cutter to stamp out 12 circles and, as soon as you cut each one, drape it over a cake. Draw on spooky faces using the black icing pen, then serve. Can be made up to a day ahead; eat leftover cakes within 1 day.

RECIPE TIPS

ICING TIPS

Make sure you roll the icing out thickly enough, especially if you're not serving them immediately. If the icing is too thin it can become soggy when it touches the apricot. The ideal thickness would be the same as a 50p coin or around 2-3mm.

More veg, less meat summer Bolognese

Prep:15 mins **Cook:**40 mins

Serves 4

Ingredients

- 2 tbsp olive oil
- 2 onions , finely chopped
- 3 carrots , finely chopped
- 4 celery sticks, finely chopped
- 2 courgettes , cut into small cubes
- 4 garlic cloves , finely chopped
- 250g pack beef mince
- 1 heaped tbsp tomato purée
- 400g can chopped tomato
- 400g fettuccine
- 200g pea , frozen or fresh
- handful parsley , roughly chopped

Method

STEP 1

Heat the oil in large deep frying pan. Add the onions, carrots, celery, courgettes and garlic. Cook for about 10 mins or until soft, adding a few splashes of water if the mixture begins to stick. Turn up the heat and add the mince. Fry for a few mins more, breaking up the mince with the back of a spoon. Stir in tomato purée, pour over the chopped tomatoes and add a can of water. Simmer for 15 mins until the sauce is thick, then season.

STEP 2

Meanwhile, cook the fettuccine following pack instructions.

STEP 3

Tip the peas into the sauce and simmer for 2 mins more until tender. Stir through the drained pasta and parsley, then serve.

Courgette muffins

Prep:35 mins **Cook:**25 mins

Makes 12

Ingredients

- 50g courgette , cut into chunks
- 1 apple , peeled and quartered
- 1 orange , halved
- 1 egg

- 75g butter, melted
- 300g self-raising flour
- ½ tsp baking powder
- ½ tsp cinnamon
- 100g golden caster sugar
- handful of sultanas
- 1 tub soft cheese mixed with 3 tbsp icing sugar, to make icing

Method

STEP 1

Brush the muffin tin with oil. **Ask your grown-up helper** to switch the oven to 190C/ 170C fan/gas 5.

STEP 2

Grate the courgettes and put them in a large bowl. Grate the apple and add to the bowl. Squeeze the orange and add the juice to the bowl.

STEP 3

Break the egg into a bowl; if any bits of shell get in, scoop them out with a spoon. Stir the butter and egg into the courgette and apple mix.

STEP 4

Sieve the flour, baking powder and cinnamon into the bowl. Add the sugar and sultanas.

STEP 5

Mix with a spoon until everything is combined, but don't worry if it is lumpy.

STEP 6

Spoon the mixture into the tin. **Ask your helper** to put it in the oven and cook for 20-25 mins. Cool in the tin, then spread some icing on each.

Super-easy fruit ice cream

Prep:20 mins

Serves 6

Ingredients

- 200g strawberries (as red as you can get), hulled
- 1 large mango, deseeded and peeled
- ¼ lemon, juiced
- 3 very ripe bananas, peeled
- 200g condensed milk

- 600ml double cream
- 4 kiwi fruit , peeled
- sprinkles or finely chopped strawberries and mango, to serve

Method

STEP 1

Mash or purée the strawberries and mango in two separate bowls. In another bowl, add the lemon juice and the banana and mash.

STEP 2

Beat the condensed milk and cream in a large bowl with an electric whisk until thick and quite stiff, a bit like clotted cream. Divide the mixture between the three bowls. Fold a fruit purée into each. Transfer each one into a freezer container and freeze until solid.

STEP 3

Purée the kiwi and sieve out any seeds if you like. Serve a scoop of each ice cream in bowls or sundae dishes and top with the kiwi sauce, sprinkles, or the chopped fruit.

Chocolate & hazelnut thumbprint cookies

Prep:20 mins **Cook:**20 mins

Makes 25

Ingredients

- 180g hazelnuts , toasted
- 100g plain flour
- 90g buckwheat flour
- 60g golden caster sugar
- 180g unsalted butter
- 100g dark chocolate , roughly chopped
- 1 tsp coconut oil (or use any flavourless oil)

Method

STEP 1

Line a baking tray with baking parchment. Tip the hazelnuts into the bowl of a food processor and pulse until finely chopped. Add the flours, sugar and a pinch of flaked sea salt, and process for 20-30 secs until fully combined. Add the butter and pulse until the mixture just starts to come together. Tip the dough out onto a work surface and knead by hand until smooth.

STEP 2

Roll the dough into 25 small balls, then transfer to the prepared baking tray. Using your thumb or the handle of a wooden spoon, make an indent in the centre of each piece of dough. Put the tray in the fridge and chill for 30 mins before baking. Heat oven to 180C/160C fan/gas 4.

STEP 3

Bake in the oven for 15-20 mins or until light golden brown. Put the chocolate and oil in a heatproof bowl and set over a pan of simmering water, stirring occasionally, until fully melted. Use a teaspoon to top each cookie with a little melted chocolate. Put aside until the chocolate has set.

You're a star sarnies

Prep:15 mins

Serves 1

Ingredients

- 2 slices wholemeal bread
- 1 tsp red pesto
- ½ tbsp cream cheese

Method

STEP 1

Use a star-shaped cutter to stamp out six bread stars from the wholemeal bread (freeze the off-cuts to make breadcrumbs). Swirl the red pesto through the cream cheese and spread onto both sides of the stars. Close, wrap in cling film and chill in the fridge if making the night before.

Sticky Stick biscuits

Prep:30 mins **Cook:**15 mins - 20 mins

Serves 16 - 20

Ingredients

- 200g salted butter
- 200g golden caster sugar
- 1 large egg
- 1 tsp vanilla bean paste
- 375g plain flour
- Mikado sticks (about 20)
- 200g milk chocolate
- 50g white ready-to-roll icing
- 25g each of black, red and green ready-to-roll icing

You will also need

- a ruler
- lolly sticks , soaked in water (16-20)

Method

STEP 1

Heat oven to 180C/160C fan/gas 4 and prepare two lined baking trays. Beat the butter and sugar together until combined then beat in the egg and vanilla. Add all of the flour and mix into a soft dough. If the dough is very soft, chill for 15 mins before shaping. You can freeze the cookie dough for a later date, but defrost thoroughly before baking.

STEP 2

Roll the dough into log shapes about 1.5cm-2cm in diameter, then cut into pieces 15cm long (using the ruler to measure).

STEP 3

Insert a soaked lolly stick into each biscuit as well as a piece of Mikado for an arm on each side. Place on the baking trays evenly spread apart.

STEP 4

Bake for 15-20 min until golden brown, but do check after 15 mins as all ovens vary. Transfer onto a wire rack to cool.

STEP 5

Break the milk chocolate into pieces and melt in a bowl set over gently simmering water, or in short bursts in the microwave. Once the biscuits are cool, use a pastry brush to gently paint the chocolate all over the back of each stick, going a little around the sides and on the back of the Mikados.

STEP 6

Once set, flip the sticks over and paint the fronts, then leave for 30 mins to completely set.

STEP 7

Mould little pieces of the icing to create his leafy coif, goggle eyes and mouth. Stick them on using a little of the leftover melted chocolate.

Honeyed carrot soup

Prep: 10 mins **Cook:** 35 mins

Serves 6

Ingredients

- 2 tbsp butter
- 2 small leeks , sliced
- 800g carrots , roughly chopped
- 2 tsp clear honey

- small pinch dried chilli flakes (optional)
- 1 bay leaf
- 2 ½l vegetable stock
- soured cream or yogurt , to serve

Method

STEP 1

Melt the butter in a large saucepan over a medium heat. Add the leeks to the pan, then cook for 3 mins until starting to soften. Add the carrots, honey, chilli (if using) and bay leaf, then cook for 2 mins.

STEP 2

Pour in the stock, bring to the boil, then simmer for 30 mins. Blend the soup in batches, return to a clean pan, then season to taste. When ready to serve, bring back to a simmer, then ladle into mugs. Add a swirl of soured cream or yogurt and serve with garlic bread or bacon butties.

Sunshine lollies

Prep: 20 mins

makes 6 x 60ml lollies

Ingredients

- 5 large carrots
- juice of 3 large oranges , zest of 1

- 1 satsuma , peeled then chopped (optional)

Method

STEP 1

Finely grate the carrots and place in the middle of a clean tea towel. Gather up the towel, and squeeze the carrot juice into a jug, discarding the pulp. Add the orange juice and top up with a little cold water if needed to make up 360ml liquid. Stir in the orange zest and satsuma pieces, if using. Pour into lolly moulds and freeze overnight.

Steak haché with pommes frites & cheat's Béarnaise sauce

Prep: 35 mins **Cook:** 45 mins

Serves 4

Ingredients

For the steak and sauce

- 1 tbsp vegetable oil
- 4 shallots , very finely chopped
- 600g freshly ground beef (ask the butcher for something with roughly 15% fat - we used chuck)
- 8 thyme sprigs , leaves picked and chopped

- 2 tsp Dijon mustard
- 2 tbsp plain flour
- 200ml crème fraîche
- 1 egg yolk
- 6 tarragon sprigs, leaves picked and finely chopped
- dressed green salad , to serve

For the pommes frites

- 4 large baking potatoes (such as Maris Piper or Russet), peeled

- 2 tbsp vegetable oil

Method

STEP 1

Heat the oil in a pan and add about 3 /4 of the shallots. Cook for 5-10 mins, stirring occasionally, until soft and starting to caramelise in places. Set aside to cool.

STEP 2

In a large bowl, combine the beef, thyme, 1 tsp Dijon and the cooled shallots. Season with black pepper but not salt at this stage (this can cause the meat to dry out). Shape into four patties and dust with flour. Put on a plate, cover with cling film and chill for at least 30 mins (or up to 2 hrs).

STEP 3

Meanwhile, prepare the frites. Slice the potatoes into skinny chips, tipping into a large bowl of cold water as you go. Drain, then transfer to a large pan and cover with fresh water, seasoning with salt.

Bring to a fast simmer, boil for 1 min, then drain well. Tip the chips onto a clean tea towel or some kitchen paper, spread in a single layer so they dry and cool quickly. Heat oven to 200C/180C fan/gas 6.

STEP 4

Tip the chips into a bowl with the vegetable oil and 1 tsp salt. Toss to coat, then spread out over two large baking trays. Cook for 45 mins or until crisp and golden.

STEP 5

When the chips are about 15 mins from being cooked, heat a large frying pan with a drizzle of oil. Season the patties with salt on both sides and cook for 3-4 mins each side, or until they have a dark brown crust but are still slightly pink inside (or cook them for a little longer if you'd prefer them well done). Transfer to a plate, cover with foil and set aside to keep warm while you make the sauce.

STEP 6

Return the pan to the heat and tip in the remaining shallots. Fry for 1-2 mins to soften, then remove the pan from the heat and stir in the crème fraîche, remaining Dijon, the egg yolk and tarragon, as well as any resting juices from the beef patties. Season well. Serve the steak with the pommes frites and a green salad, with the Béarnaise sauce on the side.

RECIPE TIPS

STEAK HACHÉ

This is a version of burger & chips minus the bun. Ask your butcher to mince the beef on the day you want to make it, so it's fresh. It's often served rare in restaurants in France, so if you'd prefer it cooked through, ask for it 'fait bien cuit'. Pommes frites are skinny chips and usually fried - however, here they're baked, so the children can help to cook them. If your kids like creamy sauces, encourage them to try the classic Béarnaise, flavoured with the beef juices and tarragon.

Simple gingerbread house

Prep: 2 hrs **Cook:** 30 mins

Makes 1 house with 12 portions

Ingredients

For the gingerbread

- 250g unsalted butter
- 200g dark muscovado sugar

- 7 tbsp golden syrup
- 600g plain flour
- 2 tsp bicarbonate of soda
- 4 tsp ground ginger

To decorate

- 200g flaked almonds
- 2 egg whites
- 500g icing sugar, plus extra to dust
- 125g mini chocolate fingers
- generous selection of sweets of your choice, choose your own colour theme
- 1 mini chocolate roll or a dipped chocolate flake
- few edible silver balls

For the house design

- template (see tips below)

Method

STEP 1

Heat the oven to 200C/180C fan/gas 6. Melt the butter, sugar and syrup in a pan. Mix the flour, bicarbonate of soda and ground ginger into a large bowl, then stir in the butter mixture to make a stiff dough. If it won't quite come together, add a tiny splash of water.

STEP 2

Cut out the template (download from the tips below). Put a sheet of baking paper on a work surface and roll about one quarter of the dough to the thickness of two £1 coins. Cut out one of the sections, then slide the gingerbread, still on its baking paper, onto a baking sheet. Repeat with remaining dough, re-rolling the trimmings, until you have two side walls, a front and back wall and two roof panels. Any leftover dough can be cut into Christmas trees, if you like.

STEP 3

Pick out the most intact flaked almonds and gently poke them into the roof sections, pointy-end first, to look like roof tiles. Bake all the sections for 12 mins or until firm and just a little darker at the edges. Leave to cool for a few minutes to firm up, then trim around the templates again to give clean, sharp edges. Leave to cool completely.

STEP 4

Put the egg whites in a large bowl, sift in the icing sugar, then stir to make a thick, smooth icing. Spoon into a piping bag with a medium nozzle. Pipe generous snakes of icing along the wall edges, one by one, to join the walls together. Use a small bowl to support the walls from the inside, then allow to dry, ideally for a few hours.

STEP 5

Once dry, remove the supports and fix the roof panels on. The angle is steep so you may need to hold these on firmly for a few mins until the icing starts to dry. Dry completely, ideally overnight. To decorate, pipe a little icing along the length of 20 mini chocolate fingers and stick these lengthways onto the side walls of the house. Use three, upright, for the door.

STEP 6

Using the icing, stick sweets around the door and on the front of the house. To make the icicles, start with the nozzle at a 90-degree angle to the roof and squeeze out a pea-sized blob of icing. Keeping the pressure on, pull the nozzle down and then off – the icing will pull away, leaving a pointy trail. Repeat all around the front of the house. Cut the chocolate mini roll or dipped Flake on an angle, then fix with icing to make a chimney. Pipe a little icing around the top. If you've made gingerbread trees, decorate these now, too, topping each with a silver ball, if using. Dust the roof with icing sugar for a snowy effect. Lay a winding path of sweets, and fix gingerbread trees around and about using blobs of icing. Your gingerbread house will be edible for about a week.

Crusty garlic bread

Prep:5 mins **Cook:**15 mins

Serves 6

Ingredients

- 60g butter, softened
- 2 garlic cloves, crushed
- 1 part-baked white baguette (about 150g)

Method

STEP 1

Put the butter in a bowl, add the garlic and mix well. Spoon the butter out onto a sheet of cling film and roll up to make a sausage-shaped log. Chill for 10 mins.

STEP 2

Heat oven to 200C/180C fan/gas 6. Slice the baguette into about 12 slices but not all the way through, leaving the base intact to hold it together.

STEP 3

Remove the cling film from the butter and thinly slice on a chopping board. Press each butter slice between the slices of bread.

STEP 4

Wrap the baguette in foil, place on a tray and bake for 5–6 mins, then peel back the foil. Cook for a further 4–5 mins to crisp up.

Sticky lemon & sesame chicken

Prep:10 mins **Cook:**35 mins

Serves 4

Ingredients

- 8-10 skinless boneless chicken thighs
- 2 tsp sesame oil
- 2 tsp cornflour
- zest and juice 2 large lemons
- 2 tbsp clear honey
- 2 tbsp soy sauce
- 2 tsp sesame seeds
- cooked noodles or rice, to serve
- cooked greens (such as sugar snap peas and pak choi), to serve

Method

STEP 1

Heat oven to 220C/200C fan/gas 7. Put the chicken in a shallow roasting tin, drizzle over the oil and season well. Roast for 25 mins.

STEP 2

Meanwhile, make the sauce. Tip the cornflour into a bowl and whisk in the lemon zest and juice until any lumps disappear. Add the honey, soy and sesame seeds and mix again.

STEP 3

Remove the chicken from the oven. Pour over the sauce, making sure every piece is well coated – it will still be very runny at this stage. Return to the oven for another 8-10 mins, spooning the sauce over the chicken every 2-3 mins as it thickens. If the sauce gets too thick, add a splash of water and scrape any sticky bits from the bottom of the tin. Serve with noodles or rice, and veg, with the extra sauce poured over the top.

Apple pie

Prep:30 mins **Cook:**20 mins - 30 mins

Serves 4

Ingredients

- 225g plain flour
- 140g butter or margarine
- 3 large cooking apples
- 2 tbsp honey
- pinch of cinnamon

- pinch of mixed spice
- 1 egg, beaten
- crème fraîche, vanilla ice cream or natural yogurt, to serve

Method

STEP 1

Heat oven to 200C/180C fan/gas 6. To make the pastry, sift the flour into a large mixing bowl and add the butter or margarine. Using your fingers, mix together until the mixture resembles breadcrumbs.

STEP 2

Add about 3 tbsp cold water – 1 tbsp at a time – to bind the mixture into a ball. Then wrap it in cling film and leave to chill in the fridge while you prepare the apples, or for 30 mins if you have time.

STEP 3

While the pastry is chilling, core the apples, then cut into even-sized chunks so they all cook in the same amount of time. Put the apples into the pie dish, drizzle over the honey and add the cinnamon, mixed spice and about 2 tbsp water.

STEP 4

Roll out the pastry on a floured work surface until it is large enough to cover the pie dish. Using the rolling pin, carefully lift the pastry and lay it over the top of the apple mixture. Carefully trim off the excess pastry (this can be rerolled and cut into shapes to decorate the pie crust if you like) and press the pastry edges onto the dish to create a seal.

STEP 5

Make a small cut in the pastry so that the air can escape during cooking, then brush with beaten egg to glaze.

STEP 6

Bake the pie in the oven for 20-30 mins until the pastry is golden and sandy in appearance and the apple filling is bubbling and hot. Serve while still warm with crème fraîche, ice cream or natural yogurt.

Printed in Great Britain
by Amazon

59838722R00147